Torture and Enhanced Interrogation

Recent Titles in the
CONTEMPORARY WORLD ISSUES
Series

Books in the **Contemporary World Issues** series address vital issues in today's society such as genetic engineering, pollution, and biodiversity. Written by professional writers, scholars, and nonacademic experts, these books are authoritative, clearly written, up-to-date, and objective. They provide a good starting point for research by high school and college students, scholars, and general readers as well as by legislators, businesspeople, activists, and others.

Each book, carefully organized and easy to use, contains an overview of the subject, a detailed chronology, biographical sketches, facts and data and/or documents and other primary source material, a forum of authoritative perspective essays, annotated lists of print and nonprint resources, and an index.

Readers of books in the Contemporary World Issues series will find the information they need in order to have a better understanding of the social, political, environmental, and economic issues facing the world today.

CONTEMPORARY WORLD ISSUES

Torture and Enhanced Interrogation

A REFERENCE HANDBOOK

Christina Ann-Marie DiEdoardo

BLOOMSBURY ACADEMIC
NEW YORK · LONDON · OXFORD · NEW DELHI · SYDNEY

BLOOMSBURY ACADEMIC
Bloomsbury Publishing Inc
1385 Broadway, New York, NY 10018, USA
50 Bedford Square, London, WC1B 3DP, UK
29 Earlsfort Terrace, Dublin 2, Ireland

BLOOMSBURY, BLOOMSBURY ACADEMIC and the Diana logo
are trademarks of Bloomsbury Publishing Plc

First published in the United States of America by ABC-CLIO 2020
Paperback edition published by Bloomsbury Academic 2025

Cover photo: Blindfolded detainees, Guantanamo, 2006.
(AF archive/Alamy)

Bloomsbury Publishing Inc does not have any control over, or responsibility for,
any third-party websites referred to or in this book. All internet addresses given
in this book were correct at the time of going to press. The author and publisher
regret any inconvenience caused if addresses have changed or sites have
ceased to exist, but can accept no responsibility for any such changes.

A catalog record for this book is available from the Library of Congress.

ISBN: HB: 978-1-4408-6227-4
        PB: 979-8-7651-4198-4
        ePDF: 978-1-4408-6228-1
        eBook: 979-8-2161-5647-5

Series: Contemporary World Issues

To find out more about our authors and books visit www.bloomsbury.com
and sign up for our newsletters.

Contents

6   RESOURCES, 293

Preface

No, torture is neither civilian nor military, nor specifically French: it is a pox which is ravaging the whole of this era. In the East as well as in the West there have been torturers. It is not so long ago that Farkas tortured the Hungarians; and the Polish do not hide the fact that their police, before Poznan, readily resorted to torture; as regards what happened in Russia when Stalin was alive, the Khrushchev report is an indispensable account; not long ago in Nasser's prisons, they "questioned" politicians who since then have been elevated, albeit with a few scars, to eminent positions. I could go on: today it is Cyprus and it is Algeria; all in all, Hitler was just a forerunner. (Sartre 1964, 2001, 35)

As Jean-Paul Sartre recognized when he wrote those words in the 1960s, just by using the terms "torture" or "enhanced interrogation" we are stating, whether consciously or otherwise, that the activity we are discussing is outside of the bounds that a consensus in society considers to be acceptable. To make things more complicated, drawing the line that sets that boundary is inherently a subjective judgment.

From Ancient Greece to Guantanamo Bay, it has sadly been the absence of torture that is a historical anomaly in human experience, rather than its presence. Justifications for its use can vary from era to era and regime to regime, but those who practiced *basanos* to compel testimony from slaves in Athens have far more in common with the police officer who beat a suspect in a station house and those who waterboarded prisoners at secret CIA facilities than any of them would probably like to admit.

What's changed over the millennia is a greater concern for appearances. The Romans, like the Greeks before them, were very open about the fact that they were engaging in torture. Their most learned judges discussed it as dispassionately as we might talk about DNA evidence or a wiretap. It was a tool for them, nothing more.

The same was true throughout most of the Middle Ages and the Renaissance in Europe. Things began to change in the eighteenth and nineteenth centuries as the Enlightenment and the development of professional police forces put pressure on governments to disavow torture and ban it from their legal codes.

Even so, it often still existed under euphemisms. Until about the middle of the twentieth century, it was generally considered acceptable for police in American cities to coerce information or confessions from prisoners by beating them senseless until they complied (DiEdoardo 2016, 95). While newspapers and commentators would use value-neutral phrases like the "third degree" to describe what these detainees suffered, few questioned the propriety of using force to intimidate a suspect into confessing or cared about the risk of prisoners confessing to acts they never committed just to make the pain stop while the real guilty parties walked free.

Not all of those who failed to take those considerations into account were monsters, though I would contend that working within a system that enables, permits, or encourages torture is a monstrous act. Some simply got caught up in the incentives associated with their position rather than see the big picture. For example, since police officers are rewarded for solving cases by producing a suspect rather than exonerating the innocent, it's not surprising that some—from San Francisco to Chicago—would use physical means of persuasion to "solve" cases by their fists rather than their brains. If one is rewarded for producing a plausible suspect, one may not care that it's the *right* suspect.

Understanding this helps explain the persistence of torture from ancient Greece to the present. While it's been known for some time that torture is usually a completely ineffective means of obtaining accurate information, this is not generally appreciated by the public or even acknowledged by some policymakers. As with the example shown here with police officers, a politician is often subject to a different set of incentives than, say, an author.

In his 2010 memoir *Decision Points*, former U.S. president George W. Bush discusses his decision to approve the waterboarding of Abu Zubaydah, a suspected al-Qaeda operative captured in Pakistan, eight years earlier.

> I knew that an interrogation program this sensitive and controversial would one day become public. When it did, we would open ourselves up to criticism that America had compromised our moral values. I would have preferred that we get the information another way. But the choice between security and values was real. Had I not authorized waterboarding on senior Al Qaeda leaders, I would have had to accept a greater risk that the country would be attacked. In the wake of 9/11, that was a risk I was unwilling to take. (Bush 2010, 169)

While Bush admits that waterboarding, which is the practice of pouring water down the breathing passages of a prisoner (Hitchens 2008), essentially a controlled drowning, was "tough" (Bush 2010, 169), he refuses to characterize it as torture. The view is far different on the receiving end, as Christopher Hitchens, who underwent the procedure as part of a story for *Vanity Fair*, discovered.

You may have read by now the official lie about this treatment, which is that it "simulates" the feeling of drowning. This is not the case. You feel that you are drowning because you are drowning—or, rather, being drowned, albeit slowly and under controlled conditions and at the mercy (or otherwise) of those who are applying the pressure. The "board" is the instrument, not the method. You are not being boarded. You are being watered. This was very rapidly brought home to me when, on top of the hood, which still admitted a few flashes of random and worrying strobe light to my vision, three layers of enveloping towel were added. In this pregnant darkness, head downward, I waited for a while until I abruptly felt a slow cascade of water going up my nose. Determined to resist if only for the honor of my navy ancestors who had so often been in peril on the sea, I held my breath for a while and then had to exhale and—as you might expect—inhale in turn. The inhalation brought the damp cloths tight against my nostrils, as if a huge, wet paw had been suddenly and annihilatingly clamped over my face. Unable to determine whether I was breathing in or out, and flooded more with sheer panic than with mere water, I triggered the prearranged signal and felt the unbelievable relief of being pulled upright and having the soaking and stifling layers pulled off me. I find I don't want to tell you how little time I lasted. (Hitchens 2008)

One could argue the differences between Bush's and Hitchens's perspectives on the issue of waterboarding are probably based on two factors. The first stems from the requirements imposed by the respective role they occupied. Since September 11, 2001, Bush has had to live with the knowledge that the CIA repeatedly tried to warn his administration that an attack by al-Qaeda on the continental United States was imminent and that his handpicked appointees failed take the proper actions to stop it (Whipple 2015). If a subsequent attack—which the intelligence community believed was likely (Whipple 2015) in the immediate aftermath of 9/11—had been successful, it's likely Bush's administration would not have survived. In contrast, Hitchens is responsible only for his own safety as an author.

The second, however, is more dispositive. Bush, according to his own statements, was willing to compromise generally accepted American principles in the interest of "security." Hitchens, on the other hand, is not.

As the foregoing suggests, it is impossible to have an objective discussion about the use of torture without recognizing the competing interests that underlay that use. In the interest of providing as much clarity as possible to that conversation, this book is divided up into seven chapters, each of which has a specific purpose.

Chapter 1 outlines the history of torture, with a focus on how it has been used by governments in Western Europe and the United States. The chapter traces how torture went from being an accepted part of criminal procedure from ancient Greece and Rome to being targeted for abolition in the eighteenth and nineteenth centuries and explores how much of the twentieth and early twenty-first centuries has been occupied by the efforts of governments, particularly democracies, to publicly decry torture while privately taking advantage of what they see as its benefits.

Chapter 2 examines the issue of torture through a discussion of the following questions: (1) How do we define torture? (2) Is torture an effective tool to reach the objectives its practitioners set for it? (3) What alternatives to torture exist? (4) Is the true abolition of torture practical on a global scale and, if so, is it desirable?

In Chapter 3, those with a personal connection to the issue of torture or with professional expertise in it tell their stories and give their perspectives. Chapter 4 profiles the key decision-makers and organizations involved in the use of torture as well as those campaigning for its abolition, while Chapter 5 focuses on the hard data and documents from which the conclusions in this book are drawn. Finally, Chapter 6 provides a detailed bibliography of resources for future research, while Chapter 7 sets forth a chronology of the events discussed in this book, followed by a glossary of key terms.

One note: this is a book on torture. Some readers may find some of the descriptions or language uncomfortable. However, it is difficult, and disingenuous, to discuss a difficult topic without including these discussions.

ACKNOWLEDGMENTS

While reading and writing about torture can be difficult, working with the amazing people at ABC-CLIO, especially Manager for Editorial Operations Robin Tutt and my editor, Catherine Lafuente, has always been a pleasure. I deeply appreciate their guidance, feedback, support, and assistance in bringing together the book you hold, whether in physical or digital form, in your hands as you read this. Most of all, thank you to my romantic partners Madeleine Ariadne Koizumi, and Katerie Whitman for all their love and support on this project. I owe you both a nice dinner at which we don't discuss *basanos*, the torture memos, or *Ad extirpanda* and promise to make that happen soon.

References

Bush, George W. *Decision Points* (New York: Random House, 2010).

DiEdoardo, Christina. *Lanza's Mob: The Mafia and San Francisco* (Santa Barbara, CA: ABC-CLIO, 2016).

Hitchens, Christopher. "Believe Me, It's Torture," *Vanity Fair*, August 2008, https://www.vanityfair.com/news/2008/08/hitchens200808 (accessed February 21, 2019).

Sartre, Jean-Paul. *Situations V* (Paris: Editions Gallimard, 1964).

Whipple, Chris. "The Attacks Will Be Spectacular," *Politico*, November 12, 2015, http://www.politico.com/magazine/story/2015/11/cia-directors-documentary-911-bush-213353 (accessed February 21, 2019).

Torture and Enhanced Interrogation

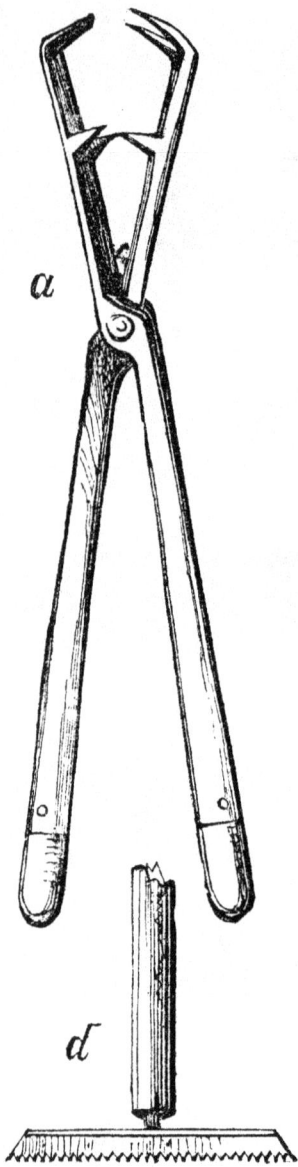
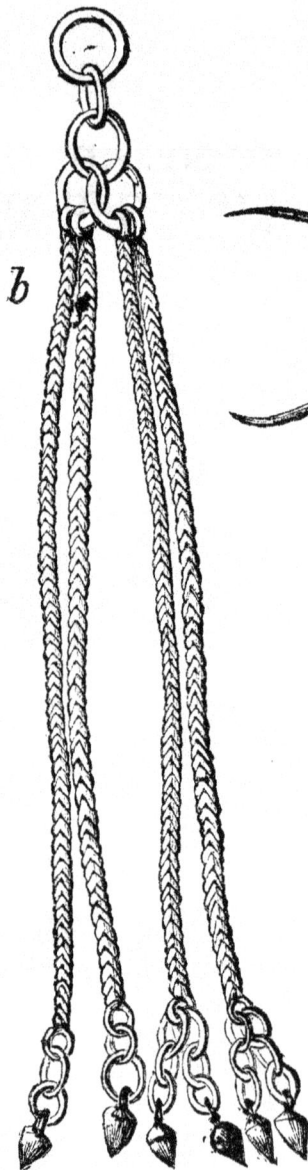

1 Background and History

By *quaestio* [torture] we are to understand the torment
and suffering of the body in order to elicit the truth. . . .
Since, therefore, *quaestio* is to be understood by force and
torment, these are the things that determine its meaning.
—Ulpian (Peters 1985: 1)

Introduction

This is a dark book about an even darker subject, so it is appropriate to subject one prevalent myth about torture to the light
of historical inquiry at the outset.

It would be comforting to believe that torture is a cruel
anomaly, perpetuated by sadists in dungeons that no government official knows about and where no judge ever treads.
While that hypothesis might help us sleep at night, it wouldn't
be true.

This is said not with an intent to normalize torture but simply to describe what has sadly been humanity's collective experience with it. While it may—or may not—be viewed as an
aberrant behavior depending on the society, who is subjected
to it, and the conditions under which it occurs, the practice

---

Torture devices or artisan crafting tools? These items, found in the Roman
Catacombs, could have been used for both purposes. The pincers (a) would
break limbs, the knotted cords (b) would lacerate the back while the claws
(c) could rip flesh from an unfortunate prisoner. Some believe they could
also have been used to work textiles. (Hilary Morgan/Alamy)

of torture has been with us since almost the beginning of re-corded history, at least in the context of Western Europe and the United States.

Ulpian, whose clinical description of judicial torture began this chapter, wasn't a brutal centurion who recognized no law other than force but one of the most prominent Roman jurists active in the third century CE and who today is considered by some scholars to have been an early advocate for human rights (Honoré 1982: ix).

From ancient Greece to Guantanamo Bay, torture has more often been the norm rather than the exception. Indeed, when seen over the perspective of the last several thousand years, it wasn't the *presence* of torture in society that is the anomaly but its general *absence* in Western Europe from about the end of the nineteenth century through the end of World War I (Peters 1985: 77), as we'll discuss in greater detail in the following pages.

Ancient Greece

From the eighth to the fifth centuries BCE, the early Greeks slowly discarded their system of what we'd consider to be justice-by-feud (*agon*) and moved toward what we'd recognize as a rudimentary system of litigation (Peters 1985: 12). Since only citizens had the privilege of being able to testify in these proceedings, the Greeks needed a means through which the evidence of noncitizens, such as slaves or those considered dishonorable, could be brought before the tribunal (Peters 1985: 14).

This posed a complicated problem. While citizens who lied under oath could be degraded in a variety of ways if caught, this deterrent to dishonesty seemed not to apply to slaves and certain unfortunate foreigners (Peters 1985: 14), who arguably had little to lose given their already marginalized status. As a re-sult, the Greeks came up with *basanos*, or torture, as one of the five "proofs" Aristotle held were available to litigants to prove their case (Peters 1985: 14).

Demosthenes lauded the practice, asserting "wherever slaves and free men are present and facts have to be found, you do not use the statements of the free witnesses, but you seek to discover the truth by applying torture [basanos] to the slaves. Quite properly, men of the jury, since witnesses have sometimes found not to have given true evidence, whereas no statements made as a result of torture have ever been proved untrue" (Wisnewski 2010: 17). As we'll see throughout this work, advocates of torture, from Demosthenes to Alan Dershowitz (2011), frequently assert that torture can be relied upon to elicit accurate testimony. Unfortunately for the backers of the use of the rack, the weight of historical evidence over the last several thousand years supports the opposite conclusion.

Indeed, a brief examination of how *basanos* worked in most cases exposes the deficiencies in the process. "The owner would normally hand over his slave to his opponent, who would administer the [*basanos*] usually in the form of whipping or beating, though the rack is also mentioned-while asking the question that had been agreed to. There was no limit to the duration of the beating or the number of blows; rather, the interrogation was supposed to continue 'until the slave seemed to tell the truth,' and at any time the owner could object to the severity or to other aspects of the interrogation and withdraw his slave" (Gagarin 1996, 1–18).

In other words, whether a slave was testifying truthfully or not, their owner *always* had the ability to terminate the interrogation, since the slaves were, after all, the owner's property. This may have been one of the reasons why the Greeks—and later, the Romans—had their doubts about the efficacy of torture as a means for compelling testimony or eliciting information (Peters 1985, 34).

The Roman Republic

In contrast to Greek practice, at first the Romans restricted the application of torture to slaves who were defendants in criminal cases (Peters 1985, 18), though this was later expanded to slaves who were witnesses in certain types of actions (Peters 1985, 18).

Unfortunately, as the sovereignty of the Roman state passed from the Senate (as a proxy for those who could vote) to the triumvirates and then ultimately to the emperor's person, protections against torture became less certain. Between 43 BCE and 31 BCE, "A praetor named Z. Gallius happened to salute Octavius while he carried a tablet under his toga. Octavius, thinking the tablet might have been a sword and Gallius the agent of conspiracy, had Gallius arrested and tortured before putting him to death" (Peters 1985, 22).

Indeed, from the reign of Emperors Tiberius through Domitian, emperors not only regularly ordered torture but often personally witnessed it (Peters 1985, 23). Methods of torture included the rack, which was "a wooden frame set on trestles in which the victim was placed with hands and feet fastened in such a way that the joints could be distended by the operation of a complex system of weights and ropes" (Peters 1985, 36). Other techniques included the use of "ungulae, hooks that lacerated the flesh [and the use of] red hot metal, flogging [and the] close constriction of the body in confinement" (Peters 1985, 35).

Ironically, while the Romans derided the Germanic tribes on the border of the empire as barbarians, the latter imposed far greater restrictions on the use of torture than Roman law did (Peters 1985, 37), at least during the years when they swung between a hot war and a cold peace with Rome. For example, while the Visigoths (who would go on to sack Rome in 410 CE) allowed free men to be tortured, that could only occur in cases where the person was accused by a peer of "homicide, adultery, offenses against the king, the people as a whole, counterfeiting, and sorcery" (Peters 1985, 38). Furthermore, they required that torture had to be judicially observed and the torturee could not lose a limb (Peters 1985, 36).

Following the collapse of the Roman Empire in 476 CE, the responsibility for prosecuting criminal offenses devolved back to the individual for approximately the next 700 years, at least in Western Europe. "Public officers did not search out and investigate crimes. Injuries were brought to the attention of the officials of justice by those who had suffered them, and it was the accuser's responsibility to see that legal officers acted" (Peters 1985, 41).

Even when those officers *did* act, what followed barely resembled what we would recognize today as a trial. Because "the oath was the strongest 'evidence' an accused party could wield" (Peters 1985, 41), if the accused could wrangle enough of their friends to swear to their good character, the case would often end there (Peters 1985, 41).

If, on the other hand, the defendant was thought to be of bad character or was accused of certain offenses believed to be especially heinous, the court could impose trial by ordeal, "a process in which the judgment of God was invoked to determine an issue rendered insolvable by the limitations of human judicial procedure," including trial by combat (Peters 1985, 42).

The change from this to a more modern legal system around the twelfth century CE unintentionally set the stage for the revival of torture on a large scale, since the new system required the extraction of confessions from the accused to function properly (Peters 1985, 42–43).

As Sir Robert Peel's creation of the first professional police force, with uniforms, indicia of office, and arrest powers, lay almost 600 years in the future, in 1829 (Stevenson 2008, 136–137)—much less a group of trained detectives, which would take even longer to come into being (Flanders 2011, 300)—it's perhaps not surprising that the authorities would return to the tools used by the ancient Greeks and Romans to force criminal suspects to talk when the latter wished to remain silent.

Western Europe

While torture as at first reserved, as with the Romans, "for known criminals and the 'lowest of men'" (Peters 1985, 47), that soon changed.

By the thirteenth century, "informal torture" (i.e., torture that wasn't performed with judicial sanction) was being used as an investigative tool by early investigators (Peters 1985, 49). In contrast, as torture became normalized through inclusion in the judicial system, its purpose was not to gain information but a confession (Peters 1985, 50).

As a result, from the mid-thirteenth century to the beginning of the nineteenth century, "torture was part of the ordinary criminal procedure of the Latin Church and of most of the states of Europe" (Peters 1985, 54). There were some procedural refinements, such as bans on measures that could kill or "permanently injure" (Peters 1985, 57) the torturee and requirements that a "medical expert . . . be present" (Peters 1985, 57), as well as "a notary . . . to make an official record of the procedure" (Peters 1985, 57). Most importantly, a confession made under torture had to be repeated in court or elsewhere for it to be valid, although this may have posed less of an issue than it initially would appear for the torturers, since a recanting defendant could be tortured *again* (Peters 1985, 57).

With most of Western Europe following a system in which a confession was considered the "queen of proofs" (Peters 1985, 58), it's not surprising that torture was often the queen's bloody handmaiden, with one "queen of torments" (Peters 1985, 69) standing out among them all. During this period, it was the *strappado*, which involved tying the detainee's hands behind their back, then attaching them to a rope "which was thrown over a beam in the ceiling, and hauled into the air, there to hang for a period of time, then let down, then raised again" (Peters 1985, 68).

Other favored methods included the leg-screw, which eventually "included a metal vice, which went around the leg and [was] tightened by a screw device, with its inner edges serrated for greater effectiveness" (Peters 1985, 68).

Given the minimal—and in some cases, nonexistent—levels of communication between Continental Western Europe and other large societies around the world during this period, it is remarkable how many followed similar paths regarding the normalization of torture. Torture was recognized in Japanese criminal procedure as early as the late 600s CE and was progressively formalized from the tenth to the sixteenth centuries (Peters 1985, 93) before being banned in 1879 (Peters 1985, 94). Islamic law follows three general schools of thought regarding the propriety of the use of torture. The first considers torture to be forbidden under all circumstances, the second permits its use against classes of proscribed persons (such as professional thieves), and the third prohibits Islamic judges—but not servants of the ruler—from engaging in it (Reza 2007, 21–28). Even so, it is perhaps not surprising that in the Ottoman Empire, as in the Christian-majority states of Western Europe, what were deemed to be the needs of the state took precedence over theological concerns (Peters 1985, 92).

To their credit, Ottoman religious officials continued to push back against its use. "In spite of the frequent use of torture and its recognition by Ottoman imperial authorities, the *muftis* consistently opposed it and even went so far to insist that if the torturer killed his victim he was obliged to pay blood money for the act, even though the civil law did not demand that he do so" (Peters 1985, 92, emphasis in original). That said, some contend these objections were more pro forma than actual. "In practice, among the Ottomans as elsewhere, the doctrine did not describe what happened" (Peters 1985, 93).

More recent scholarship has tentatively indicated that at least in some cases in the twelfth and thirteenth centuries in Spain, those who converted from Islam to Christianity may be have been exempted from the tortures they would have otherwise been subjected to by Spanish civil authorities as a part of the judicial process (Myers, forthcoming).

As for Russia, torture was practiced there from at least 1100 CE and was prevalent from 1497 CE until Czar Alexander I banned the practice in 1801 (Peters 1985, 95–96). Despite his decree, torture in Russia would outlive both the Romanovs and their successors (Peters 1985, 96–97).

Things were little better in the areas conquered by European colonizers in Africa and elsewhere. Since those invaders brought their legal system with them, torture often infected the lands they appropriated, even in places where it didn't already exist. From 1652 until the British captured South Africa in 1795, the Dutch colonial authorities engaged in torture (Peters 1985, 135). While the practice was officially banned from 1795 until 1961, when South Africa gained its independence, by 1964 police constables were being tried for torturing suspects who "had been beaten, subjected to electric shocks, struck with a *sjambok* [a dreaded whip made of rhinoceros hide] and partially suffocated by plastic bags" (Peters 1985, 136).

England

England was a partial exception to the general prevalence of torture during this period for mixed reasons of policy and legal procedure. In 1166, King Henry II created a process where grand juries presented evidence to royal justices who rode circuit around the realm. If the royal justices believed there was sufficient evidence that a crime had been committed, they would impanel a jury of local residents to try the case.

Since that jury could consider circumstantial evidence in a way that wasn't then possible on the Continent, there was less of a need for confessions and, thus, for torture, which "became generally irrelevant" after 1166 (Peters 1985, 59). Even so, "although torture seems to have made little headway in common law, it made considerable headway during the sixteenth century in royal orders or Orders in Council, particularly . . . in the case of political crimes" (Peters 1985, 80). As with "informal" torture on the Continent, in England, torture was more an investigatory tool than a way to get confessions during this period (Peters 1985, 80).

Church Courts

As we saw in ancient Greece and Rome (and will see again in later historical contexts), in Continental Europe "once torture had been admitted as a routine part of procedure, privilege tended to become weaker" (Peters 1985, 61). As a result, members of previously favored classes who had been exempted from the torturer's ministrations quickly discovered that this was no longer true if they had the misfortune to be accused of certain crimes, such as "heresy, magical practices, counterfeiting, and certain kinds of homicide and treason" (Peters 1985, 61). The breakdown of the division between secular and church courts enhanced this trend, particularly since secular courts had powers their religious counterparts lacked in many places (Peters 1985, 64).

That said, one can't say the ecclesiastical courts were squeamish on the subject. In 1252, Pope Innocent IV, who was also a lawyer, approved the use of torture by the Inquisition against heretics by equating the latter to "literal thieves and murderers" (Peters 1985, 65).

Advances in Criminology

Even so, while the pace of change seems glacial in retrospect, reforms were making their way forward. By the fourteenth century, French law on torture had evolved to explicitly distinguish between torture used to gain a confession and torture used after a confession to gain the names of the subject's accomplices (Peters 1985, 66). In 1754, Prussia became the first European state to bar the use of torture for all purposes (Peters 1985, 90), and shortly thereafter Italian criminologist Cesare Beccaria sounded the call to ban torture across the Continent.

In his "An Essay on Crimes and Punishments," Beccaria recast torture as a manifest abuse of the sovereign's authority, rather than as a tool in the sovereign's arsenal. "What right, then, but that of power, can authorize the punishment of a citizen so long as there remains any doubt of his guilt?" (Beccaria and Ingraham 1819, 59), he wrote.

As Beccaria noted, "This dilemma is frequent. [A defendant] is either guilty or is not guilty. If guilty, he should only suffer the punishment ordained by the laws, and torture becomes useless, as his confession is unnecessary. If he be not guilty, you torture the innocent; for in the eye of the law, every man is innocent whose crime has not been proved" (Beccaria and Ingraham 1819, 59–60).

More significantly, he mounted a frontal assault on the philosophical justifications for the use of torture by judicial officers. "It is confounding all relations to expect that a man should be both the accuser and accused; and that pain should be the test of truth, as if truth resided in the muscles and fibres of a wretch in torture. By this method, the robust will escape and the feeble be condemned" (Beccaria and Ingraham 1819, 60). To Beccaria, it was impossible to discuss torture without acknowledging that "these are the inconveniencies of this pretended test of truth, worthy only of a cannibal" (Beccaria and Ingraham 1819, 60).

Beyond his moral objections to torture, Beccaria contended it was singularly ineffective as a means of deterring criminal activity or changing behavior.

"What is the political intention of punishments?" he wrote. "To terrify and be an example to others. Is this intention answered by thus privately torturing the guilty and the innocent? It is doubtless of importance that no crime should remain unpunished; but it is useless to make a public example of the author of a crime hid in darkness. A crime already committed, and for which there can be no remedy, can only be punished by a political society with an intention that no hopes of impunity should induce others to commit the same" (Beccaria and Ingraham, 1819, 60).

He further mocked what he termed the other "ridiculous motive for torture, namely, to *purge a man from infamy*. Ought such an abuse to be tolerated in the eighteenth century? Can pain, which is a sensation, have any connection with a moral sentiment, a matter of opinion? Perhaps the rack may be considered as the refiner's furnace" (Beccaria and Ingraham 1819, 61; emphasis in original).

Five years after Beccaria penned those words, English legal commentator William Blackstone declared the use of torture to be "an engine of the state, not of law" and held it should be excluded from criminal procedure (Peters 1985, 103), which was starting to happen across Western Europe.

As the eighteenth century reached its end and nation-states developed professional police forces, pressure increased on their governments to drop torture as "part and parcel of a world not only overthrown, but utterly destroyed. In the light of reason and humanity [torture] could not come again" (Peters 1985, 99–100). By the nineteenth century, this ideal seemed to have come true on the surface, and most historians thought the use of torture by courts and police had been condemned to history's dustbin (Peters 1985, 77), never to be spoken of except as an anachronism.

They couldn't have been more wrong, mainly because the practice of torture never really went completely away, especially in dark rooms in police stations across that nation which Ronald Reagan famously termed a "City on a Hill" (Reagan 1980) because of the moral example it supposedly set for the world: the United States.

The United States

Some of this had to do with the way American police forces were established. Some departments in the South began as slave-catching patrols, while others, such as the St. Louis Police Department, were organized to "protect" white settlers from Indigenous Americans (Kappeler 2014). Given these organizational lineages, it is not surprising that police in the United States have rarely prioritized the welfare and civil rights of prisoners in their operations.

Worse, since most local law enforcement agencies in the United States are decentralized and until the middle of the twentieth century had little formal accountability, "American police [were] generally free to operate as they wished, often restrained less by principle and judicial supervision than by political and social pressure" (Peters 1985, 111). As New York Police Department inspector Alexander "Clubber" Williams pithily quipped in the 1870s, "There is more law at the end of a policeman's night stick than in any ruling of the U.S. Supreme Court" (Brands 1997, 277).

Williams is also credited for coining the term "tenderloin" to describe the area around Sixth Avenue and 27th Street in New York City, mainly because it was "a district so full of saloons, deadfalls and coney snares (brothels, to put it plainly), gambling halls, music halls, bully boys, steerers and what the diarist, George Templeton Strong, called the 'noctivagous strumpetocracy' that, in comparison, Times Square [in 1979] displays a sort of mean innocence." Once Williams took charge of the precinct, he proclaimed, "I've had nothing but chuck steak for a long time and now I'm going to get a little of the tenderloin" ("In the Tenderloin" 1979).

Thanks to the plethora of illegal businesses in his new domain ripe for police extortion, Williams ultimately "retired rich" ("In the Tenderloin" 1979) from the NYPD in 1895 (Czitrom 2016, 310), but enough of his colleagues remained who shared his views to make both abuse of suspects and corruption perennial problems in the city its residents call the Big Apple to this day.

Indeed, from New York to San Francisco, the law of the nightstick and the curse of the torturer often spoke louder in station houses than the Bill of Rights and the emollient words of the Founding Fathers. As *The New York Times* delicately put it in 1902, "The chief reason that so little is heard of the 'third degree' as it is really practiced by the police of the different large cities in the United States is that those upon whom it is practiced to the full extent of its brutality are of that class that would not be believed even when they tell the truth, and of course those who practice it would not care to have the public know of the delicate arts of their profession" ("To Abolish the Third Degree" 1902, 23).

Even so, the *Times* was aware in 1902 that "there is an apartment in the Tombs Prison known as the 'dark cell' which is typical of the cells used for putting prisoners through the 'third degree'.... The gate or door to the cell is composed of massive iron bars covered with a series of screens arranged so as to prevent the penetration of the slightest ray of light" ("To Abolish the Third Degree" 1902, 23). It apparently only took "a few hours in the 'dark cell' before the boldest of the bad prisoners are as meek as lambs, bleating to get out" ("To Abolish the Third Degree" 1902, 23).

By 1910, U.S. senator Frank Brandegee was leading a Senate Select Committee on the use of the "third degree" by police forces, which included everything from feeding prisoners excessively salted food and then denying them water to striking prisoners with "hidden blows," depriving them of sleep, confining them in "sweat boxes," and releasing vermin, such as rats, in their cells (Watkins 1910, SM3). Brandegee's scope was limited to the acts of federal officers and U.S. attorneys (Seligman 2018, 87), likely because the U.S. Supreme Court had held in 1890 in *In Re Kemmler* that the Eighth Amendment's ban on cruel and unusual punishment didn't apply to state officers and officials, a position that didn't change for decades.

In 1929, the term "third degree" was sufficiently well known to make it into the *Encyclopedia Britannica*, which defined it as "the employment of brutal methods by police or prosecuting authorities to extort information or confessions from persons in custody" (Encyclopedia Britannica 1929, 135). Furthermore, "The phrase as often employed includes not only the use of physical violence, but also forms of torture as depriving a prisoner of food, drink, sleep and toilet facilities and the prolonged and uninterrupted interrogation of him when exhausted, suffering and broken down by such deprivations. It is more commonly applied however to those forms of physical assault (such as beating with a rubber hose) which produce pain but leave no traces" (Encyclopedia Britannica 1929, 135).

As we'll see later, the refinement of methods which didn't leave obvious marks would eventually be America's biggest contribution, if one can call it that, to the pool of human knowledge on torture. One can almost draw a line connecting what went on in the back rooms of American police stations in the late nineteenth and early twentieth centuries to the dungeons operated by the security services of American client states in the Cold War to the secret prisons and "black sites" (Siems 2017) (so named because they officially didn't exist) run by the Central Intelligence Agency (CIA) in Afghanistan and elsewhere after the 9/11 attacks on New York and the Pentagon.

There are other parallels worth noting between these periods. Torture was used against members or suspected members of groups that the state had dehumanized, so whether those targeted were deemed to be "criminals," "communists," or "terrorists" mattered less than the fact that they were viewed as lesser humans.

Indeed, suspected criminals were arguably *worse* off than the unlucky slaves and foreigners in Ancient Greece who were subjected to *basanos*, since the latter's torture was at least partially governed by the metes and bounds of a judicial proceeding, while the extent of the torment of those in police custody was largely dependent upon the whims of their captors.

Things had gotten so bad by 1931 that the Wickersham Commission had enough evidence not only to title their report "Lawlessness in Law Enforcement" but also to "recoun[t] in enormous and grisly detail the arbitrary coercive character of police practices in the USA" (Peters 1985 112).

World War II

Meanwhile, European nations were returning to their old habits. Seven years after Benito Mussolini seized power in Italy in 1922, his OVRA secret police used "torture regularly upon suspected enemies of state, party and people" (Peters 1985, 122). Even in supposedly free France, police began to adopt the methods of their American colleagues in administering the "third degree" to suspects and prisoners in their custody after 1929 (Peters 1985, 112). Later, French police in occupied

Paris assisted the Nazi Gestapo in running "twelve torture chambers . . . functioning twenty-four hours a day" (Cahill 2006, 219), while in Vichy (and later in occupied France) the *Milice* paramilitary force set up by French Nazi collaborators "was in many ways a French Gestapo and its name became as synonymous with execution and brutality as its German model" (Cahill 2006, 307).

In the Soviet Union, statutory bans on torture, such as the one set forth in the Soviet Criminal Code, were widely ignored (Peters 1985, 129–130). Felix Dzerzhinsky, founder of the Cheka and the OGPU, the first two secret services to protect the Soviet state, appeared to find concerns over the propriety of torture misguided, if not outright silly. "We stand for organized terror—this should be frankly stated—terror being absolutely indispensable in current revolutionary conditions" (Peters 1985, 128).

By his orders, "suspects might be arrested late at night, verbally and physically abused, rushed into a prison, threatened with death (and even led to a place of execution several times, only to be returned to prison) and were tried by no regular procedure, with no defence permitted" (Peters 1985, 128).

Dzerzhinsky found his imitators in Nazi Germany after Adolf Hitler was named chancellor in 1933. Within a short time, the Nazi regime, through "the creation of special tribunals, the widening definition of political crimes, and the intensification of methods of interrogation and punishment" (Peters 1985, 123), increasingly normalized torture.

A complete examination of the use of torture in the Third Reich is beyond the scope of this book, but there are some salient points which should be discussed, as they are relevant to our narrative.

By 1942, Henrich Himmler, in his capacity as *Reichsführer* of the Nazi *Schutzstaffel*, or SS, a paramilitary and security force, was explicitly ordering the use of the "third degree" (i.e., "bread and water, close confinement, extraordinary exercises, hidden cells, deprivation of sleep, and beatings")

(Peters 1985, 124–125) against "communists, Marxists, Jehovah's Witnesses, saboteurs, terrorists, members of resistance movements, antisocial elements, refractory elements, or Polish or Soviet vagabonds" (Peters 1985, 125). While Himmler decreed that "in all other cases, preliminary authorization is necessary [for the use of torture]" (Peters 1985, 125), there's no indication that authorization was often refused when it was sought.

While Hitler's minions, like their colleagues in the Soviet Union, fascist Italy, or France, used torture to obtain information or to punish political enemies of their regime, Nazi torturers went far beyond the comparatively limited objectives of torture in those countries and expanded it into a means of achieving state policy. Beginning in 1934, they forcibly sterilized between 300,000 and 400,000 people they considered physically or mentally unfit to reproduce (United States Holocaust Museum 2018) as a way of putting their racist eugenic theories into practice. Around 1937, Himmler's subordinates coined the term "*Verschärfte Vernehmung*," or "enhanced interrogation" (Sullivan 2007), in order "to describe a form of torture that would leave no marks, and hence save the embarrassment pre-war Nazi officials were experiencing as their wounded torture victims ended up in court" (Sullivan 2007).

Initially, *Verschärfte Vernehmung* resembled the "third degree" of American police practice, with prisoners being placed on restricted diets, being denied sleep, and being beaten by the guards (Sullivan 2007). However, consistent with previous historical experience, torture in Nazi Germany and in the areas occupied by the German *Wehrmacht* soon outgrew these bounds and expanded into the waterboarding of prisoners and attempts to induce hypothermia (Sullivan 2007).

French philosopher and historian Jean Paul-Sartre vividly describes what those days were like for those in occupied France.

In 1943, in the Rue Lauriston [the Gestapo headquarters in Paris] Frenchmen were screaming in agony and pain; all

France could hear them. In those days the outcome of the war was uncertain and we did not want to think about the future. Only one thing seemed impossible in any circumstances: that one day men should be made to scream by those acting in our name. (Peters 1985, 133)

Ironically, Hanns Joachim Scharff—the man considered by many to be the best interrogator the Nazis possessed—eschewed these methods. Scharff interviewed over 500 captured Allied pilots and "successfully elicited useful information from all but about 20 of them" (Wilber 2016).

The irony of Scharff's success is that he was placed in his job by a random event.

Without formal training as an interrogator he was unconstrained by standard procedures. Scharff was actually an enlisted administrative specialist who was pressed into service as an interrogator only when the officer responsible for interrogating Allied fighter pilots was killed in an aircraft accident. After observing the high-pressure, threat-based techniques used with limited success by his predecessor, Scharff sought to create an environment that might make the POW momentarily forget he was being interrogated. In addition to being questioned in an office environment, for example, Scharff would take a given POW for a walk through a nearby forest or for drinks at the officer's club. (Granhag et al. 2016, 135)

Pär Anders Granhag, a psychology professor at the University of Gothenburg in Sweden whose research is focused on the detection of deception, eyewitness testimony, and investigative psychology, summed up Scharff's technique in five points: "(1) Employ a friendly approach . . . (2) Do not press for information . . . (3) [Maintain] the illusion of knowing it all . . . (4) [Use] confirmations/disconfirmations . . . (5) Ignore new information" (Granhag et al. 2016, 137–138). After the war, Scharff assisted the Pentagon with developing programs to train American military personnel to resist the tactics he had pioneered before his death in 1992 (Wilber 2016). Since then, Granhag and others have taught those same techniques to the FBI (Granhag et al., 2016, 137).

The United Nations

The immediate aftermath of World War II offered some justification for the hope that torture might be soon banished from human experience. In 1948, of the sixty nations that were then members of the United Nations (UN), forty-eight voted in favor (while eight abstained and two did not vote) of the Universal Declaration of Human Rights (United Nations 1948, PV 183), whose Article 5 explicitly declared that "no one shall be subjected to torture or to cruel, inhuman or degrading treatment or punishment" (United Nations 1948).

Herbert Vere Evatt, who presided over the General Assembly and had a hand in the Declaration's drafting, praised it as the "first occasion on which the organized community of nations had made a declaration of human rights and fundamental freedoms" (United Nations 1948, PV 183). Even so, he was quick to recognize that "the Declaration only marked a first step since it was not a convention by which States would be bound to carry out and give effect to the fundamental human rights; nor would it provide for enforcement" (United Nations 1948, PV 183).

Two years later, the Council of Europe passed the European Convention on Human Rights, which also banned torture (Peters 1985, 144), but unlike the Declaration, it could be enforced through the European Court of Human Rights.

However, events were soon to demonstrate the gap between what national governments committed to do before the UN or the Council of Europe and what their servants did on the ground. Thirteen years after their people had been subjected to torture at the hands of the Nazi Gestapo (as Sartre described) and its Vichy French collaborators, French officials began to torture those opposed to French colonial rule in Algeria (Peters 1985, 133).

Algeria

According to Edward Behr, who covered the Algerian War for Independence from France as a foreign correspondent, "As in occupied Paris, when some houses were taken over by the Gestapo as interrogation centers, so several villas in Algiers came to have a deservedly sinister reputation. How many people died under torture will never be known, but the figure was certainly in the thousands, perhaps in the tens of thousands if one includes those 'shot while trying to escape' after the torture sessions" (Behr 1986, 119).

Far more people than those who died were affected by the torture campaign, however. To Behr, who had served in the Indian army under the British toward the end of World War II before becoming a journalist, "perhaps the most appalling aspect of the war was the French troops' habit of picking up civilians at random, questioning them, torturing them and then letting them go. It wasn't difficult, as a result, to talk to Algerians who had actually been tortured" (Behr 1986, 122).

During this period, torture practices included, but were not limited to, what the French army called *la baignoire*, or "the bath"—what we'd know today as waterboarding (Behr 1986, 122). According to other authorities, the French followed five rules when they tortured prisoners. "1. It is necessary that torture be properly conducted. 2. It must not take place in front of children. 3. It must not be performed by sadists. 4. It must be *humane*, that is it should cease immediately when the type [sic] confesses. And above all, it must leave no marks" (Peters 1985, 178).

It's hardly surprising that Sartre would say of this period thus: "Torture is neither civilian nor military, nor is it specifically French; it is a plague infecting our whole era" (Peters 1985, 134).

While there is much truth to what Sartre says, it's important to understand that the way torture was employed in Algeria by the French colonial authorities distinguishes it from some of the earlier examples of torture we've seen elsewhere. As sociologist Marnia Lazreg points out, "Torture . . . appears as a political practice that unfolds in a social *situation* from which it is inseparable. In this respect, the stated end of torture, intelligence, does not and cannot define torture: Torture in Algeria was not primarily about information, although some useful information was collected. Information can be had without the use of torture as a French intelligence officer found out" (Lazreg and Weitz 2008, 7, emphasis in original).

To Lazreg, "the democratic state in crisis is especially attracted to torture because it is pure power, and affords absolute control. Although politically onerous, engaging in torture for liberal democracies also provides an expedient and instantaneous response to a crisis defined as one of 'security'. Tapping into torture-power is, for the state, a matter of re-sourcing itself, rejuvenating itself by re-creating itself, refashioning its existence as the power of instrumental reason" (Lazreg and Weitz 2008, 7).

Not only was torture ultimately insufficient to maintain France's colonial hold on Algeria, an argument can be made that the use of it encouraged the breakdown of discipline among French soldiers stationed there, which contributed both to the May 1958 seizure of Algiers by the army (which brought down the Fourth Republic and paved the way for retired Gen. Charles de Gaulle to return to power) (Behr 1986, 165–170) and to the French army's unsuccessful military coup in Algiers in April 1961 (Behr 1986, 181, 186, 188).

Later in 1961, British lawyer Peter Benenson formed Amnesty International (AI) to advocate for "prisoners of conscience." AI would go on to become one of the most effective grassroots voices against torture in the pre-Internet age by orchestrating mail-in campaigns from around the world to get political prisoners released.

One of the organization's first big tests would come in Greece, where—six years after the failed Algiers *putsch*—the Greek military overthrew its civilian masters in a right-wing coup and thereby brought torture back to the land discussing which we began this chapter.

Modern Greece

Thanks in large part to AI's work on this subject, Greece withdrew from the Council of Europe in 1969 before it was expelled from that body (Ginger 1969, 1), but it would take the fall of the military regime in 1975 and the subsequent criminal proceedings described in AI's book *Torture in Greece: The First Torturer's Trial 1975*, which some have called "one of the classic works on the documentation and techniques of torture in the late twentieth century" (Peters 1985, 158), for the remaining facts to come out.

As with the French experience in Algeria, torture was used for multiple purposes by the new regime.

> From the first day of the Junta's rule, torture was an integral part of the state machinery for suppressing opposition. It should be stressed, however, that during the seven years of dictatorship it was used for different purposes at different periods. During the period 1967–71, the purposes of torture were to extract information about resistance activities and to deter the population from political activity. . . . [During this period] [t]he policy was to avoid leaving marks, or at least not to allow detainees any contact with the outside until such marks had disappeared. During the period 1971–74, however, the purpose of torture increasingly became intimidation and terrorisation, with the specific aim of destroying the student movement. To a large extent torture was conducted by military police conscripts who were encouraged by their officers to leave marks on the victim. (Amnesty International 1977, 11)

In either case, a prisoner's journey usually started by their being snatched off the street and "were often accompanied by a beating" (Amnesty International 1977, 16). "On arrival at headquarters, the detainee would . . . usually be taken to the commanding officer and verbally threatened with imminent and severe violence. In order to intimidate him, he might be shut into a guardroom where there were clubs, whips, and canes hanging on the wall" (Amnesty International 1977, 16).

Typically, there wasn't a long wait before the real violence began.

"At the outset of the . . . torture routine, prisoners would be deprived of both food and drink. They would be told to remain standing in the corner of their cell, sometimes on one foot but usually at attention. This ordeal would last several days. It would often be interspersed with more beatings—standings and beatings together known as a 'tea party with toast'" (Amnesty International 1977, 16–17).

Like the practitioners of the "third degree" in the United States, Greek torturers sometimes adulterated the food they gave their prisoners with salt (Amnesty International 1977, 17). On other occasions, they put soap in the water they gave to torture victims to make it undrinkable (Amnesty International 1977, 17).

Sometimes, the guards went further and threatened or carried out sexual assaults on the detainees, including the insertion of "an iron needle" up a male prisoner's urethra (Amnesty International 1977, 32).

To Amnesty, indications that such activities appear to have been aberrations (or innovations, depending on one's point of view as to the propriety of torture) missed the fundamental point. "Although such sexual aberrations among torturers often attract considerable attention and deserved condemnation from well-meaning opponents of torture, it is important to see that these individual perversions are not the cause of a system of torture. Rather, once a system of torture has been created to support the political needs of those in power, the rulers' agents will exhibit patterns of behaviour that they would not otherwise be in a position to do. Social jealousy and sexual aggression are two cases in point" (Amnesty International 1977, 32).

Torture in Greece also sheds light on another question: can torturers be "made" or does being an effective torturer require a particular psychological makeup that not every person possesses?

In the Greek context, given that between 400 and 600 conscript soldiers were assigned to the torture centers at any one time and about 4,000 draftees had worked there at some point during their service, with the overwhelming majority having brutalized prisoners (Amnesty International 1977, 36), the answer would appear to be the former.

According to one expert, "torturers are deliberately trained in such a way as to alter their personalities, make them accept a fabricated political reality in which their victims have been set outside the pale of humanity, and sustain this illusion by both coercion and reward" (Peters 1985, 184).

According to testimony from one soldier-defendant at the 1975 torturers trial, the regime trained its torturers by torturing them too. "From the moment we arrived . . . from the Basic Training Centre, the torture began. They snatched us from the army lorries and threw us down like sacks. The beating began and they made us eat the straps from our berets. . . . They beat us with belts and clubs. . . . The beating never stopped. . . . They beat us in the lorries, in the lecture halls and during the lessons" (Amnesty International 1977, 38). As another soldier-defendant told the court that it was "nothing" to beat a prisoner five times "when you've had sixty from your comrades" (Amnesty International 1977, 38).

Perhaps the greatest irony in the Greek context was that while torture has been against the Greek constitution since the early 1800s, "under Greek law, torture *per se* is not a crime. The [1975] trial was held, therefore, within the limits of the only possible charges. These concerned 'insults,' 'abuse of authority,' and 'bodily injury,' which in Greek law are misdemeanours. It was only because some of the torture victims were officers superior in rank to the defendants that stiff sentences were imposed" (Amnesty International 1977, 58).

How "stiff" those sentences truly were may be a matter of debate given the gravity of the conduct, even given the limitations imposed by Greek law as it was at the time. While four defendants received prison terms of fifteen years or more, most of the others got off lighter and several were acquitted entirely (Amnesty International 1977, 72).

Even so, AI believes that that Greek experience of the first torturer's trial in 1975 helped spur the adoption of the "Declaration on the Protection of All Persons from Being Subjected to Torture and Other Cruel, Inhuman or Degrading Treatment or Punishment" by the UN's General Assembly in December of that year, which will be discussed in greater detail later in this chapter (Amnesty International 1977, 8).

Before we get there, it's important to note that Greece wasn't the only country in Europe where both torture and attempts to stop it through the legal system were taking place during this period.

Ireland and the U.K.

In 1971, Ireland brought a case against the United Kingdom (Coogan 2002, 438) at the European Court of Human Rights regarding the British government's treatment of persons believed to be members of the Provisional Irish Republican Army (IRA), an armed insurgent group that sought to expel the British from Ireland and unify the island under one government.

After seven years of deliberation, the Court delivered its ruling in 1978 and "found that the following five techniques were used: 1. hooding the detainees except during interrogation; 2. making them stand continuously against a wall in a spreadeagled and painful posture for prolonged periods of some hours; 3. submitting them to continuous and monotonous noise;

4. depriving them of sleep; and 5. restricting them to a diet of [a] round of bread and one pint of water at six-hourly intervals" (Coogan 2002, 438).

While in a 16–1 vote the Court found that such tactics were "inhuman and degrading," it also found in a separate 13–4 vote that they did not constitute "torture" within the meaning of Article 3 of the Convention (Coogan 2002, 438).

Comparing the Greek case with that of Northern Ireland illustrates some interesting parallels and important differences. Placing prisoners in "stress positions" (whether by the Greek method of forcing them to stand at attention or the British method of spread-eagling) is a popular torture technique, primarily because it requires little infrastructure and leaves no marks. The same can be said of restricting the intake of food and drink (or, in the Greek case, at least on occasion, restricting the intake of food and drink and adulterating the food the prisoner did get).

However, the difference is more important for our analysis. Once the regime the Greek torturers served had fallen, they had outlived their political usefulness and lost their immunity from prosecution, even if only a small proportion were ultimately brought to justice. In contrast, the British government not only remains in power, but British rule in Northern Ireland continues as of this writing, despite the IRA's ceasefire in July 1997 (Rowan 2017).

In other words, so long as the government which gave the orders to those who turn the screws of torture remains in existence, that government has little practical incentive to voluntarily hold those who carried out those orders to account. While this disinclination to act can be countered by public and international pressure, overcoming it is far from easy.

The United States in the Civil Rights Era

The 1960s brought some positive change on the torture front in America, where the "third degree"—though not completely

eliminated—became less common due to certain changes in
criminal procedure.

In May 1961, California repealed its "vagrancy" statute,
which had allowed the police to arrest those without visible
means of support (DiEdoardo 2016, xxiii). In practice—and
especially in San Francisco—it had been one of the tools used
by police to round up members of groups they didn't like, ranging from suspected members of the Italian mafia (DiEdoardo
2016, 95) to lesbian, gay, bisexual, transgender, and intersex
or asexual individuals (Boyd 2003, 216) to persons of color
(Boyd 2003, 217) without having to establish probable cause
that any of these detainees had committed a crime, as the U.S.
Constitution would require. Fewer members of marginalized
communities who could be arrested on dubious constitutional
grounds meant a smaller population of potential victims of the
"third degree."

More significantly, the U.S. Supreme Court's decisions in
Mapp v. Ohio in 1961 (which required state courts to exclude evidence the police obtained through illegal searches)
and *Miranda v. Arizona* in 1965 (which barred the use of
statements made by prisoners to their interrogators if the
prisoners hadn't been informed of their right to consult with
an attorney) removed much of the motivation for police to
torture prisoners.

Indeed, the "third degree" was directly on the mind of
Chief Justice Earl Warren, who wrote the majority opinion in
Miranda.

> An understanding of the nature and setting of this in-
> custody interrogation is essential to our decisions today.
> The difficulty in depicting what transpires at such inter-
> rogations stems from the fact that, in this country, they
> have largely taken place incommunicado. From extensive
> factual studies undertaken in the early 1930's, including
> the famous Wickersham Report to Congress by a Presi-
> dential Commission, it is clear that police violence and

the "third degree" flourished at that time. In a series of cases decided by this Court long after these studies, the police resorted to physical brutality—beating, hanging, whipping—and to sustained and protracted questioning incommunicado in order to extort confessions. The Commission on Civil Rights in 1961 found much evidence to indicate that "some policemen still resort to physical force to obtain confessions," 1961 Comm'n on Civil Rights Rep. Justice, pt. 5, 17. The use of physical brutality and violence is not, unfortunately, relegated to the past or to any part of the country. Only recently in Kings County, New York, the police brutally beat, kicked and placed lighted cigarette butts on the back of a potential witness under interrogation for the purpose of securing a statement incriminating a third party. *People v. Portelli,* 15 N.Y.2d 235, 205 N.E.2d 857, 257 N.Y.S.2d 931 (1965). The examples given above are undoubtedly the exception now, but they are sufficiently widespread to be the object of concern. Unless a proper limitation upon custodial interrogation is achieved—such as these decisions will advance—there can be no assurance that practices of this nature will be eradicated in the foreseeable future. (*Miranda* 1966, 445–447)

Warren went on to approvingly quote from the Wickersham Report of 1931:

Not only does the use of the third degree involve a flagrant violation of law by the officers of the law, but it involves also the dangers of false confessions, and it tends to make police and prosecutors less zealous in the search for objective evidence. As the New York prosecutor quoted in the report said, "It is a short-cut, and makes the police lazy and unenterprising." Or, as another official quoted remarked: "If you use your fists, you are not so likely to use your wits." We agree with the conclusion expressed in the report, that "The third degree brutalizes the police, hardens the prisoner against society, and lowers the esteem in which the administration of Justice is held by the public." (*Miranda* 1966, 447–448)

As the previous selections make clear, while *Miranda* is best known as the decision that required police to advise suspects and prisoners they had a right to remain silent, its author was primarily concerned with ending the practice of the "third degree" in station houses across America. In that light, *Miranda* can be viewed as one of the most important anti-torture decisions in American jurisprudence of the twentieth century.

Yet while America was reducing the prevalence of torture at home, its soldiers and secret police were spreading it abroad, supposedly in the name of fighting communism.

American Use of Torture Abroad

The CIA's involvement with torture—or, if one prefers, "enhanced interrogation"—began in 1949 with Project Bluebird (McCoy 2012, 17), which was supposed to train its agents to withstand interrogation by their opposite numbers, including adversaries whose tactics resembled the "third degree" instead of those used by Scharff.

The CIA's concern about what could happen to its agents (and more directly, whether they would keep the secrets they knew) if they fell into the hands of the secret or political police in the Eastern Bloc was understandable, as a 1951 Agency report on the Hungarian State Protection Authority (AVH) interrogation procedures showed.

When a suspect is first brought in for questioning, he is met by a Colonel of Political Police. Without further ado, the suspect is punched in the face, hit on the head with the butt of a heavy service pistol, and then kicked in the pit of the stomach. With this sudden introduction to

60 Andrassy Ut, the prisoner is then dragged bleeding down into the cellar. There he is stripped naked and placed on two chairs. For at least ten agonizing minutes, the victim's feet are unmercifully beaten with heavy galvanized rubber hoses. It is after this preliminary torture that the suspect is first questioned. He is now asked for the first time whether or not he is guilty of the crime as charged. If the unfortunate victim does not admit guilt, he is then flung to the hard floor. A chair is placed on his chest. The interrogating officer then sits on the chair and begins striking the prisoner in the head with a heavy instrument. If he still refuses to admit his guilt, a tin, electric-wired head gear is placed on his battered head and the current is released. After one of these introductory questionings at 60 Andrassy Ut, the suspect is about 80% broken not only in mind, but in body as well. (Central Intelligence Agency 1951, CD No. 50X1-HUM)

Ironically, the AVH's former headquarters at 60 Andrassy Ut. in Budapest is now the home of the Museum of Terror, which documents torture and other atrocities committed in Hungary when it was under Communist rule, as well as the Fascist government that preceded it.

While the 1951 report was based on "unevaluated" human source information (Central Intelligence Agency 1951, CD No. 50X1-HUM) at the time, the Agency appeared to have taken it seriously. In 1956, a CIA report titled "Communist Control Techniques" classified secret at the time, declared,

The effects of isolation, anxiety, fatigue, lack of sleep, uncomfortable temperatures, and chronic hunger produce disturbances of mood, attitudes, and behavior in nearly all prisoners. The living organism cannot entirely withstand such assaults. The Communists do not look upon these assaults as "torture." Undoubtedly, they use the methods which they do in order to conform, in a typical legalistic manner to overt Communist principles which demand that "no force or torture be used in extracting information from prisoners." *But these methods do, of course, constitute torture and physical coercion. All of them lead to serious disturbances of many bodily processes.* (Central Intelligence Agency 1956, 25X1A8a; emphasis added)

By the time the aforementioned report was written, the CIA's focus had moved from teaching its agents to withstand torture to instructing them on how to engage in it, beginning in 1951 with the agency's Project Artichoke, which was designed to develop "any method by which we can get information from a person against his will and without his knowledge" (McCoy 2012, 18).

Shortly after Project Artichoke began, "the agency had acquired secret prisons in the Canal Zone, West Germany and Japan, and was dispatching Artichoke teams overseas for interrogations with drugs, hypnosis, 'psychological harassment' and 'special interrogation techniques'" (McCoy 2012, 18).

Researching Torture

After a 1951 meeting between members of British and Canadian intelligence, as well as the CIA, in Montreal, the Canadian Research Board gave McGill University professor Donald O. Hebb a grant "to explore 'sensory isolation' as a means for 'intervention in the individual mind'" (McCoy 2012, 20). Through the use of paid volunteers, who were students at the university, Hebb learned that he could induce virtual psychosis in twenty-four to forty-eight hours just by depriving the subjects of sensory stimuli (McCoy 2012, 20).

Of course, the staff who ran the "dark cell" (To Abolish the Third Degree 1902, 23) at the Tombs in New York City in 1902 had already figured out that keeping prisoners in the dark without sound was usually sufficient to break them in a "few hours" (To Abolish the Third Degree 1902, 23), but Hebb helped the agency understand the physical and mental factors that typically caused this to happen.

Around the same time, researchers on the CIA payroll at Cornell University "found . . . that the KGB's most devasting torture technique involved not brutal beatings but simply enforced standing. When victims were forced to remain immobile for days at a time, legs swelled, skin sometimes erupted in suppurating lesions, and hallucinations began—all incredibly painful. This procedure became integral to the CIA's psychological paradigm and is now called 'stress positions'" (McCoy 2012, 20).

From then until 1962, the CIA would spend billions to "unlock the mysteries of the human mind, searching for methods that would make spies reveal their secrets, turn enemy agents into double agents, and persuade millions through a subtle psychological warfare" (McCoy 2012, 16).

As Professor Alfred W. McCoy, a historian specializing in Southeast Asia and the CIA, pointed out, the agency's work in this area may have been the first "advance" in the state of the torture art for four centuries.

> If we can attribute any genius to these discoveries, [then] the CIA's development of no-touch torture was the first real revolution in the cruel science of pain since the sixteenth century. Throughout two thousand years of Western judicial torture, the same problem had persisted—the strong defied pain, while the weak blurted out whatever was necessary to stop it. By contrast, the CIA's psychological paradigm fused two new methods, the sensory disorientation discovered by Hebb and the self-inflicted pain documented by Cornell researchers, in a combination that would, in theory, cause victims to feel responsible for their own suffering and feel subservient to their inquisitors. (McCoy 2012, 22)

The CIA codified its interrogation procedures in its 1963 *KUBARK Counterintelligence Interrogation Manual* (Central

Intelligence Agency 1963, C01297486), with KUBARK being the Agency's code name for itself (Hajjar 2012), and some of its conclusions make for fascinating, if disturbing, reading.

> It has been plausibly suggested that, whereas pain inflicted on a person from outside himself may actually focus or intensify his will to resist, his resistance is likelier to be sapped by pain which he seems to inflict upon himself. In the simple torture situation the contest is one between the individual and his tormentor (and he can frequently endure). (Central Intelligence Agency 1963, 94)

In contrast, when a detainee was forced into a stress position,

> An intervening factor is introduced. The immediate source of pain is not the interrogator but the victim himself. The motivational strength of the individual is likely to exhaust itself in this internal encounter. . . . As long as the subject remains standing, he is attributing to his captor the power to do something worse to him, but there is actually no showdown of the ability of the interrogator to do so. (Central Intelligence Agency 1963, 94)

On a deeper level, the Agency recognized the truth Beccaria had argued for over 200 years ago—that is, that physical torture is often counterproductive if one's goal is to elicit information.

> Interrogatees who are withholding but who feel qualms of guilt and a secret desire to yield are likely to become intractable if made to endure pain. The reason is that they can then interpret the pain as punishment and hence as expiation. There are also persons who enjoy pain and its anticipation and who will keep back information that they might otherwise divulge if they are given reason to expect that withholding will result in the punishment

that they want. Persons of considerable moral or intellectual stature often find in pain inflicted by others a confirmation of the belief that they are in the hands of
inferiors, and their resolve not to submit is strengthened.
Intense pain is quite likely to produce false confessions,
concocted as a means of escaping from distress. A time-
consuming delay results, while investigation is conducted
and the admissions are proven untrue. During this respite
the interrogatee can pull himself together. He may even
use the time to think up new, more complex "admissions"
that take still longer to disprove. (Central Intelligence
Agency 1963, 94)

The Agency discovered that *threats* to inflict pain or administer
narcotics to the detainee were often more effective in terms
of eliciting information than physically torturing prisoners
or actually giving them drugs (Central Intelligence Agency
1963, 98). That said, it did find that "drugs can be effective
in overcoming resistance not dissolved by other techniques. As
has already been noted, the so-called silent drug (a pharma-
cologically potent substance given to a person unaware of its
administration) can make possible the induction of hypnotic
trance in a previously unwilling subject" (Central Intelligence
Agency 1963, 99). Even when an Agency interrogator wasn't
using hypnosis, "the drug provides an excellent rationalization
of helplessness for the interrogatee who wants to yield but has
hitherto been unable to violate his own values or loyalties"
(Central Intelligence Agency 1963, 100).

   The manual concludes with the following five points (Central Intelligence Agency 1963, 103):

1. The principal coercive techniques are arrest, detention, the
    deprivation of sensory stimuli, threats and fear, debility,
    pain, heightened suggestibility and hypnosis, and drugs.
2. If a coercive technique is to be used, or if two or more
    are to be employed jointly, they should be chosen for their

effect upon the individual and carefully selected to match his personality.

3. The usual effect of coercion is regression. The interrogatee's mature defenses [crumble] as he becomes more childlike. During the process of regression the subject may experience feelings of guilt, and it is usually useful to intensify these.

4. When regression has proceeded far enough so that the subject's desire to yield begins to overbalance his resistance, the interrogator should supply a face-saving rationalization. Like the coercive technique, the rationalization must be carefully chosen to fit the subject's personality.

5. The pressures of duress should be slackened or lifted after compliance has been obtained so that the interrogatee's voluntary cooperation will not be impeded.

Perhaps the two most illuminating points about the *KUBARK Manual* are its implicit admission that the only difference between the CIA and Eastern Bloc interrogations is that the former usually does not try to "convert" the subject and its suggestion that Agency interrogators imitate their KGB counterparts in this area: "If the interrogatee remains semi-hostile or remorseful after a successful interrogation has ended, less time may be required to complete his conversion (and conceivably to create an enduring asset) than might be needed to deal with his antagonism if he is merely squeezed and forgotten" (Central Intelligence Agency 1963, 104).

In less than thirteen years, the CIA had gone from trying to teach its agents to withstand interrogation by the KGB and other hostile intelligence services to codifying and improving the KGB's techniques to create a more refined and effective CIA interrogation policy.

The difference? To the CIA, as to those who defended the methods used by the British in Ireland, so-called no-touch torture was not torture at all. In an era where reports about the use of torture frequently found their way into public discourse, by claiming torture which left no obvious marks was not actually torture, its proponents and perpetrators sought, and largely succeeded, in avoiding accountability for their actions (McCoy 2012, 23).

Banning Torture

After Amnesty International launched a campaign in 1972 to ban torture around the world, it ended up being banned from using UNESCO facilities in Paris as a meeting location because of AI's criticism of "more than sixty countries, from democracies to police states, that used torture systematically" (Peters 1985, 159–160). Even so, the 1970s offered some bright spots to those who wanted to make torture anachronistic again. In 1975, the UN General Assembly adopted the "Declaration of the Protection of All Persons from Being Subjected to Torture and Other Cruel, Inhuman or Degrading Treatment or Punishment" (Peters 1985, 142). An annex to the resolution further defined torture as "any act which by severe pain or suffering, whether physical or mental, is intentionally inflicted by or at the instigation of a public official on a person for such purposes as obtaining from him or a third person information or confession, punishing him for an act he has committed or is suspected of having committed, or intimidating him or other persons" (Peters 1985, 143).

Other than resolutions that deal with "the institutional framework and administrative and financial administration of the [United Nations]," most UN General Assembly resolutions "are recommendatory in nature and are thus not legally binding even on those Members that vote in favour of the resolutions or decisions in question" (United Nations 1994, 274–275). The 1975 Declaration was no exception to this rule, but it did signal the way the winds of international opinion were blowing, at least in the public statements of member governments.

A year later, the 1966 International Covenant on Civil and Political Rights, which banned torture and medical experimentation, came into force (Peters 1985, 143). As of May 2018, the Covenant has been ratified by 170 countries (including the United States and all members of the European Union) with another 6 having signed the Covenant but not ratified it and 21 others taking no action (United Nations, "Status of Ratification International Dashboard," Human Rights Office of the High Commissioner, http://indicators.ohchr.org/, accessed May 20, 2018).

Unlike the Declaration, the Covenant requires those countries that have ratified it to provide the Human Rights Committee with periodic reports as to their compliance with the Covenant's obligations, which are then made publicly available on the Committee's website. While any state can accuse another signatory state of violating the Covenant and have that allegation heard by the Committee, it can hear complaints from private citizens only if their country has signed and ratified the Optional Protocol. As of May 2018, 116 signatories to the Covenant have done so, but neither the United States nor the U.K. are among them, leaving their citizens with no private right to inform the Committee of violations of the Covenant committed in or by either country (United Nations, "Optional Protocol to the International Covenant on Civil and Political Rights," http://www.ohchr.org/EN/ProfessionalInterest/Pages/OPCCPR1.aspx).

South America

As the *détente* between the United States and the USSR of the 1970s gave way to the 1980s and the last act of competition and conflict of the Cold War, governmental views on torture swung between two extremes.

According to James Lemoyne's "Testifying to Torture" expose, which appeared in *The New York Times*,

> When the Reagan Administration came into office in 1981, ending the guerrilla war in El Salvador was high on its agenda. Honduras, an utterly impoverished country situated between El Salvador and Nicaragua, quickly became a key base for American efforts in the region. Administration officials vowed to cut off arms they said were being

sent from Nicaragua to the Salvadoran rebels. In fact, several weapons shipments from Nicaragua were intercepted in Honduras between 1980 and 1982. At the same time, the Reagan Administration was preparing to use Honduras to launch the contra guerrilla war against the Sandinistas.

By the beginning of 1981, according to American and Honduran officials, the C.I.A. had helped bring Argentine Army officers to Honduras to train the contras and Honduran intelligence units. The Argentines were led by Col. Osvaldo Ribeiro, who, a Honduran officer said, had learned and practiced secret murder during the "dirty war" in the mid-1970's, in which an estimated 12,000 or more Argentines "disappeared" in a state-directed campaign of elimination known in Central America as "the Argentine method." At the same time, according to American and Honduran officials, the C.I.A. pushed for the rapid rise of a Honduran Army colonel, Gustavo Alvarez Martinez. (Lemoyne 1988)

Martinez and his allies within the CIA and the Honduran government soon went to work.

In 1982, with strong American encouragement, Honduras's newly-elected civilian President, Roberto Suazo Cordova, promoted Alvarez to general and named him commander of the army. Even before his promotion, Alvarez was organizing a new army intelligence unit with C.I.A. support, which would be known as Battalion 316. Sgt. Florencio Caballero, who had already received American training, says he was among the first of those recruited to serve in the new unit.

"I was taken to Texas with 24 others for six months between 1979 and 1980," Mr. Caballero told me. . . . In Texas, said Mr. Caballero, the Americans "taught me interrogation, in order to end physical torture in Honduras. They taught us psychological methods—to study the fears and weaknesses of a prisoner. Make him stand up, don't let him sleep, keep him naked and isolated, put rats and cockroaches in his cell, give him bad food, serve him dead animals, throw cold water on him, change the temperature." (Lemoyne 1988)

As often happens when torture is employed, things quickly got out of hand. "'The Americans didn't accept physical torture, they didn't accept kidnapping—they said to arrest people using a judicial order,' Mr. Caballero said. 'But guerrillas don't wait there with a pen to sign a judicial order. Our commander ordered us to kill them. We hid people from the Americans, interrogated them, then gave them to a death squad to kill'" (Lemoyne 1988).

By the time he sat down with *The New York Times*, Caballero and his death squad had tortured and murdered nearly 120 people, including an American priest, Father James Carney, who had backed the guerillas (Lemoyne 1988), all with Washington's tacit approval.

According to Lemoyne "[s]ome American officials, as well as several Honduran military officers I talked to, expressed a frank willingness to use power to achieve political goals, even if people are killed. The elimination of suspected leftists in Honduras was perhaps unfortunate, they said. But they argued that it was limited in scope—and it 'worked.' The guerrilla networks were destroyed, they contended, and the Government was given a chance to improve its performance and win public support before new guerrillas gained a foothold" (Lemoyne 1988).

By the time Caballero's revelations came to light in 1988, the CIA had already switched gears on the issue. Four years earlier, the Agency told clients like the Honduran military that coercive methods of interrogation were now "deplored" and that "[e]xtreme deprivation of sensory stimuli induces unbearable stress and anxiety and is a form of torture" (McCoy 2012, 28–29).

Meanwhile, at the United Nations, diplomats were crafting yet another treaty against torture, though unlike most of its predecessors, this one would have considerable practical effects in the United States and elsewhere.

The Convention against Torture

On December 10, 1984, the General Assembly unanimously approved the Convention against Torture ("Yes, Declaim against Torture" 1984), which attempted to incorporate the provisions of the 1966 Covenant on Civil and Political Rights and the 1975 Declaration against torture while simultaneously closing loopholes exploited by those who wanted to publicly support a ban on torture while privately evading it.

First, while the Convention's definition of torture is similar to that articulated in the annex to the Declaration, it differs from it in one key respect. Under the Declaration and annex, an act did not qualify as torture unless it was "inflicted by or at the instigation of a public official" (Peters 1985, 143).

In contrast, under the Convention,

> the term "torture" means any act by which severe pain or suffering, whether physical or mental, is intentionally inflicted on a person for such purposes as obtaining from him or a third person information or a confession, punishing him for an act he or a third person has committed or is suspected of having committed, or intimidating or coercing him or a third person, or for any reason based on discrimination of any kind, *when such pain or suffering is inflicted by or at the instigation of or with the consent or acquiescence of a public official or other person acting in an official capacity.* (United Nations 1984; emphasis added)

This expanded the reach of the Convention to cover not only acts of torture committed by members of nongovernmental organizations (like death squads) but those by private citizens, so long as the acts of torture were encouraged or tolerated by the government.

Second, the Convention provided that "no exceptional circumstances whatsoever, whether a state of war or a threat of war, internal political instability or any other public emergency, may be invoked as a justification of torture" (United Nations 1984), an apparent attempt to avoid repeats of one of the U.K.'s defenses against Ireland before the European Court of Human Rights, where Britain had claimed conditions caused by the troubles in Northern Ireland justified its special measures because of "a public emergency threatening the life of the nation" (*Ireland v. United Kingdom*, Sec. 205–206).

While such conditions were not an excuse for torture under the European Convention on Human Rights either, in that case they may have provided cover for the Court to justify its finding that the British measures, although "inhuman and degrading" (Coogan 2002, 438), did not rise to the level of torture.

Third, the Convention against Torture banned signatory states from extraditing or returning persons to other countries "where there are substantial grounds for believing that [they] would be in danger of being subjected to torture" (United Nations 1984). This is a powerful weapon for immigration attorneys in the United States, as it can bar the government from expelling non-U.S. citizens who are otherwise ineligible to remain in the country.

Fourth, the Convention obligates states to criminalize torture if they have not already done so, thereby avoiding the problem faced by the post-military regime in Greece that lacked the statutory tools to hold the practitioners of *basanos* accountable.

Fifth, the Convention provides that states are obligated to initiate torture cases not only when the acts occur within their borders but also when they are committed on their ships and vessels or by their citizens and makes torture an extraditable offense.

As of May 2018, 163 countries have ratified the Convention, including all major world powers with the exception of

India (which has been an unratified signatory since 1997). It is not uncommon for there to be a long lag time between signing the Convention and ratifying it, as shown by the example of the United States, which joined the Convention in 1988 under President Ronald Reagan but didn't ratify until halfway through President Bill Clinton's first term in 1994.

U.S. Reaction to the Convention against Torture

When a country ratifies a treaty like the CAT, it can do so without reservations, in which case it is bound by the text of the document, or "with reservations," where it conditions its ratification on its interpretation of what certain terms in the document mean or how it interacts with its national law.

In America's case, its reservations to the CAT "narrowed the standard for psychological torture by requiring that 'prolonged mental harm' be caused by just four specific acts[:] '(1) the intentional infliction or threatened infliction of severe physical pain or suffering; (2) the administration or application, or threatened administration or application, of mind altering substances or other procedures calculated to disrupt profoundly the senses or the personality; (3) the threat of imminent death; or (4) the threat that other person will imminently be subjected to death, severe physical pain or suffering, or the administration . . . of mind altering substances'" (McCoy 2012, 31–32).

At a stroke, the United States had reduced the Convention's intended broad coverage of mental torture to a sliver and provided a road map for its interrogators to *continue* engaging in mental torture, so long as whatever they did could be described as something that didn't fit within the four categories of the reservation.

However, this seemed more of a theoretical than a practical problem at the time. After all, in the summer of 1996, the United States did something it had never attempted before: imposed criminal penalties under domestic law for "grave breaches" of the Geneva Conventions, which included—but were not limited to—torture.

The War Crimes Act of 1996

Given the congressional deadlock that became routine in the early twenty-first century, what may be the most remarkable thing about the War Crimes Act of 1996 is that it went from being introduced in the House by a Republican congressman to being signed into law by Democratic president in less than three months.

Although the United States had ratified the Geneva Conventions, until the Act, it had not passed any legislation to allow for the prosecution of those who violated it. As a result, there were interesting anomalies, such as the federal statute banning torture, which only applies to acts committed *outside* the United States.

After the Act became law, any member of the U.S. military or U.S. national who committed a "grave breach" of the Geneva Conventions (including torture) *anywhere* in the world "shall be fined under this title or imprisoned for life or any term of years, or both, and if death results to the victim, shall also be subject to the penalty of death" (War Crimes Act of 1996). Through a series of amendments passed between 1997 and 2006, Congress expanded the reach of the War Crimes Act to cover other breaches of international law, but the penalties remain the same.

Because of the Act, at least before 9/11, "U.S. intelligence has generally favored psychological methods that did not cross the line into the physical and thus the criminal" (McCoy 2012, 27). Unfortunately, the law was insufficient to stop federal officials from violating a key provision of the Convention against Torture.

From 1995 through the end of President Clinton's term in January 2001, the United States violated CAT's prohibition against rendition by transferring terror suspects to countries where they were likely to be tortured (McCoy 2012, 32).

During the Clinton era, "strict procedures governed the program. First, the receiving country had to have issued an arrest warrant for the person. Second, the administration scrutinized each rendition before senior government officials granted approval. Third, the CIA notified the local government, and obtained an assurance from the receiving government that it would not ill-treat the individual" (Weissbrodt and Bergquist 2006, 589).

Notwithstanding this, to some legal observers, "In most instances extraordinary rendition . . . constitutes a criminal conspiracy to commit torture in violation of the Torture Statute" (Weissbrodt and Bergquist 2006, 618). Eight months after Clinton left office, this pattern of CAT violations would seem almost quaint in retrospect.

9/11 and America's Response

In a cruel twist of irony, George W. Bush thought he was going to be the education president. When he declared at his inauguration on January 20, 2001, that "[t]ogether we will reclaim America's schools before ignorance and apathy claim more young lives" (Government Printing Office 2001), many observers were concerned that a presidency that had failed to win a popular vote—and which won the electoral college only through the intervention of the U.S. Supreme Court in *Bush v. Gore*—would step back from international commitments to focus on domestic issues instead.

Instead, around 8:14 A.M. on September 11, 2001, a team of al-Qaeda hijackers led by Mohamed Atta seized control of American Airlines Flight 11 (Kean and Hamilton 2004, 4). Just over thirty minutes later, Atta intentionally crashed the plane into the North Tower of the World Trade Center, instantly killing everyone on the flight (and many in the tower) (Kean and Hamilton 2004, 7).

In quick succession, other al-Qaeda teams took control of United Flight 175 (Kean and Hamilton 2004, 7), American Airlines Flight 77 (Kean and Hamilton 2004, 8), and United

Flight 93 (Kean and Hamilton 2004, 11). Shortly thereafter, the hijackers plunged United Flight 175 into the South Tower of the World Trade Center (Kean and Hamilton 2004, 8) and American Airlines Flight 77 into the Pentagon (Kean and Hamilton 2004 10). Only a successful uprising by the doomed (and unarmed) passengers on United Flight 93 prevented al-Qaeda from plunging the plane into their intended target, which many believed was either the White House or the U.S. Capitol building (Kean and Hamilton 2004, 13–14).

Before the clock struck twelve on the East Coast that day, 2,996 people (including the hijackers) were dead and over 6,000 injured (Plumer 2013). In less than four hours, Atta and al-Qaeda had carried out the deadliest domestic terrorist attack in American history, toppled the iconic towers of the World Trade Center, and severely damaged the Pentagon.

While the public didn't know it at the time, there was another victim that day. America's commitment to end the use of torture by its public servants, lukewarm at the best of times, finally burned to ashes for almost a decade.

Appropriately for the man who wanted to be the education president, Bush was told the second plane had hit the World Trade Center while he was literally reading "The Pet Goat" to a group of first graders in Emma E. Booker Elementary School in Sarasota County, Florida (Glass 2015). Later that evening, however, there was nothing juvenile about his response.

"The pictures of airplanes flying into buildings, fires burning, huge structures collapsing have filled us with disbelief, terrible sadness, and a quiet, unyielding anger," he told millions of Americans on a televised address. "The search is underway for those who are behind these evil acts" (Bush 2001).

The president didn't wait long to put his anger into action. On September 17, 2001, Bush gave the CIA power to detain suspected terrorists for extended periods at sites outside of the United States (Peralta 2014). Within two months, "CIA officers had begun researching potential legal defenses for using interrogation techniques that were considered torture by foreign governments and a non-governmental organization" (U.S. Congress 2012 19). Among others, these included what Dershowitz would later term the "ticking time bomb" scenario, where the "CIA could argue that the torture was necessary to prevent imminent, significant, physical harm to persons, where there is no other available means to prevent the harm" (U.S. Congress 2012, 19). Alas, for the Agency, for Dershowitz, and for those who agreed with them, nothing in the CAT allows for the suspension of its provisions no matter what the circumstances may be, but no one seemed to have been concerned about this detail.

The Agency was returning to the days of Project Artichoke and the *KUBARK Counterintelligence Interrogation Manual*, despite having decided in the late 1980s that "[p]hysical abuse or other degrading treatment was rejected not only because it is wrong, but because it has historically proven to be ineffective" (U.S. Congress 2012, 18).

Still, the CIA weren't the only ones who wanted to ignore America's treaty obligations. In the aftermath of the quick collapse of the Taliban regime in Afghanistan, which had given sanctuary to al-Qaeda founder Osama bin Laden, the United States had to decide what to do with Taliban and al-Qaeda prisoners and whether to treat them as prisoners of war.

In a January 2002 memo, Department of Justice attorney John Yoo argued that the Geneva Conventions didn't apply to either al-Qaeda (because they were a "violent political or organization and not a nation state" [Yoo 2002, 1]) or the Taliban (because "Afghanistan was not—even prior to the beginning of the present conflict—a functioning State" [Yoo 2002, 2]). Accordingly, in Yoo's mind, so long as the American soldiers didn't torture their Taliban or al-Qaeda prisoners or force them into military service, they could escape criminal liability under the War Crimes Act (Yoo 2002, 6).

Bush reportedly agreed with Yoo but faced strong opposition from Secretary of State Colin Powell and the State Department to any suspension of the Geneva Convention protections for al-Qaeda and Taliban prisoners (*The New York Times*, https://archive.nytimes.com/www.nytimes.com/ref/in ternational/24MEMO-GUIDE.html, accessed May 26, 2018).

Later that month, White House Counsel Alberto Gonzales adopted Yoo's reasoning in his own memo to Bush, particularly the section on avoiding criminal prosecution under the Act by arguing the Geneva Conventions didn't apply (Gonzales 2002, 2).

On February 7, 2002, Bush took the step he had been inching toward since the Twin Towers fell, declaring that none of the provisions of the Geneva Conventions applied to al-Qaeda prisoners and that common Article III of the Geneva Convention (which bars torture) didn't apply to either Taliban or al-Qaeda detainees but that he ordered they be treated "humanely" (Bush 2002).

The CIA could read between the lines. A month later, they had their first test subject under the new interrogation regime after Pakistan captured Abu Zubaydah and turned him over to American custody (U.S. Congress 2012, 21).

At the time, the Agency thought Zubaydah was a senior official in al-Qaeda (U.S. Congress 2012, 21, f. 60) and that the Khalden training camp he allegedly administered in Afghanistan was also controlled by the group (U.S. Congress 2012, 21, f. 60).

On its editorial page, *The New York Times* called Zubaydah "the head of operations for Al Qaeda and a chief of recruitment and terror training for the group" who "likely has a map in his head of sleeper cells and terrorist operations around the world" ("A Master Terrorist Is Nabbed" 2002, A14).

FBI agents were the first to interrogate Zubaydah using noncoercive tactics. Although they obtained critical pieces of intelligence, including the role of Khalid Shaikh Mohammed in the planning of the 9/11 attacks, at the behest of the CIA's leadership, they were replaced by Agency interrogators, who waterboarded Zubaydah eighty-three times without securing any comparable successes (McCoy 2012, 36–37).

The Agency also came close to killing him on several occasions. "The waterboarding technique was physically harmful, inducing convulsions and vomiting. Abu Zubaydah . . . became 'completely unresponsive, with bubbles rising through his open, full mouth'" (U.S. Congress 2012, 3). This is less surprising once one realizes that the Agency had "'enhanced' the practice of waterboarding by creating 'a special gurney with the perfect angle to flood the lungs with water, using saline solution to avoid death by 'hyponatremia' from excessive ingestion of water, necessary since agency interrogators were allowed three 'applications' [of waterboarding on prisoners] per hour'" (McCoy 2012, 39). Furthermore, "Detainees were also fed special liquid diets to prevent suffocation during vomiting induced by waterboarding. Interrogators were encouraged, in the pursuit of technical perfection, to record their torture sessions in log books" (McCoy 2012, 39). Other tactics included "walling," which—like it sounds—involved "slamming detainees against a wall" (U.S. Congress 2012, 3) and a combination of sleep deprivation and placing Zubaydah in a stress position, where he was kept "awake for up to 180 hours, usually standing" sometimes with his wrists "shackled above [his] head" (U.S. Congress 2012, 3).

After this torture proved fruitless, the FBI resumed its interrogation of Zubaydah and through the use of noncoercive means learned "important intelligence that 'included the details of Jose Padilla, the so-called "dirty bomber." But then . . . [the] CIA team took control once more, moving to 'the next stage in the force continuum' by placing Aby Zubaydah 'in a confinement box.' Convinced that the CIA's methods were becoming 'borderline torture,' [the FBI interrogator] filed a protest with his FBI Director Robert Mueller, and 'was pulled out'" (McCoy 2012, 36–37).

Zubaydah would spend the next four years being transferred between CIA black sites in Thailand (where he lost an eye because of CIA torture [Pilkington 2017]), Poland, Lithuania, Afghanistan and elsewhere (Black and Raphael 2015), before being finally transferred to U.S. military custody at Guantanamo Bay, Cuba, on December 5, 2006 (The Rendition Project). Later, Zubaydah said, "I was told during this period that I was one of the first to receive these interrogation techniques, so no rules applied. It felt like they were experimenting and trying out techniques to be used later on other people" (Bikundo 2016, 114).

As the U.S. Senate Select Committee on Intelligence would discover a decade later, Zubaydah's reported importance and involvement with al-Qaeda were both "significantly overstated" (U.S. Congress 2012, *y*, 21).

During his detainee review in 2007 at Guantanamo Bay, Zubaydah asserted that the truth was far more nuanced, testifying that he had only handled logistics—in Pakistan—to get recruits to and from the insurgent training camp at Khalden (which was on such bad terms with al-Qaeda that the Taliban closed it as a favor to the group), that he supported "defensive," rather than "offensive" jihad, and that he had opposed attacks on "innocent civilians" like those at the World Trade Center (Verbatim Transcript 2007, 8–11).

On February 12, 2014, in a response to a Freedom of Information Act request by investigative reporter Jason Leopold, the U.S. Department of Defense confirmed that Zubaydah was part of a group of seventy-one Guantanamo detainees who were eligible for Periodic Review Board appearances to determine if they could be released (Jacobsmeyer 2014). Later that year, the European Court of Human Rights (ECHR) ordered the Polish government to pay Zubaydah $135,000 in damages for assisting the CIA in violation of Article Three of the European Convention on Human Rights, which prohibits torture (British Broadcasting Corporation 2014). On May 31, 2018, the ECHR found Lithuania and Romania complicit in Zubaydah's torture because both countries hosted CIA black sites on their soil and ordered each to pay him $117,000 in damages (British Broadcasting Corporation 2018). As of mid-2018, Zubaydah remains in custody at Guantanamo Bay, with neither a trial nor a release date on his horizon.

On August 1, 2002, the Bush administration crossed a second line. Previously, the CIA had been concerned how it could justify tactics like waterboarding if its personnel were ever held to account under 18 U.S.C. 2340, which bans torture by Americans outside the United States. Assistant Attorney General Jay Bybee set their collective minds at ease by arguing that the law and the Convention against Torture (1) only applied to "extreme" breaches of the Convention and (2) even if such an "extreme" breach took place, prosecution "may be barred because enforcement of the statute would represent an unconstitutional infringement of the President's authority to conduct war" (Bybee 2002).

The memo removed whatever restraints remained on the CIA's interrogators. In November 2002, al-Qaeda operative Abd al-Rahim al-Nashiri, who allegedly organized the attack on the U.S.S. *Cole* in 2000, was captured in the United Arab Emirates and turned over to the United States (Department of Defense 2006, 3–6). He was "subjected to the CIA's enhanced interrogation techniques during at least four separate periods" (U.S. Cogress 2012, 67), which included "total light deprivation, loud continuous music, isolation, and dietary manipulation" (U.S. Congress 2012, 67, f. 338) as well as waterboarding (*The New York Times*, https://www.nytimes.com/interactive/projects/guantanamo/detainees/10015-abd-al-rahim-al-nashiri, accessed May 27, 2018). Not satisfied with the results they were getting from al-Nashiri, his interrogators decided to get creative and use techniques that hadn't been approved by the Agency.

According to the Senate Select Committee on Intelligence's report, "[CIA Officer 2] placed al-Nashiri in a 'standing stress position' with 'his hands affixed over his head' for approximately two-and-a-half days. Later, during the course of al-Nashiri's debriefings, while he was blindfolded, [CIA Officer 2] placed a pistol near al-Nashiri's head and operated a cordless drill near al-Nashiri's body" (U.S. Congress 2012, y, 69).

Later on, "The Office of Inspector General later described additional allegations of unauthorized techniques used against al-Nashiri by [CIA Officer 2] and other interrogators, including slapping al-Nashiri multiple times on the back of the head during interrogations, implying that his mother would be brought before him and sexually abused; blowing cigar smoke in al-Nashiri's face; giving al-Nashiri a forced bath using a stiff brush; and using improvised stress positions that caused cuts and bruises resulting in the intervention of a medical officer, who was concerned that al-Nashiri's shoulders would be dislocated using the stress positions" (U.S. Congress 2012, y, 70).

On July 25, 2014, the ECHR ruled that Poland had been complicit in the CIA's torture of al-Nashiri because of the black site on its soil and ordered Poland to pay him $135,000 in damages (British Broadcasting Corporation 2014). Four years later, it issued a similar ruling against Romania and Lithuania, ordering those countries to pay al-Nashiri $117,000 for his injuries (British Broadcasting Corporation 2018).

In some ways, al-Nashiri was lucky. In November 2002, Gul Rahman died while in CIA custody, probably from hypothermia, after a CIA interrogator manacled him to the wall and forced him to sit on a cold concrete floor while wearing only a sweatshirt (U.S. Congress 2012, y, 54). Similarly, after the CIA took custody of Khalid Sheikh Mohammed (deemed the "principal architect of the 9/11 attacks" by the 9/11 Commission (Kean and Hamilton 2004, 145), he was reportedly waterboarded 183 times in March 2003 alone (McCoy 2012, 42).

Like Zubaydah and Khalid Sheikh Mohammed, al-Nashiri was transferred to and interrogated at multiple CIA black sites until being turned over to military custody at Guantanamo Bay on September 4, 2006 (Department of Defense 2006, 6). His case is pending before a Military Commission at Guantanamo that could impose the death penalty if he is found guilty, but his trial has been delayed for years, most recently on February 16, 2018, when it was suspending following revelations that the government may have been illegally monitoring al-Nashiri's communications with his lawyers (Jindia 2018).

Abu Ghraib

Following the American invasion of Iraq in 2003 and the collapse of President Saddam Hussein's Baath Party government, the U.S. Army took over one of Saddam's most notorious prisons, Abu Ghraib, located about twenty miles west of Baghdad. It didn't take long for the U.S. Army and the CIA to write their own dark chapter in the facility's history.

On April 18, 2004, CBS News reported that prisoners in U.S. custody at the facility were being tortured on a massive scale (Peters 1985, 16), with photographic evidence to prove it. Among other things, it later came out that CIA interrogators appeared to have killed Iraqi insurgent Manadel al-Jamadi by putting him in a stress position during interrogation, despite the five broken ribs he had suffered during his earlier capture by Navy SEALs (McChesney 2005). Worse, one American soldier posed in front of al-Jamadi's body while giving a "thumbs up" sign (McChesney 2005).

Ultimately, nine enlisted soldiers—most famously, Pfc. Lynndie England, who had been photographed next to naked prisoners—were court-martialed for their roles in the abuse (Salon Staff 2006). A 2008 report from members of the Senate Armed Services Committee declared that former secretary of defense Donald Rumsfeld bore ultimate responsibility for the abuses, a conclusion Rumsfeld rejected (Scott and Mazzetti 2008, A14).

Just over a year after the Abu Ghraib scandal broke, *The Washington Post* exposed the CIA's secret prison network (Priest 2005). A few days later, CIA National Clandestine

Service Director Jose Rodriguez ordered "the destruction of videotapes depicting the use of the CIA's coercive interrogation techniques, including waterboarding, against Abu Zubaydah and al-Nashiri from 2002" (Berenson 2014).

While newspapers investigated, and the CIA destroyed evidence, Congress was also acting. On December 30, 2005, it passed the Detainee Treatment Act of 2005 (DTA), which barred the military from using interrogation techniques "not authorized by and listed in the Army Field Manual on Intelligence Interrogation." The DTA also provided that "no individual in the custody or physical control of the United States Government . . . shall be subject to cruel, inhuman, or degrading treatment or punishment" (Detainee Treatment Act 2005), which was further defined as actions "prohibited by the Fifth, Eighth and Fourteenth Amendments to the Constitution of the United States, as defined by the United States Reservations, Declarations and Understandings to the United Nations Convention against Torture" (Detainee Treatment Act 2005).

In one of history's great ironies, the efforts of Bush's legal team to claim that neither the War Crimes Act of 1996 nor the Convention against Torture applied to what the CIA and the military were doing to detainees had spurred Congress to codify the Convention's provisions, albeit without penalties for violators. Still, the administration thought it could take comfort in the fact that the DTA at least limited the ability of federal courts to hear petitions for habeas corpus (which would allow a civilian court to order the release of a detainee) from prisoners at Guantanamo Bay.

Six months later, on June 29, 2006, the U.S. Supreme Court not only dashed that hope (at least for the current case) but also held in *Hamdan v. Rumsfeld* that Bush's military commissions were unconstitutional and violated the Geneva Conventions, including Article Three's provisions against torture, which *applied* to all suspected terrorists in American military custody, thereby eviscerating Yoo's and Bybee's previous advice to the contrary.

The onetime education president could read the writing on the wall. On September 7, 2006, Bush admitted the existence of the CIA's secret prisons, called on Congress to establish military commissions to try the prisoners, and acknowledged the Geneva Conventions *did* apply to them. He also stated all detainees had now been transferred to Guantanamo and noted that while the CIA had used "alternative" means of interrogation, "the US does not torture. I have not authorized it and I will not" (British Broadcasting Corporation 2006).

Of course, the problem for Bush was that neither of those statements was true. It was his executive orders and the black sites set up with his knowledge and approval that set the stage for the tortures inflicted around the world on persons held in military or CIA custody.

In any case, Congress responded to *Hamdan* and Bush's request by passing the Military Commissions Act (MCA) of 2006 that October, which repeated Bush's earlier attempt to restrict habeas relief for detainees and—strangely enough, given Bush's statements and the law's claim that the military commissions qualified as a "regularly constituted court" under Article 3 of the Geneva Conventions (Military Commissions Act 2006)—also provided that "no alien unlawful enemy combatant subject to trial by military commission under this chapter may invoke the Geneva Conventions as a source of rights" (Military Commissions Act 2006).

On July 20, 2007, Bush issued Executive Order 13440, where he defined "cruel, inhuman, or degrading treatment or punishment" as acts "prohibited by the Fifth, Eighth, and Fourteenth Amendments to the Constitution of the United States" (Bush 2007, Sec. 2(c)) (though not the CAT) and certified that the CIA's new techniques were in compliance with the Geneva Conventions and did not constitute torture (Bush 2007, Sec. 3).

In the end, it didn't matter. Since the MCA repeated Bush's earlier attempt to restrict access to habeas relief for detainees, the U.S. Supreme Court struck down the jurisdiction-stripping provisions of the law in *Boumediene v. Bush* in June 2008. Seven months later, the United States had a new president who—on his second full day in office—revoked Executive Order 13440 and the CIA's detention powers, ordered the agency to close any remaining prisons, and restricted the Agency to using the interrogation techniques in the Army Field Manual (Obama 2009a).

The Obama Administration

From the first moments of his presidency, Barack Obama promised major changes in the way the United States treated detainees. No one who watched his inaugural address on January 20, 2009, can forget the moment, about halfway through the speech, when he declared, "As for our common defense, we reject as false the choice between our safety and our ideals" (Phillips 2009), let alone the tortured look on Bush's face when Obama followed up with, "Our Founding Fathers, faced with perils that we can scarcely imagine, drafted a charter to assure the rule of law and the rights of man—a charter expanded by the blood of generations. Those ideals still light the world, and we will not give them up for expedience sake" (Phillips 2009).

Besides revoking Bush's Executive Order 13440, Obama ordered the closure of the Guantanamo Bay prison "as soon as practicable, and no later than 1 year from the date of this order" (Obama 2009b), or January 22, 2010. As for the remaining detainees, they were to be "returned to their home country, released, transferred to a third country, or transferred to another United States detention facility in a manner consistent with law and the national security and foreign policy interests of the United States" (Obama 2009b).

For a variety of reasons, ranging from resistance from Congress and the military, a reluctance of some countries to accept former prisoners and his administration's preoccupation with other issues, it never happened (Bruck 2016). Guantanamo

Bay remained in operation on Obama's last day in office in 2017, with his successor not only declining to close it, but being on record promising to "load it up with some bad dudes" (Bruck 2016).

Obama not only failed to close the Guantanamo Bay detention facility but also failed to hold any of those who had carried out acts of torture under Bush's presidency accountable. In June 2011, Attorney General Eric Holder announced that his office had investigated about one hundred cases of detainee mistreatment and had declined to bring charges against their captors in any of them ("No Penalty for Torture" 2012). In the late summer of 2012, Holder announced that he would not prosecute anyone for the deaths of Rahman in Afghanistan and al-Jamadi in Iraq while both were in American custody ("No Penalty for Torture" 2012). Meanwhile, the Obama administration, like the Bush and Clinton administrations that preceded it, continued to violate the Convention against Torture by engaging in extraordinary rendition of prisoners (McCoy 2012, 47).

In fairness, Obama was at heart a technocratic centrist, rather than the liberal both his admirers and detractors wanted him to be. His administration set a record for the use of the Espionage Act to prosecute both leakers and those journalists who published what the leakers disclosed to them (Gomez 2017), including Chelsea Manning, whose treatment while in military detention illustrated how the tolerance of torture during the Bush years had infected soldiers in the United States.

Chelsea Manning and WikiLeaks

On October 22, 2010, WikiLeaks, a website dedicated to the dissemination of leaked government documents, released 391,832 "Significant Action" reports prepared by U.S. Army personnel during the Iraq War from 2004 through 2009 (WikiLeaks 2010). According to WikiLeaks founder Julian Assange, the documents provided "compelling evidence of war crimes" (Pitzke 2010), including the intentional slaughter of surrendering insurgents by a U.S. Army Apache helicopter (Baram 2010) and "303 allegations of abuse by coalition forces . . . after 2004" (Baram 2010), that is, after the Abu Ghraib torture scandal had come to light. A spokesman for an enraged Pentagon declared, "This security breach could very well get our troops and those they are fighting with killed" (Thompson 2010).

Manning had been Assange's source (Alexander 2017). She obtained the documents while serving as an intelligence analyst in Iraq as an enlisted soldier with the U.S. Army (Alexander 2017).

Arrested on May 29, 2010, she was transferred to the U.S. Marine base at Quantico, Virginia, in July 2010, where she was held "in conditions that aroused widespread condemnation, including being held in solitary confinement for 23 hours a day and being made to strip naked at night" (Pilkington 2012). In February 2012, the U.N. Special Rapporteur on Torture formally informed the United States that such conditions, particularly the solitary confinement aspect, could "amount to a breach of article 7 of the International Covenant on Civil and Political Rights, and to an act defined in article 1 or article 16 of the Convention against Torture" (Mendez 2012). Indeed, when Manning was finally brought to trial in 2013, the military judge hearing the case awarded her an additional 112 days of custody credit because of the abuse she had suffered at Quantico (Tate 2013).

Manning was ultimately acquitted of the most serious charge against her—that of "aiding the enemy"—but convicted of seventeen other violations in July 2013, in a verdict condemned by human rights groups around the world (Pilkington 2013). Originally sentenced to thirty-five years in prison (Tate 2013) in August 2013, years of advocacy by her supporters ultimately persuaded Obama to commute her sentence on January 17, 2017, just before he left office (Pilkington et al. 2017). She was released on May 17, 2017.

Manning has worked as an activist for digital privacy after she was freed. At one of her first public speaking appearances after her release at the Aaron Swartz Day commemoration in San Francisco at the Internet Archive's headquarters, she told the audience, "I think it's really important to remember, especially at a time like this, that institutions which matter, and which make decisions about us . . . can, and regularly do, fail. Whenever systems fail, you do have power" (DiEdoardo 2017, 9).

Swartz was a legendary computer hacker and developer who is credited with helping to create the online community Reddit, among other endeavors (Gustin 2013). In 2011, the U.S. government accused him of wire fraud and violating the Computer Fraud and Abuse Act after Swartz connected a computer to MIT's network to automatically download academic journal articles using a login credential he legitimately possessed. Facing the potential of decades behind bars, Swartz killed himself in 2013 (Gustin 2013). His life and work, as well as that of those who were inspired by him, have been celebrated at the "Aaron Swatrz Day" hackathon in San Francisco every year since his death.

On March 8, 2019, U.S. District Judge Claude Hilton had Manning arrested after she refused to testify before a federal grand jury believed to be investigating WikiLeaks (British Broadcasting Corporation 2019). Manning told the court she had already disclosed all she knows about WikiLeaks during her 2013 court martial (British Broadcasting Corporation 2019). In a prepared statement, Manning said, "I will not participate in a secret process that I morally object to, particularly one that has been historically used to entrap and persecute activists for protected political speech" (Manning 2019). On May 9, 2019, Manning was released from custody after the term of the grand jury for which she was subpoenaed expired (Cameron 2019). However, the United States quickly subpoenaed her for a successor grand jury.

On May 16, 2019, after she repeated her refusal to testify, U.S. District Judge Anthony Trenga returned her to custody on contempt charges and fined her $500 for every day she was in custody up to thirty days—and $1,000 a day for every day she spent in custody defying the order to testify after that. As of November 2019, she remained in custody based on her refusal to testify.

The Future of Torture

Although Donald Trump promised to "bring back waterboarding, and . . . bring back a hell of a lot worse than waterboarding" (Bruck 2016) as a candidate, as of May 2018, he has done far less since assuming power in this area than might have been expected, at least on the surface. In January 2018, he issued an executive order (Trump 2018) that revoked that part of Obama's Executive Order 13492 that called for the closure of Guantanamo Bay by 2010, though this provision had arguably lapsed long before. Even so, it's notable that Trump's Executive Order 13823 provides that "detention operations at U.S. Naval Station Guantánamo Bay shall continue to be conducted consistent with all applicable United States and international law, including the Detainee Treatment Act of 2005" (Trump 2018), which would include by reference the Convention against Torture.

On the other hand, Trump may be uncharacteristically playing a long game. During his first two years in power, he managed to place Neil Gorsuch—who helped defend Bush's interrogation policies while at the Office of Legal Counsel (Williams 2017)—on the U.S. Supreme Court (Gordon 2017) and install torture supporter (Osborne 2017) Mike Pompeo first as CIA director and then as secretary of state (McCaskill 2018). He even managed to get the Senate to confirm Gina Haspel, who not only ran the CIA's black site in Thailand but drafted the cable Rodriguez sent to destroy videotapes of waterboarding and other interrogations, as CIA director (Taddonio 2018).

Furthermore, Trump arguably expanded the use of torture into new domestic arenas with his "family separation" policy, which attempted to deter undocumented immigration by stripping children from their families and holding them in different immigration detention facilities (Stuart 2019).

These facilities are anything but safe, especially for members of vulnerable groups. According to a 2018 report from the Center for American Progress, LGBTQ immigrants were 97 percent more likely to be sexually assaulted while in Immigration and Customs Enforcement (ICE) custody than straight immigrants (Moreau 2018). Worse, at least twenty-two immigrants have died in ICE custody since 2017 (Seville et al. 2019), including Roxana Hernandez, a transgender woman from Honduras who sought asylum in the United States as part of a caravan (Seville et al. 2019).

In an eerie parallel to the treatment handed out to Gul Rahman, Hernandez died after being confined for five days in a freezing cell (Green 2018). According to an independent autopsy ordered by the Transgender Law Center, "before [Hernandez] died, she was beaten by 'a baton or similar object while she was restrained by handcuffs'" (Lawler 2018). To a casual observer, it might seem ironic that practices that Bush exported to CIA black sites around the world had found their way back to the United States under Trump, but a student of the field knows history teaches one lesson when it comes to torture: tolerance of torture ensures its expansion. Several thousand years after Aristotle declaimed about the uses of *basanos*, torture remains with us, despite the best efforts of diplomats, lawyers, judges, and politicians.

References

Alexander, Harriet. "Who Is Chelsea Manning and Why Is She Being Released from Prison?" *Telegraph*, May 17, 2017, https://www.telegraph.co.uk/news/2017/05/17/chelsea-manning-released-prison/ (accessed May 28, 2018).

Amnesty International. *Torture in Greece: The First Torturers' Trial 1975* (London: Amnesty International Publications, 1977).

Baram, Marcus. "WikiLeaks' Iraq War Logs: U.S. Troops Abused Prisoners for Years after Abu Ghraib," *Huffington Post*, October 22, 2010, https://www.huffingtonpost.com/2010/10/22/wikileaks-iraq-war-logs-i_n_772658.html (accessed May 28, 2018).

Beccaria, Cesare, and Edward D. Ingraham (Trans.). *An Essay on Crimes and Punishments* (Philadelphia: Philip H. Nicklin, 1819).

Behr, Edward. *Anyone Here Been Raped & Speaks English? A Foreign Correspondent's Life Behind the Lines* (London: Hodder & Stoughton, 1986).

Berenson, Tessa. "A Timeline of the Interrogation Program," *Time*, December 9, 2014, http://time.com/3625181/senate-torture-report-timeline/ (accessed May 28, 2018).

Bikundo, Edwin. *International Criminal Law: Using or Abusing Legality* (Abingdon: Routledge, 2016).

Black, Crofton, and Sam Raphael. "Revealed: The Boom and Bust of the CIA's Secret Torture Sites," *The Bureau of Investigative Journalism*, October 14, 2015, https://www.thebureauinvestigates.com/stories/2015-10-14/revealed-the-boom-and-bust-of-the-cias-secret-torture-sites (accessed May 27, 2018).

Boyd, Nan Alamilla. *Wide Open Town: A History of Queer San Francisco to 1965* (University of California Press, Berkeley, 2003).

Brands, H. W. *T.R.: The Last Romantic* (New York: Basic Books, 1997).

British Broadcasting Corporation. "Bush Admits to CIA Secret Prisons," September 7, 2006, http://news.bbc.co.uk/2/hi/5321606.stm (accessed May 28, 2018).

British Broadcasting Corporation. "Poland 'Helped in CIA Rendition,' European Court Rules," July 24, 2014, http://www.bbc.com/news/world-europe-28460628 (accessed May 27, 2018).

British Broadcasting Corporation. "Lithuania and Romania Complicit in CIA Torture—European Court," May 31, 2018, http://www.bbc.com/news/world-europe-44313905 (accessed May 31, 2018).

British Broadcasting Corporation. "Chelsea Manning: Wikileaks Source Jailed for Refusing to Testify," March 8, 2019, https://www.bbc.com/news/world-us-canada-47501 763 (accessed March 10, 2019).

Bruck, Connie. "Why Obama Has Failed to Close Guantánamo," *The New Yorker*, August 1, 2016, https://www.newyorker.com/magazine/2016/08/01/why-obama-has-failed-to-close-guantanamo (accessed May 28, 2018).

Bush, George W. "Inaugural Address," January 20, 2001, http://www.presidency.ucsb.edu/ws/?pid=25853 (accessed May 25, 2018).

Bush, George W. "Humane Treatment of al Queda and Taliban Detainees" (The White House, 2002).

Bush, George W. "Interpretation of the Geneva Conventions Common Article 3 as Applied to a Program of Detention and Interrogation Operated by the Central Intelligence Agency," EO 13440, Sec. 2 (c), July 20, 2007.

Bybee, Jay. "Memorandum for Alberto R. Gonzalez, Counsel to the President" (United States Department of Justice, Office of Legal Counsel, August 1, 2002).

Cahill, Carmen. *Bad Faith: A Forgotten History of Family, Fatherland and Vichy France* (New York: Alfred A. Knopf, 2006).

Cameron, Dell. "Chelsea Manning Has Been Released from Jail," *Gizmodo*, May 9, 2019, https://gizmodo.com/chelsea-manning-has-been-released-from-jail-1834656732 (accessed May 9, 2019).

Central Intelligence Agency. Information Report, CD No. 50X1-HUM, Dec. 51, CIA-RDP80–00926A004400 050027; Declassified in Part, Sanitized Copy Approved for Release January 22, 2013. https://www.cia.gov/library/ readingroom/docs/CIA-RDP80-00926A004400050027-1 .pdf (accessed November 3, 2019)

Central Intelligence Agency. "Communist Control Techniques: An Analysis of the Methods Used by Communist State Police in the Arrest, Interrogation and Indoctrination of Persons Regarded as 'Enemies of the State,'" 25X1A8a, April 2, 1956, SECRET, Approved for Release September 26, 2000.

Central Intelligence Agency. "Kubark Counterintelligence Interrogation," C01297486, July 1963, Secret, Approved for Release February 25, 2014 (copy in author's possession).

Coogan, Tim Pat. *The IRA* (London: Palgrave, 2002).

Czitrom, Daniel. *New York Exposed: The Gilded Age Scandal That Launched the Progressive Era* (Oxford University Press, 2016).

Dershowitz, Alan. "The Case for Torture Warrants," The Great Debate, 2011, http://blogs.reuters.com/great-debate/ 2011/09/07/the-case-for-torture-warrants/ (accessed April 21, 2018).

Detainee Treatment Act of 2005, Pub. Law 109-148, 119 Stat. 2739 (109th Cong).

DiEdoardo, Christina Ann Marie. *Lanza's Mob: The Mafia and San Francisco* (Santa Barbara, CA: ABC-CLIO, 2016).

DiEdoardo, Christina A. "Resist: 'We Got This.'" Bay Area Reporter, November 16, 2017, p. 22.

Encyclopedia Britannica, 14th Ed. (London: The Encyclopedia Britannica Co., 1929).

European Court of Human Rights (ECHR). *Case of Ireland v. the United Kingdom.* Judgement of 18 January 1978 (N° 91).

Flanders, Judith. *The Invention of Murder: How the Victorians Reveled in Death and Detection and Created Modern Crime* (New York: St. Martin's Press, 2011).

Gagarin, Michael. "The Torture of Slaves in Athenian Law." *Classical Philology* 91 (1): 1–18 (1996).

Ginger, Henry. "Greece, Facing Expulsion, Quits Council of Europe," *The New York Times*, December 13, 1969, p. 1.

Glass, Andrew. "Bush Reads 'The Pet Goat' to Schoolchildren, Sept. 11, 2001," *Politico*, September 11, 2015, https://www.politico.com/story/2015/09/bush-reads-the-pet-goat-to-schoolchildren-sept-11-2001-213544 (accessed May 26, 2018).

Gomez, Luis. "Before Trump's Crackdown on Leaks, Obama Went after 10 Leakers, Journalists," *San Diego Union-Tribune*, August 4, 2017, http://www.sandiegouniontribune.com/opinion/the-conversation/sd-before-trump-obama-prosecuted-leaks-20170804-htmlstory.html (accessed May 28, 2018).

Gonzales, Alberto R. "Decision re Application of the Geneva Convention on Prisoners of War to the Conflict with Al Queda and the Taliban," January 25, 2002.

Gordon, Rebecca. "Donald Trump Has a Passionate Desire to Bring Back Torture," *The Nation*, April 6, 2017, https://www.thenation.com/article/donald-trump-has-a-passionate-desire-to-bring-back-torture/ (accessed May 28, 2018).

Government Printing Office. *Public Papers of the Presidents of the United States: George W. Bush* (2001, Book II) (September 11, 2001).

Granhag, Pär Anders, Steven Kleinman, and Simon Oleszkuewicz. "The Scharff Technique: On How to Effectively Elicit Intelligence from Human Sources." *International Journal of Intelligence and CounterIntelligence* 29 (1): 135 (January 2016).

Green, Carla. "Transgender Honduran Woman's Death in US 'Ice Box' Detention Prompts Outcry," *The Guardian*, May 31, 2018, https://www.theguardian.com/us-news/2018/may/31/roxana-hernandez-transgender-honduran-woman-dies-us-ice-box (accessed March 11, 2019).

"The Guantanamo Docket: Abd al Rahim al Nashiri," *The New York Times*, https://www.nytimes.com/interactive/projects/guantanamo/detainees/10015-abd-al-rahim-al-nashiri (accessed May 27, 2018).

"A Guide to the Memos on Torture," *The New York Times*, https://archive.nytimes.com/www.nytimes.com/ref/international/24MEMO-GUIDE.html (accessed May 26, 2018).

Gustin, Sam. "Aaron Swartz, Tech Prodigy and Internet Activist, Is Dead at 26," *Time*, January 13, 2013, http://business.time.com/2013/01/13/tech-prodigy-and-internet-activist-aaron-swartz-commits-suicide/ (accessed November 3, 2019).

Hajjar, Lisa. "CIA: KUBARK'S Very Long Shadow," *Al Jazeera*, August 6, 2012, https://www.aljazeera.com/indepth/opinion/2012/08/201285121033592843.html (accessed May 19, 2018).

Honoré, Tony. *Ulpian: Pioneer of Human Rights*, 2nd ed. (Oxford University Press, 1982, 2002).

"In the Tenderloin," *The New York Times*, May 20, 1979, https://www.nytimes.com/1979/05/20/archives/in-the-tenderloin.html (accessed May 2, 2018).

"IRA Ceasefire 20 Years on: Internal Battles, Peace Talks, New Hope," *BBC News*, July 20, 2017, http://www.bbc.com/news/uk-northern-ireland-40656954 (accessed May 14, 2018).

Jindia, Shilpa. "Secret Surveillance and the Legacy of Torture Have Paralyzed the USS Cole Bombing Trial at Guantanamo," The Intercept, March 5, 2018, https://theintercept.com/2018/03/05/guantanamo-trials-abd-al-rahim-al-nashiri/ (accessed May 27, 2018).

Kappeler, Victor E. "A Brief History of Slavery and the Origins of American Policing," 2014, http://plsonline.eku .edu/insidelook/brief-history-slavery-and-origins-american-policing (accessed May 1, 2018).

Jacobsmeyer, Paul J., Chief, Department of Defense Office of Freedom of Information. Letter to Jason Leopold, 13-F-1139, February 12, 2014, https://www.document cloud.org/documents/1020057-guantanamo-parole-list .html (accessed May 27, 2018).

Kean, Thomas H., and Lee Hamilton. "The 9/11 Commission Report: Final Report of the National Commission on Terrorist Attacks Upon the United States" (National Commission on Terrorist Attacks Upon the United States, 2004).

Lawler, Orpheli Garcia. "What Happened to Roxana Hernández, the Trans Woman Who Died in ICE Custody?" *New York Magazine: The Cut*, December 5, 2018, https://www.thecut.com/2018/12/roxana-hernndez-a-transgender-woman-died-in-ice-custody.html (accessed November 3, 2019).

Lazreg, Marnia, and Eric Weitz. *Torture and the Twilight of Empire: From Algiers to Baghdad* (Princeton University Press, 2008).

Lemoyne, James. "Testifying to Torture," *The New York Times*, June 5, 1988.

Manning, Chelsea. Twitter post, March 8, 2019, 10:58 A.M., https://twitter.com/xychelsea/status/110409417095057 8177.

"A Master Terrorist Is Nabbed." *The New York Times*, April 6, 2002.

McCaskill, Nolan D. "Pompeo Confirmed as Secretary of State," *Politico*, April 26, 2018, https://www.politico.com/ story/2018/04/26/pompeo-clears-key-senate-hurdle-to-be-secretary-of-state-555908 (accessed May 28, 2018).

McChesney, John. "The Death of an Iraqi Prisoner," *National Public Radio*, October 27, 2005, https://www.npr.org/templates/story/story.php?storyId=4977986 (accessed May 27, 2018).

McCoy, Alfred W. *Torture and Impunity: The U.S. Doctrine of Coercive Interrogation* (University of Wisconsin Press, 2012).

Mendez, Juan E. "Report of the Special Rapporteur on Torture and Other Cruel, Inhuman or Degrading Treatment or Punishment, Addendum Observations on Communications Transmitted to Governments and Replies Received," A/HRC/19/61/Add. 4, February 29, 2012.

Military Commissions Act of 2006, Pub. L. 109–366, 120 Stat 2602 (109th Congress).

Miranda v. Arizona, 384 U.S. 436 (1966).

Moreau, Julie. "LGBTQ Migrants 97 Times More Likely to Be Sexually Assaulted in Detention, Report Says," NBC News, June 6, 2018, https://www.nbcnews.com/feature/nbc-out/lgbtq-migrants-97-times-more-likely-be-sexually-assaulted-detention-n880101 (accessed March 11, 2019).

Myers, Ariana Natalie. "I Once Was Lost: Between Christian and Muslim in the Crown of Aragon, 1225–1330" (PhD Dissertation, Princeton University, Forthcoming).

"No Penalty for Torture." *The New York Times*, September 5, 2012.

Obama, Barack H. "Ensuring Lawful Interrogations," EO 13491, January 22, 2009a.

Obama, Barack H. "Review and Disposition of Individuals Detained at the Guantánamo Bay Naval Base and Closure of Detention Facilities," EO 13492, January 22, 2009b.

Osborne, Samuel. "Americas Donald Trump's CIA Director Nominee Mike Pompeo Is Open to Waterboarding,"

The Independent, January 23, 2017, https://www
.independent.co.uk/news/world/americas/donald-trump-
cia-director-mike-pompeo-open-waterboarding-enhanced-
interrogation-torture-a7541026.html (accessed May 28,
2018).

Peralta, Eyder. "'Torture Report': A Closer Look at When
and What President Bush Knew," *National Public Radio*,
December 16, 2014, https://www.npr.org/sections/thetwo-
way/2014/12/16/369876047/torture-report-a-closer-look-
at-when-and-what-president-bush-knew (accessed May 25,
2018).

Peters, Edward. *Torture* (University of Pennsylvania Press,
1985, 1999).

Phillips, Macon. "President Barack Obama's Inaugural
Address," 2009, https://obamawhitehouse.archives.gov/
blog/2009/01/21/president-barack-obamas-inaugural-
address (accessed May 28, 2018).

Pilkington, Ed. "Bradley Manning's Treatment Was Cruel
and Inhuman, UN Torture Chief Rules," *The Guardian*,
March 12, 2012, https://www.theguardian.com/world/
2012/mar/12/bradley-manning-cruel-inhuman-treatment-
un (accessed May 28, 2018).

Pilkington, Ed. "Bradley Manning Verdict: Cleared of 'Aiding
the Enemy' but Guilty of Other Charges," *The Guardian*,
July 31, 2013, https://www.theguardian.com/world/2013/
jul/30/bradley-manning-wikileaks-judge-verdict (accessed
May 28, 2018).

Pilkington, Ed. "Guantánamo Detainee to Testify on
'Unspeakable Torture' by CIA Agents," *The Guardian*,
May 10, 2017, https://www.theguardian.com/us-news/
2017/may/10/guantanamo-detainee-abu-zubaydah-cia-
torture-hearing (accessed May 27, 2018).

Pilkington, Ed, David Smith, and Lauren Gambino.
"Chelsea Manning's Prison Sentence Commuted by

Barack Obama," *The Guardian*, January 18, 2017, https://www.theguardian.com/us-news/2017/jan/17/chelsea-manning-sentence-commuted-barack-obama (accessed May 28, 2018).

Pitzke, Marc. "Outrage, Applause, Indifference: US Reacts to WikiLeaks Iraq Documents," *Spiegel Online*, October 23, 2010, http://www.spiegel.de/international/world/outrage-applause-indifference-us-reacts-to-wikileaks-iraq-documents-a-724974.html (accessed May 28, 2018).

Plumer, Brad. "Nine Facts about Terrorism in the United States Since 9/11," Wonkblog, *The Washington Post*, September 11, 2013, https://www.washingtonpost.com/news/wonk/wp/2013/09/11/nine-facts-about-terrorism-in-the-united-states-since-911/ (accessed May 25, 2018).

Priest, Dana. "CIA Holds Terror Suspects in Secret Prisons," *The Washington Post*, November 2, 2005, http://www.washingtonpost.com/wp-dyn/content/article/2005/11/01/AR2005110101644.html (accessed May 28, 2018).

Reagan, Ronald. "A Vision for America," November 3, 1980, http://www.presidency.ucsb.edu/ws/?pid=85199 (accessed May 1, 2018).

The Rendition Project. "Abu Zubaydah," https://www.therenditionproject.org.uk/prisoners/zubaydah.html (accessed May 27, 2018).

Reza, Sadiq. "Torture and Islamic Law," *Chicago Journal of International Law* 8 (1): Article 4 (2007). Available at: https://chicagounbound.uchicago.edu/cjil/vol8/iss1/4 (accessed October 28, 2019) Rowan, Brian.

Salon Staff. "Prosecutions and Convictions," March 14, 2006, https://www.salon.com/2006/03/14/prosecutions_convictions/ (accessed May 27, 2018).

Scott, Shane, and Mark Mazzetti. "Senate Panel Report Links Top Bush Administration Officials to Abuse of Detainees," *The New York Times*, December 12, 2008.

Seligman, Scott D. *The Third Degree: The Triple Murder That Shook Washington and Changed American Criminal Justice* (University of Nebraska Press, 2018).

Seville, Lisa Riordan, Hannah Rappleye, and Andrew W. Lehren. "22 Immigrants Died in ICE Detention Centers during the Past 2 Years," *NBC News*, January 6, 2019, https://www.nbcnews.com/politics/immigration/22-immigrants-died-ice-detention-centers-during-past-2-years-n954781 (accessed March 11, 2019).

Siems, Larry. "Inside the CIA's Black Site Torture Room," *The Guardian*, October 9, 2017, https://www.theguardian.com/us-news/ng-interactive/2017/oct/09/cia-torture-black-site-enhanced-interrogation (accessed May 2, 2018).

Stevenson, Leonard. *Policing in America: A Reference Handbook* (Santa Barbara, CA: ABC-CLIO, 2008).

Stuart, Tessa. "Trump's Family Separation Policy Was Exponentially Worse Than Previously Known," *Rolling Stone*, January 17, 2019, https://www.rollingstone.com/politics/politics-news/family-separation-thousands-779254/ (accessed March 10, 2019).

Sullivan, Andrew. "Verschärfte Vernehmung," *The Atlantic*, May 29, 2007, https://www.theatlantic.com/daily-dish/archive/2007/05/-versch-auml-rfte-vernehmung/228158/ (accessed May 4, 2018).

Taddonio, Patrice. "CIA Director Nominee Supported Destruction of Torture Tapes," *PBS Frontline*, May 9, 2018, https://www.pbs.org/wgbh/frontline/article/cia-director-nominee-supported-destruction-of-torture-tapes/.

Tate, Julie. "Bradley Manning Sentenced to 35 Years in WikiLeaks Case," *The Washington Post*, August 21, 2013, https://www.washingtonpost.com/world/national-security/judge-to-sentence-bradley-manning-today/2013/08/20/85bee184-09d0-11e3-b87c-476db8ac34cd_story.html (accessed May 28, 2018).

Tate, Julie, and Ellen Nakashima. "Judge Refuses to Dismiss Charges against WikiLeaks Suspect Bradley Manning," *The Washington Post*, January 8, 2013, https://www.washingtonpost.com/world/national-security/judge-refuses-to-dismiss-charges-against-wikileaks-suspect-bradley-manning/2013/01/08/2eab1f62-59cb-11e2-beee-6e38f5215402_story.html (accessed May 28, 2018).

Thompson, Mark. "WikiLeaks Releases Iraq War Logs," *Time*, October 22, 2010, http://nation.time.com/2010/10/22/wikileaks-releases-iraq-war-logs/ (accessed May 28, 2018).

"To Abolish the Third Degree," *The New York Times*, July 6, 1902, p. 23.

Trump, Donald J. "Protecting America through Lawful Detention of Terrorists," EO 13823, January 30, 2018.

United Nations. 183rd Plenary Meeting, PV 183, December 10, 1948, 933, http://undocs.org/A/PV.183 (accessed May 6, 2018).

United Nations. "Universal Declaration of Human Rights," http://www.ohchr.org/EN/UDHR/Documents/UDHR_Translations/eng.pdf (accessed May 6, 2018).

United Nations. "Convention against Torture and Other Cruel, Inhuman or Degrading Treatment or Punishment," Human Rights Office of the High Commissioner, General Assembly Resolution 39/46 of December 10, 1984, http://www.ohchr.org/EN/ProfessionalInterest/Pages/CAT.aspx (accessed May 22, 2018).

United Nations Office of Legal Affairs. *United Nations Juridical Yearbook 1986* (United Nations, 1994).

United Nations. "Status of Ratification International Dashboard," Human Rights Office of the High Commissioner, http://indicators.ohchr.org/ (accessed May 20, 2018).

United Nations. "Human Rights Committee-Introduction," Human Rights Office of the High Commissioner, http://www.ohchr.org/EN/HRBodies/CCPR/Pages/CCPRIntro.aspx (accessed May 20, 2018).

United Nations. "Optional Protocol to the International Covenant on Civil and Political Rights," http://www.ohchr .org/EN/ProfessionalInterest/Pages/OPCCPR1.aspx (accessed May 20, 2018).

United States Holocaust Museum. "Forced Sterilization," https://www.ushmm.org/learn/students/learning-materials-and-resources/mentally-and-physically-handicapped-victims-of-the-nazi-era/forced-sterilization (accessed May 4, 2018).

United States Senate Select Committee on Intelligence. "Committee Study of the Central Intelligence Agency's Detention and Interrogation Program," Findings and Conclusions, Executive Summary (2012).

U.S. Department of Defense. "JTF-GTMO Detainee Assessment," December 8, 2006, JTF-GTMO-CDR, 20311208, pp. 3–6. Available at https://www.theren ditionproject.org.uk/pdf/PDF%20443%20[JTF-GTMO%20Detainee%20Assessment,%20Abd%20al-Rahim%20al-Nashiri%20(8%20December%202006)].pdf (accessed November 24, 2019)

"Verbatim Transcript of Combatant Status Review Tribunal Hearing for ISN 10016." March 27, 2007, 8–11, https://www.aclu.org/legal-document/verbatim-transcript-combatant-status-review-tribunal-csrt-hearing-abu-zubaydah (accessed March 7, 2019).

War Crimes Act of 1996, Pub.L. 104–192, 110 Stat. 2104 (104th Congress).

Watkins, John Elfreth. "Charges of the Third Degree Ordeal," *San Francisco Chronicle*, October 16, 1910.

Weissbrodt, David, and Amy Bergquist. "Extraordinary Rendition and the Torture Convention." *Va. J. Int'l L* 46: 585, 589 (2006).

WikiLeaks. "Iraq War Logs," https://wikileaks.org/irq/ (accessed May 28, 2018).

Wilber, Del Quintin. "FBI Gets an Unexpected Lesson from a Former Interrogator for The Nazis," *Los Angeles Times*, June 10, 2016, http://www.latimes.com/nation/la-na-fbi-nazi-interrogator-20160610-snap-story.html (accessed May 6, 2018).

Williams, Joseph P. "Gorsuch Questioned Early on Torture Memo," *U.S. News & World Report*, March 21, 2017, https://www.usnews.com/news/politics/articles/2017-03-21/gorsuch-questioned-early-on-torture-memo (accessed May 28, 2018).

Wisnewski, J. Jeremy. *Understanding Torture* (Edinburgh University Press, 2010).

"Yes, Declaim against Torture," *The New York Times*, December 15, 1984.

Yoo, John. "Application of Treaties and Laws to al Qaeda and Taliban Detainees," U.S. Department of Justice, Office of Legal Counsel, January 9, 2002.

2 Problems, Controversies, Solutions

While knowing the history of torture is important, to fully understand why politicians from Emperor Augustus to Donald Trump insist on keeping it in their arsenals, it's necessary to examine the following questions: (1) How do we define torture? (2) Is torture an effective tool to reach the objectives its practitioners set for it? (3) What alternatives to torture exist? (4) Is the true abolition of torture practical on a global scale, and if so is it desirable?

How Do We Define Torture?

In many ways, the answer to this question depends on whether we are speaking about American law—or the law the rest of the world follows.

Since the mid-1980s, the United Nations has defined torture as

> any act by which severe pain or suffering, whether physical or mental, is intentionally inflicted on a person for such purposes as obtaining from him or a third person information or a confession, punishing him for an act he or a third person has committed or is suspected of having committed, or intimidating or coercing him or a third

---

Protesters demanding the closure of the U.S. prison camp at Guantanamo Bay, Cuba gather in front of the American Embassy in London. Note that they are wearing orange jumpsuits, googles, and face masks to show solidarity with the Guantanamo detainees. (Shutterstock)

person, or for any reason based on discrimination of any kind, when such pain or suffering is inflicted by or at the instigation of or with the consent or acquiescence of a public official or other person acting in an official capacity. ("Convention against Torture" 1984)

American law views the matter very differently. Under the reservations to the Convention against Torture (CAT) stated by the Senate in its ratification message to the United States,

In order to constitute torture, an act must be specifically intended to inflict severe physical or mental pain or suffering and that mental pain or suffering refers to prolonged mental harm caused by or resulting from: (1) the intentional infliction or threatened infliction of severe physical pain or suffering; (2) the administration or application, or threatened administration or application, of mind altering substances or other procedures calculated to disrupt profoundly the senses or the personality, (3) the threat of imminent death, (4) the threat that another person will imminently be subjected to death, severe physical pain or suffering, or the administration or application of mind altering substances or other procedures calculated to disrupt profoundly the senses or personality. (U.S. Congress 1990)

The contrast between the two approaches is striking. The goal of the CAT, which the U.N. General Assembly approved unanimously in 1984 and which entered into force in 1987, is to provide the widest possible protection against torture by defining, as broadly as possible, what behaviors and acts are proscribed. In contrast, the United States, in its reservation to the ratification of the CAT and in subsequent domestic legislation, such as the War Crimes Act of 1996 (18 U.S.C. 2441 (d)(1)(a)), has seemingly sought to narrow the scope of behavior considered to be torture (and which therefore is supposed to be banned under the CAT). Indeed, the most recent amendments to the Act, which were passed in 2006 after the CIA's (Central Intelligence Agency's) and the military's involvement in the torture of detainees at various sites around the world came to light, adopt the restrictive approach pioneered in the reservations to the CAT (Pub. L 109–366, 120 Stat. 2633).

It wasn't always this way. In *U.S. v. Karl Brandt et al.*, the so-called Doctors' Trial, and the first case brought by the International Military Tribunal at Nuremberg after the end of World War II, the United States specifically charged several Nazi doctors and scientists who had conducted high-altitude experiments on concentration-camp prisoners, which constituted torture (Office of the Military Government for Germany 1946, 6–7).

In the *Brandt* case, the United States argued that carrying out experiments "in a low-pressure chamber in which the atmospheric conditions and pressures prevailing at high altitude (up to 68,000 feet) could be duplicated" (Office of the Military Government for Germany 1946, 6) constituted torture, especially since "many victims died as a result of these experiments and others suffered grave injury" (Office of the Military Government for Germany 1946, 6–7).

The *Brandt* case is a prime example of how a restrictive definition of torture can impede prosecutions. If the case had arisen in 1992, when the operative definition of torture in the United States was the language in the U.S. Senate's reservation to the CAT, instead of the 1946 definition, the Nazi doctors could have plausibly argued that their intent on subjecting the prisoners to human experimentation was to advance their knowledge of science, rather than to intentionally inflict "severe physical pain or suffering" on their subjects, thereby disqualifying their actions from being considered as torture under the reservation to the CAT. Nevertheless, Brandt and several others were found guilty and sentenced to death, while others received long sentences.

Two years later, forty-eight of the then sixty members of the United Nations approved the Universal Declaration of Human Rights, whose Article 5 provided that "no one shall be subjected to torture or to cruel, inhuman or degrading treatment or punishment" ("Universal Declaration of Human Rights" 1948). While the Declaration drew a distinction, troubling in the light of later experience, between "torture" and "cruel, inhuman or degrading treatment," it did appear to offer a public sign that there was an international consensus against either type of behavior.

Unfortunately, in the area of torture it is often more important to look at what governments are really doing behind closed doors than what they proclaim they are doing in international forums. As the ideological freeze of the Cold War settled in across Europe, the CIA began with trying to teach its agents to withstand the torture they could expect to receive if captured behind the Iron Curtain and ended up adopting the same techniques used by its opposite numbers in the Russian Ministry of State Security and its successor, the KGB. As we saw in the previous chapter, the CIA continued to use some of those techniques—like placing prisoners in stress positions—more than halfway through the first decade of the twenty-first century.

The United States was not unique, of course, in following what might appear to be a hypocritical policy regarding torture in these years, even among other Western democracies. While it did not acknowledge doing so until September 2018, France engaged in torture on a massive scale in its efforts to suppress those fighting for the independence of Algeria (McAuley 2018) despite being a signatory to the European Convention on Human Rights. Similarly, during the early to mid-1970s, the UK—also a signatory to the European Convention on Human Rights—subjected suspected members of the Irish Republican Army to what the European Court of Human Rights termed "inhuman and degrading treatment" (Coogan 2002, 438).

The primary objective of American policymakers in this area has been to secure the maximum freedom of action for American soldiers and spies with regard to interrogation and treatment of prisoners, while simultaneously reducing, to the lowest likelihood possible, the chance that the said soldiers and spies will face prosecution in the United States or abroad for their acts. Specifically, as long as its servants do not threaten prisoners or someone else with "imminent" death, administer (or threaten to administer) mind-altering drugs, or intend to inflict "severe" physical or mental pain and suffering, they can plausibly (at least in American eyes) claim they haven't engaged in "torture" for the purposes of sanctions under the CAT or the War Crimes Act of 1996.

On the one hand, this strategy has the benefit of candor. Because of the reservation, the United States isn't making an unconditional promise to refrain from the behaviors targeted by the CAT but is explicitly carving out a space where its agents can still use techniques like stress positions, notwithstanding the fact that the CIA has known for decades how dangerous they can be for the prisoner. On the other hand, the approach leaves the United States open to criticism that it is attempting to evade its obligations under the CAT by articulating reservations that essentially strip the prohibition against torture of any meaning.

On a more practical note, following an interpretation of the definition of "torture" that isn't widely accepted by the rest of the world causes concrete problems of its own. In 2009, an Italian court convicted twenty-three Americans—including Robert Seldon Lady, the former CIA station chief in Milan—in absentia for kidnapping Osama Moustafa Hassan Nasr, a.k.a. Abu Omar, who was later transferred to Egyptian custody, where he was allegedly tortured (Donadio 2009).

While the CIA and military personnel in the case have received prison sentences and are technically fugitives from justice, the odds are good that none will serve any time in jail, unless a future Italian government demands that they be extradited. Even so, Lady was briefly detained in Panama in 2013 before being released due to Panama's not having an extradition treaty with Italy. In 2015, Italian president Sergio Mattarella pardoned Lady and another defendant in the case ("Italian President Pardons CIA Kidnappers" 2015).

Meanwhile, outside the United States, the law on CAT continues to advance in fits and starts, as discussed in the following sections.

United Nations

From 1989 through mid-2018, the Committee against Torture, the U.N. body charged with investigating and adjudicating claims of violations of the CAT's terms, received 873 complaints against 39 countries. According to the Committee, 257 of these were discontinued (presumably by the claimant) prior to a decision and 101 were rejected as inadmissible. Of the 348 cases where it reached a decision, the Committee found a violation of the CAT in less than half (142) of them, and another148 cases remain pending (United Nations 2018, 11).

Although a country can avoid a finding of liability simply by objecting to the Committee's jurisdiction, perhaps what's most surprising about the Committee's jurisprudence is that *more* nations don't do so, even given the fact that most of the cases involving torture that are not connected to immigration denials tend to originate from the Global South, whose nations may face consequences that are less of a concern to other powers, such as potential cuts in trade or aid, for rejecting the Committee's jurisdiction.

As the majority of cases that do reach a decision concerning torture before the Committee tend to involve allegations of fairly severe physical assaults that might qualify as torture even under the more restrictive American definition, there is little practical guidance on what forms, if any, of mental coercion constitute torture under the CAT based on the Committee's jurisprudence to date. Proceedings before other multinational bodies and tribunals tell a similar story, as we'll see in the following sections.

European Commission/European Union

In 1968, the European Commission "adopted a general approach that distinguished between 'torture,' 'inhuman' and 'degrading' treatment. The European Court and Commission, unlike some of their international and regional counterparts, have continued to follow this approach of distinguishing between the different forms of ill-treatment. While the definitions have been refined since these early cases, torture continues to carry a special stigma which distinguishes it from other forms of ill-treatment" (Association for the Prevention of Torture, Center for Justice and International Law 2008, 56–57; APT). The Court and the Commission were not always consistent with these definitions— backsliding somewhat in Ireland's case against the UK regarding the treatment of suspected IRA detainees by the British, where it found an action had to inflict "serious and cruel suffering" to be torture (APT 2008, 57), but finding in *Aydin v Turkey* that rape could constitute torture (APT 2008, 58). In 1999, two years after *Aydin*, the Court finally adopted the CAT's definition of torture in *Selmouni v France* and in doing so "re-emphasised the purposive element of torture, which had been marginalised since *The Greek Case*" (APT 2008, 59).

In 2003, some observers condensed four decades of case law into a three-pronged test, where, in order for an act to constitute torture under EU law, it apparently must involve (1) "the infliction of severe mental or physical pain or suffering"; (2) "the intentional or deliberate infliction of the pain"; and (3) "the pursuit of a specific purpose, such as gaining information, punishment or intimidation" (Reidy 2003, 12).

Organization of American States

Although an Inter-American Convention to Prevent and Punish Torture became effective in 1987 (APT 2008, 94), only eighteen of the thirty-five countries that are members of the Organization of American States have signed the convention and either ratified or acceded to its terms ("Inter-American Convention to Prevent and Punish Torture" 1985)—and the United States and Canada are notably not among them, which limits the convention's utility. Even so, it is worth discussing because it takes a different approach to defining torture than the CAT, the EU, or U.S. law does.

Under Article 2 of the Convention, "torture shall be understood to be any act intentionally performed whereby physical or mental pain or suffering is inflicted on a person for purposes of criminal investigation, as a means of intimidation, as personal punishment, as a preventive measure, as a penalty, or for any other purpose. Torture shall also be understood to be the use of methods upon a person intended to obliterate the personality of the victim or to diminish his physical or mental capacities, even if they do not cause physical pain or mental anguish" (OAS, Treaty Series, No. 67).

As commentators have noted, "This definition goes further than that of the UNCAT in that it does not require that the pain or suffering be 'severe,' makes reference to 'any other purpose' rather than 'such purposes as' (as in the UNCAT) and includes methods intended to obliterate the personality of the victim or diminish his capacities, independently of whether such methods cause pain or suffering" (APT 2008, 96). Moreover, under the Inter-American Convention, the intent (or lack thereof) of the perpetrator to cause harm is irrelevant if the other requirements are met (APT 2008, 96–97). Under this standard, those engaged in behavior, like the Nazi doctors discussed earlier, probably would be held liable for torture, while they might escape punishment under American law if they successfully argued they didn't *intend* to cause harm by their actions.

Accordingly, it is not surprising that "the Inter-American Commission became the first international adjudicatory body to recognise rape as torture in *Raquel Martí de Mejía v Peru.* . . . The Inter-American Court and Commission have thus shown greater flexibility than other international instances in adopting an expansive definition of torture and State responsibility, based on the need to guarantee fundamental principles" (APT 2008, 98). Furthermore, the Court and Commission have gone further than other bodies in declaring solitary confinement to constitute "inhuman" (and thus banned) treatment under the Convention (APT 2008, 117).

African Commission

Under Article 5 of the African Charter on Human and Peoples' Rights (1981, 5; ACHPR), "All forms of exploitation and degradation of man particularly slavery, slave trade, torture, cruel, inhuman or degrading punishment and treatment" are banned. Unfortunately, "there is no enforcement mechanism for the Commission's decisions and recommendations, which have been widely ignored by States" (APT 2008, 126).

As with their European counterparts, it is rare for the African Commission on Human and Peoples' Rights to issue a positive decision on the merits on a claim that a member state has engaged in torture. Even when the Commission does, its inability to enforce its decisions can lead to tragicomic results.

In *Dawit Isaak v Republic of Eritrea*, the Commission pointed out "that the rights and obligations of the parties were duly determined in *Article 19 v Eritrea*. The Commission also notes that the present Communication is consequent to the Respondent State's failure to implement its decision, which has led to the Complainant being held incommunicado for about 13 years now" (*Dawit Isaak v Republic of Eritrea*, para 59). However, notwithstanding Eritrea's continuing failure to comply with the Commission's directives, it ended up dismissing the latest case because "any decision on the present Communication will add no value other than to reaffirm what was previously settled" (*Dawit Isaak v Republic of Eritrea*, para 60).

While the African Union, the successor organization to the Organization of African Unity, does not appear to specifically define torture under the African Charter, pursuant to the Robben Island Guidelines for the Prohibition and Prevention of Torture in Africa, African Union member states are expected to ratify the CAT "without reservations," among other things ("Robben Island Guidelines for the Prohibition and Prevention of Torture in Africa" 2002). This suggests that the African Union's intention was to follow CAT jurisprudence in this area, but as there is presently no way of bringing the offending states to book, it may be a moot question.

Association of Southeast Asian Nations

While the United Nations' jurisprudence may be riddled with loopholes and the African Union is weakened by the lack of any enforcement mechanism when it comes to torture cases, both appear robust when compared with the situation within the Association of Southeast Asian Nations (ASEAN).

While ASEAN has been more successful than the two prior associative efforts by nations in the region after World War II ("Cooperation in Asia" 1967), to many observers this has largely been due to ASEAN's explicit policy of noninterference with the policies of its member states, as set forth in its Treaty of Amity and Cooperation ("Treaty of Amity and Cooperation in Southeast Asia" 1976).

Indeed, under Article 10 of the Treaty, each member state "shall not in any manner or form participate in any activity which shall constitute a threat to the political and economic stability, sovereignty, or territorial integrity of another High Contracting Party" ("Treaty of Amity and Cooperation in Southeast Asia" 1976).

This provision offers little space for a prohibition on torture to even be publicly articulated, let alone enforced, since any state that chose to engage in torture could easily claim criticism of its behavior presented a "threat" to its stability. Seen in that light, the surprise is not that the organization waited until 2012 to issue the ASEAN Human Rights Declaration (AHRD), but that it did so at all.

While Section 14 of the AHRD bans torture using familiar language, stating that "no person shall be subject to torture or to cruel, inhuman or degrading treatment or punishment" ("ASEAN Human Rights Declaration" 2012), Section 40's disclaimer that the Declaration gives no "state, group or person any right to perform any act aimed at undermining the purposes and principles of ASEAN" ("ASEAN Human Rights Declaration" 2012) appears to strip Section 14 of any force it might have had.

To some observers, "as long as ASEAN remains an intergovernmental body and not a people-powered institution, the 'ASEAN way' will remain one of noninterference, and it is improbable that the protection of human rights will be paid little more than lip service" (Leader 2012). Sometimes, not even that is paid. As Human Rights Watch pointed out before a 2018 summit between ASEAN and Australia, "Almost all ASEAN leaders invited to Sydney preside over governments that deny basic liberties and fundamental freedoms to their citizens" ("Human Rights in Southeast Asia: Briefing Materials for the ASEAN-Australia Summit" 2018, 2).

While this is likely to be of little comfort to their victims, the decision by those heads of state whose governments practice torture and which are members of ASEAN not to address the issue may backfire on them in the end, as doing so simply deprives ASEAN of its best opportunity to contribute to its own definitions of what torture is and what it isn't. Lacking an ASEAN-specific definition of torture, which currently does not exists, the jurisprudence of the United Nations, at least for those nations that are signatories to the CAT, would appear to be the best source of persuasive legal authority, if and when the torturers within the ASEAN area are ever brought to account.

Summary

With one exception, a strong argument can be made that the 165 nations that have ratified the CAT represent a consensus—at least on paper—that international law favors the adoption of an expansive definition of torture to at least cover both physical and mental abuse, so long as the abuse is sufficiently severe. The Organization of American States adopts an even more expansive standard, while the African Union, pursuant to its Robben Island Guidelines, has demanded that its members ratify the CAT without any reservation of rights to its terms and that the European Union's definition of torture, apart from the additional requirement that the abuse be motivated by a specific purpose, is functionally identical to the CAT's. Similarly, while ASEAN does not specifically define torture in its AHRD, all its members other than Malaysia and Myanmar have signed and ratified the CAT. However, the position of the United States, which requires that abuse be "prolonged" and "severe" to constitute torture, bucks this trend.

The dichotomy between the approach of the CAT and that of the United States is not accidental and represents the tension between two irreconcilable public policy goals. If one's overriding priority is to reduce, if not eradicate, the use of torture, a clear, broad, and commonly accepted definition, like the CAT's, is the preferred starting point. If, on the other hand, one's priority is to insulate government officials, employees, and contractors from accountability and in so doing maximize the scope of choice for future policymakers, then a tight definition of torture riddled with exceptions is the way to go. While their actions have not always matched their paper commitments, since the 1980s most governments in the world have chosen the first goal, while the United States has pursued the second.

Is Torture an Effective Tool?

To evaluate the effectiveness of torture, we must first examine what those who practice it are trying to accomplish.

As set forth in greater detail later, if one's goal is to elicit information the use of torture is akin to using a sledgehammer to kill a fly that's resting on an expensive and fragile glass goblet. If the hammer makes contact, the fly will probably die—but the consequential damage to the goblet makes this a Pyrrhic victory at best for the one swinging the hammer. Moreover, while the fly may evade the swing and survive, the goblet assuredly will not.

From Nazi Germany to the CIA's black sites in the early part of the twenty-first century, experience has shown that interrogation of prisoners without the use of physical or psychological torture is a more effective way of eliciting accurate and useful information.

Why then do policymakers and their servants, who are presumably aware of this, continue to engage in torture? One reason is that, in many cases, obtaining information is a secondary objective to their real goal, which can include anything from extrajudicial punishment of a targeted population to compelling changes in human behavior.

World War II: Noor Inayat-Khan and the Gestapo

When the British Special Operations executive trained Noor Inayat-Khan to be one of the first female wireless operators inserted into occupied France during World War II to enable the Allies to work with the French resistance, they didn't mince words. "She was warned that interrogation was impossible to resist if the torturers knew their business and were willing to be patient. Agents, deprived of their L [suicide] pills, sometimes broke down and revealed their security checks. These included meaningless questions from Bletchley to which should be given meaningless answers. Thus, to the challenge 'Have you washed?' the correct answer would be 'The trees blossom'" (Stevenson 1978, 242). Furthermore, "if an agent was in captivity and forced to transmit under German supervision, she need only omit a meaningless letter or number that was regularly included in her transmissions while at liberty" (Stevenson 1978, 242).

Given her prewar background as an author of children's books (Stevenson 1978, 236) and her "terrified" reactions during practice interrogations (Stevenson 1978, 241), both Noor's comrades and some of her instructors had qualms about her being dropped into Nazi-occupied France (Stevenson 1978, 243–244). She went anyway and evaded capture for three-and-half months before the Nazis caught up with her (Stevenson 1978, 253).

Rather than breaking quickly under Gestapo interrogation, Noor "was almost killed in one attempt to escape" (Stevenson 1978, 250). After her second bid for freedom, the Gestapo shipped her first to a prison in Germany, where she "was handcuffed and chained day and night in a crouching position so that she depended on male jailers to deal with her sanitary and feeding problems. In this manner, chained like a vicious animal in total isolation, she was held for ten months" (Stevenson 1978, 253).

Despite all this, Noor refused to talk, so "she was taken with three others to Dachau Camp on the 12th September 1944. . . . On arrival, she was taken to the crematorium and shot" (Stevenson 1978, 253). Even so, "Noor had one last moment of defiance, uttering the word 'Liberté' before [her executioner] pulled the trigger" (Vargo 2012, 105). In a rare point of agreement, both the Nazis (Vargo 2012, 100–101) and the British (Stevenson 1978, 253) agree she never gave the Gestapo any useful information.

As the Noor case study shows, an individual's resources to resist physical and mental torture are not always easy to judge ahead of the event. The best efforts of the Gestapo, even using methods like putting her in stress positions, were unavailing, and Noor took her secrets to the grave.

The Korean War

While there were documented instances of torture by North Korean forces against captured American soldiers—a 1954 report by the U.S. Senate's Subcommittee on Korean War Atrocities identified the Bamboo Spear case in December 1950, when several captured flyers had their flesh punctured by "heated, sharpened bamboo sticks" (U.S. Senate, S. Rep. 848, 6–7), and another in July 1950, when North Korean soldiers burned the feet of an American prisoner with cigarette butts and stuck a can opener into "his open shoulder wound" (U.S. Senate, S. Rep., 848, 9)—both incidents do not appear to have occurred as part of an interrogation.

In contrast, Chinese interrogators relied on a different set of tools when questioning American and other U.N. prisoners.

In the Chinese prison the individual interrogator is still important and in occasional cases the management of the prisoner may quite closely duplicate that of the KGB. But in most instances the efforts of the interrogator are supplemented by the effects of the interaction between the prisoner and 6 or 8 of his fellow prisoners with whom he is incarcerated in a crowded cell. Here the group replaces the interrogator as the focus of the prisoner's relationships. In this setting of complete lack of privacy there is an unremitting routine of self-criticism sessions, group discussion sessions, rote learning, and constant repetition of Communist viewpoints, and the repeated rewriting and rejection of autobiographical essays. The group exploits the feeling of emotional nakedness and unworthiness which the self-criticism sessions engender, dwelling upon items obtained from the prisoner's life history during those sessions which arouse in him guilt, conflict and anxiety. (U.S. Congress 1956, 33)

Indeed, under the Chinese system "physical violence is not approved officially, and if a jailer or an interrogator happens to strike a man it is not condoned except where it is not known" (U.S. Congress 1956, 26). Some of the reason for that was because "the additional Chinese goal is to produce a long-lasting change in the basic attitude and behavior of the prisoner" (U.S. Congress 1956, 24).

When describing the Chinese approach toward interrogation and attempts to induce false confessions, a U.S. Air Force sociologist noted that he was excluding "torture from the outline to emphasize that inflicting physical pain is not a necessary nor particularly effective method of inducing compliance. While many of our people did encounter physical violence, this rarely occurred as part of a systematic effort to elicit a false confession" (Biderman 1957, 618–620). Indeed, "where physical violence *was* inflicted during the course of such an attempt, the attempt was particularly likely to fail completely" (Biderman 1957, 620; emphasis in original). Even so, placing prisoners in stress positions, such as forcing them to stand for extended periods in the same position, was a popular tool for many Chinese interrogators (Biderman 1957, 620).

To Biderman (1957, 620–621), "For the interrogator, forced standing has still further advantages. It is consistent with formal principles of legality and humaneness important to the Communists. These principles are important in the interrogation—particularly in facilitating the adoption of a positive attitude by the prisoner toward the interrogator and the forces he represents. Adherence to these mythical principles also protects the interrogator from potential punishment at some future time for mistreating prisoners."

While Biderman (1957, 625) believes the North Koreans obtained false confessions from air force personnel more "quickly and economically" than the Chinese did, he attributes this to the fact that the North Koreans did rely on self-criticism sessions as much as the Chinese did.

> Among the Air Force prisoners pressured for false confessions in North Korea and in Communist China, there are cases of simply incredible heroism, fortitude and attachment to principle in the face of particularly intensive Communist coercion. There are also cases—far fewer in number although far more publicized—of a surprising inability to withstand coercion. Nonetheless, depending upon how one chooses to draw the line, it is possible for us to say truthfully that all who were really involved resisted, or that all complied, for in truth the behavior of all involved at some point a mixture of compliance and resistance. (Biderman 1957, 625)

The Vietnam War

Officially, the government of North Vietnam banned the use of torture by its interrogators in 1951 (Stein 2014). However, American soldiers, sailors, and pilots quickly learned that a different set of rules often applied on the ground. By the end of American involvement in the Vietnam conflict, "nearly six hundred U.S. prisoners, including 25 civilians" had been captured by North Vietnamese government forces or the Viet Cong in

South Vietnam (Rochester 2010, 1). Worse, "characterizing the fallen aviators and captured ground personnel as 'air pirates' and mercenaries, the enemy denied them the protection of the Geneva wartime conventions and at one point threatened to put the prisoners on trial for war crimes" (Rochester 2010, 2). In multiple cases, pilots reported that the North Vietnamese used physical torture as an aid to interrogation and to attempt to coerce prisoners to make "confessions" for the media—but in a pre-Internet era, this did not always go as planned.

> In a ruse that became legendary in POW lore, Tanner and his backseater, Lieutenant Ross Terry, got off the hook at their initial torture session by "confessing" that fellow carrier pilots Lieutenant Commander Ben Casey [a fictional TV doctor] and Lieutenant Clark Kent had been court-martialed for refusing to fly their missions. Not only did the Vietnamese excitedly accept the claim, but they then had the aviators repeat the story in a televised interview with a Japanese journalist. Only when excerpts of the interview aired in the West, to howls of amusement, did Hanoi realize its blunder. As a result, Tanner spent a record 123 days in irons. (Rochester 2010, 29)

Sometimes, it did, as Lieutenant Commodore John S. McCain (2008) found out:

> They bounced me from pillar to post, kicking and laughing and scratching. After a few hours of that, ropes were put on me and I sat that night bound with ropes. Then I was taken to a small room. For punishment they would almost always take you to another room where you didn't have a mosquito net or a bed or any clothes. For the next four days, I was beaten every two to three hours by different guards. My left arm was broken again and my ribs were cracked. They wanted a statement saying that I was sorry for the crimes that I had committed against North

Vietnamese people and that I was grateful for the treatment that I had received from them. . . .

I held out for four days. Finally, I reached the lowest point of my 5½ years in North Vietnam. I was at the point of suicide, because I saw that I was reaching the end of my rope. I said, O.K., I'll write for them.

They took me up into one of the interrogation rooms, and for the next 12 hours we wrote and rewrote. The North Vietnamese interrogator, who was pretty stupid, wrote the final confession, and I signed it. It was in their language, and spoke about black crimes, and other generalities. It was unacceptable to them. But I felt just terrible about it. I kept saying to myself, "Oh, God, I really didn't have any choice." I had learned what we all learned over there: Every man has his breaking point. I had reached mine.

On a later recording of that statement, McCain said, "I, as a U.S. airman, am guilty of crimes against the Vietnamese country and people. I bombed their cities, towns and villages and caused many injuries, even death, to the people of Vietnam" (Nowicki 2016).

While this may have been gratifying to his captors and their political masters at the time, it is questionable how much, if at all, confessions like McCain's helped advance North Vietnam's main political objective of turning American public opinion against the war, especially given their obviously coerced nature.

It is interesting to speculate whether North Vietnam would have gotten better results by use of the approach favored by Hanns Joachim Scharff as discussed in Chapter 1 (and later in this chapter). While such tactics might not have worked on particularly ideologically committed pilots like McCain— who was, after all, the son of a high-ranking naval officer and a Naval Academy graduate—they could have reaped dividends when applied to prisoners who were less motivated.

In any event, because of his POW experiences, McCain would go on to become one of the strongest Republican voices against the use of torture by the Bush and Trump administrations during his time in the U.S. Senate until his death in August 2018.

The CIA's *KUBARK* Manual

In 1963, the CIA noted in its *KUBARK* interrogation manual that "all good interrogators avoid coercive techniques whenever the necessary information can be gained without them. *In other words, physical or psychological duress is counter-productive* when employed against a source whose voluntary cooperation can be enlisted without pressure" (Central Intelligence Agency 1963, 18; emphasis added).

Among other things, their use risks turning a temporarily "broken" enemy into a permanent embittered one.

> If coercion must be used and is successful, the temporary effect upon a hostile penetration agent . . . or provocateur is the creation of a vacuum in his loyalties. He is likely to feel drained and apathetic. If the interrogator (or his service) restores the source's self-esteem at this point by supplying an acceptable rationalization or conversion to anti-Communist beliefs, the source will continue to volunteer cooperation. But if he has been compelled to divulge through the use of pressures exceeding his resistance (for example, narcosis or hypnosis), and if his motives are ignored once his information has been mined, he is likely to revert to the role of antagonist and try to cause us trouble by any means available to him. (Central Intelligence Agency 1963, 18)

That didn't mean the Agency was squeamish about the practice.

> All coercive techniques are designed to induce regression. As Hinkle notes . . . the result of external pressures of sufficient intensity is the loss of those defenses most recently acquired by civilized man: ". . . the capacity to carry out

the highest creative activities, to meet new, challenging, and complex situations, to deal with trying interpersonal relations, and to cope with repeated frustrations. Relatively small degrees of homeostatic derangement, fatigue, pain, sleep loss, or anxiety may impair these functions." As a result, "most people who are exposed to coercive procedures will talk and usually reveal some information that they might not have revealed otherwise." (Central Intelligence Agency 1963, 83)

It's not so much that the CIA was ignorant about the possibility that prisoners might provide false information just to end a torture session but that the agency saw it as a tolerable risk.

Psychologists and others who write about physical or psychological duress frequently object that under sufficient pressure subjects usually yield but that their ability to recall and communicate information accurately is as impaired as the will to resist. This pragmatic objection has somewhat the same validity for a counterintelligence interrogation as for any other. But there is one significant difference. Confession is a necessary prelude to the CI interrogation of a hitherto unresponsive or concealing source. And the use of coercive techniques will rarely or never confuse an interrogatee so completely that he does not know whether his own confession is true or false. He does not need full mastery of all his powers of resistance and discrimination to know whether he is a spy or not. Only subjects who have reached a point where they are under delusions are likely to make false confessions that they believe. (Central Intelligence Agency 1963, 84)

The CIA used the *KUBARK* methods, "including sensory deprivation techniques and forced standing" (U.S. Congress

2012, 33), when it interrogated KGB lieutenant colonel Yuri Nosenko following his defection in the late 1960s. Based on fears Nosenko was a double-agent, the CIA confined and periodically tortured him for three years before being convinced of his bona fides (Shapira 2017). Parts of the *KUBARK* manual were later used by the CIA to train security forces in Latin America in the early 1980s (U.S. Congress 2012, 33).

Thus, despite ample empirical evidence that physical coercion was not an effective means of obtaining either compliance or information, the agency retained its belief in *KUBARK*, which helped set the stage for the techniques the Agency used at so-called black sites around the world following the 9/11 attacks on New York, Washington, and Pennsylvania. As the U.S. Senate's Select Committee on Intelligence later determined, the Agency would have been better off if it had listened to the naysaying psychologists.

> The Committee finds, based on a review of CIA interrogation records, that the use of the CIA's enhanced interrogation techniques was not an effective means of obtaining accurate information or gaining detainee cooperation. For example, according to CIA records, seven of the 39 CIA detainees known to have been subjected to the CIA's enhanced interrogation techniques produced no intelligence while in CIA custody. CIA detainees who were subjected to the techniques immediately after being rendered to CIA custody. Other detainees provided significant accurate intelligence prior to, or without having been subjected to these techniques. (U.S. Congress 2012, 3)

Indeed, the Committee found the CIA's methods were not just useless, but actively counterproductive. "While being subjected to the CIA's enhanced interrogation techniques and afterwards, multiple CIA detainees fabricated information, resulting in faulty intelligence. Detainees provided fabricated information on critical intelligence issues, including the terrorist threats which the CIA identified as its highest priorities" (U.S. Congress 2012, 3).

Assuming what one wants is accurate information, physical torture has been shown not to be effective in a domestic context as well. Peter Neufeld, who co-founded The Innocence Project, declared in 2012 that "quite simply, what Cooperstown is to baseball Chicago is to false confessions. . . . It is the hall of fame" (Davis 2018). Indeed, "of the 29 wrongful conviction rulings involving false confessions in the United States in 2017, 13 were in Cook County, where the court system covers Chicago, according to the National Registry of Exonerations" (Davis 2018).

Police in Chicago have a long history of using extrajudicial violent methods to harass those they don't like—this is the department, after all, whose detective shot Al Capone's successor, Frank Nitto, better known as Frank Nitti, three times during a raid "for no apparent reason" (Eghigian 2006, xvi), and who later went on to book Nitto long after the shooting on "general principles" (Eghigian 2006), rather than something as pedestrian as a criminal charge. Even so, according to Davis (2018), a spike in the use of the third degree beginning in the late twentieth century, which he attributes to a rise in crime rates and corresponding pressure to secure convictions, was in a class by itself:

> Chicago police have long grappled with a reputation for torturing suspects into confessing, due in large part to the notorious detective Jon Burge, who along with his "midnight crew" has been found responsible for beating, electrocuting and intimidating suspects from the 1970s to the '90s. The city has paid out more than $100 million in settlements and reparations in Burge-related cases alone and more than $500 million altogether in the past decade to settle police misconduct and wrongful conviction lawsuits, according to a report from the Better Government Association.

Beyond the monetary cost to the city, of course, is the price paid by innocent people who in some cases spent decades of their lives behind bars for crimes they had not committed (Davis 2018), to say nothing of the corrosive effect on the confidence of city residents in their police and justice system, without which a police force is nothing but an occupying army.

Of course, this does not answer the question of whether the methods used by Burge and others were "effective" in the sense of reducing overall crime (at the cost, of course, of violating the constitutional rights of those in their custody). Dean Angelo, who once ran the police union in Chicago, lauded Burge after his death this way: "Jon Burge put a lot of bad guys in prison that belonged . . . in prison. People picked a career apart that was considered for a long time to be an honorable career and a very effective career. I don't know that Jon Burge got a fair shake based on the years and years of service that he gave the city. But we'll have to wait and see how that eventually plays out in history" (Sobol et al. 2018).

As best we can tell there does not appear to be any strong correlation between the methods of police officers like Burge who engaged in torture and a reduction in the crime rate in Chicago, particularly in the area of violent crimes. While it is true that the homicide rate in Chicago peaked at around thirty-three murders for every 100,000 residents in the early 1990s (which most observers blame on the initial spread of crack cocaine) before gradually declining to 15 or so per 100,000 in the early 2000s (Univ. of Chicago Crime Lab 2016, 5), other cities experienced similar or greater declines without resorting to the use of police torture, at least on the scale performed by Burge and his colleagues. For example, San Francisco's murder rate dropped from 18 per 100,000 people in 1992 to 6 per 100,000 in 2002, while San Diego's went from 14 per 100,000 to 4 per 100,000 in the same period (Friedman et al. 2017, 5).

All of this leads us to a fundamental question: if torture is not an effective means of gaining information or of securing compliance, why do some policymakers continue to support it or turn away when their subordinates engage in it? Paradoxically, this may be because torture is more about the practitioner than about their victim.

As was noted in the previous chapter, some sociologists believe that, in some cases, servants of so-called liberal democracies renew their faith in the power of the state by engaging in torture (Lazreg and Weitz 2008, 7). As Lazreg and Weitz (2008, 7) have found, this is especially true when a government is struggling against an indigenous resistance that it can hurt, but not completely suppress, using military force.

However, torture can also be about the desire of interrogators and their political masters to build cover for themselves, as shown in the most recent American experience with torture from 2001 through 2009 of Taliban and al-Qaeda detainees.

While both Franklin Delano Roosevelt and George W. Bush were presidents during an attack on the United States that caused mass casualties, thanks to changes in technology and access to the presidency, they are remembered in very different ways. The image of Roosevelt most usually connected with Pearl Harbor is that of him addressing Congress the next day when he declared that December 7, 1941, was a "date which will live in infamy" before asking for a declaration of war against Japan. In contrast, Bush will forever be saddled with the photo depicting his blank expression as an aide whispers word about the second plane hitting the World Trade Center while he read "The Pet Goat" to children (Glass 2015).

Similarly, while both Roosevelt's and Bush's governments had received warnings prior to the attacks, those given to Roosevelt were only declassified long after his death (Persico 2004), while the 9/11 Commission established by Congress ensured that many of the warnings given to Bush came out during his first term. Given this background, it is hard to imagine a situation where the Bush presidency could have survived politically if there had been another mass-casualty attack on the United States after 9/11 on his watch.

For these reasons, it's not hard to see why Bush was receptive to the idea of subjecting detainees to the kind of abusive treatment the United States had prosecuted the Nazis for at Nuremberg. If the use of torture provided intelligence that prevented another attack, he'd look like a hero. If terrorists struck anyway, he could claim that he'd done all he could to get the information that would have prevented it.

As noted in the Senate's report, the use of torture likely made the problem worse, as it gave detainees a motive to fabricate information and cause the government to waste resources chasing false leads. However, since the report wasn't made publicly available until long after he was out of office, its effect on Bush was negligible. Indeed, an argument can be made that engaging in torture helped defuse criticism from those members of his party even further to the right than he was and thereby *helped* Bush politically, particularly since his successor declined to prosecute anyone who engaged in torture on Bush's watch.

While it would be superficial in accord with some of his public statements, it does not appear that Bush was attracted by the idea of using torture on Taliban and al-Qaeda prisoners as a means of extrajudicial punishment or deterrence, for one key reason. For that approach to work, others would need to know about what was done to the prisoners, ideally from their own lips, which directly conflicted with the administration's desire to keep exactly what was going on at the CIA's black sites a secret.

Moreover, the ability of relatively open and democratic societies to effect change in the behavior of their opponents by using harsh methods ranges from limited to nonexistent, according to some scholars.

"Can we terrorize the terrorists into stopping their terror? This counter-terrorism is what we mean when we speak of fighting fire with fire. If by 'effectiveness' we mean successful and permanent elimination of a crisis, then we should ask—is it common sense to argue that democracy can "effectively" turn the terrorists into law-abiding and peace-loving citizens, by using the instruments of fear and force? Of course not!" (Naidu 1995, 6).

Naidu was writing about the Canadian experience in October 1970, when the Front de libération du Québec (FLQ) kidnapped British trade representative James Richard Cross and Quebec minister of labour Pierre Laporte. Ultimately, the FLQ wanted an independent Quebec with a Marxist-oriented economy (FLQ Manifesto 1970), but in exchange for their release of the officials, the FLQ demanded the release of multiple prisoners and $500,000 in ransom, among other things (Canadian Broadcasting Corporation 2010).

Instead, on October 13th, Canadian prime minister Pierre Elliott Trudeau called out the Canadian military to protect government buildings in Ottawa, before quipping to a Canadian Broadcasting Corporation reporter, "There's a lot of bleeding hearts around who don't like to see people with helmets and guns. All I can say is 'go ahead and bleed' but it's more important to keep law and order in this society than to be worried about weak-kneed people who don't like the looks [of a soldier]" (Canadian Broadcasting Corporation 2018). When asked by the media how far he would go in this regard, Trudeau replied, "Just watch me" (Canadian Broadcasting Corporation 2018).

On October 16, 1970, Trudeau invoked the War Measures Act for the first time in Canada's peacetime history, which suspended civil liberties across Quebec. According to the now-declassified portions of his cabinet meeting the day before, the government expected that "approximately 200 people could be arrested during the first round of action by the police and perhaps another thousand all told eventually" as a result of the Act ("The FLQ Situation," 4). Ultimately, while 497 people were rounded up on suspicion of association with the FLQ, the vast majority (435) were never charged with a crime (Smith et al. 2013, 2018). Some, like Nicolas Galipeau, were as young as fifteen and whose only crime was "having the wrong parents," in his case, ones sympathetic to Quebec separatism (Peritz 2000).

Shortly thereafter, the FLQ killed Laporte, but Cross was located "after routine police work" rather than information gathered through the War Measures Act (Bélanger 2000a) and after Cross's kidnappers were given a safe-conduct to Cuba in exchange for his release, the tension began to ease (Bélanger 2000b).

In November 1970, the president of the Quebec Civil Liberties Union declared that he had visited about one-half of the 118 people who were still in custody and that "none had been tortured, although some had complained that they had been subjected to questioning techniques that were 'absolutely unacceptable'" (Tetley 2000, Appendix D, 31). While details of what these techniques were are hard to come by, it should be remembered that the crisis occurred during an era when one Montreal police officer "secured a rape confession by publicly stripping off the suspect's clothes" in a nonpolitical case (Ha 2016), so the force's *standard* interrogation practices sometimes strayed into the realm of what we would consider torture today in nonpolitical cases. It does not seem fanciful to imagine that they might have been tempted to go even further after the prime minister had essentially proclaimed that Quebec was in danger of falling to an insurrection.

Indeed, by July 1971—six months after Canadian military forces had vacated the province at the end of the crisis—Quebec's Ombudsman would advise the provincial government that 103 of the 238 complaints of mistreatment that arose under the War Measures Act were justified and could merit financial compensation (Tetley, Appendix E, 3).

Two further ironies had to wait for the passage of time to be uncovered. First, "several years later, after extensive investigation, it became apparent that the FLQ was not the major paramilitary organization many had believed. . . . At the time of the October Crisis, the group had no more than thirty-five members" (Canadian Broadcasting Corporation 2001).

Thus, despite arresting over ten times as many people—most of whom turned out to be innocent—as the FLQ had members, the Canadian and Quebec governments still had to rely on standard police techniques and investigation to locate and free Cross.

Second, six years after Trudeau's death in 2000, Canadian historians Max and Monique Nemni (2006, 173–182), who had been given unprecedented access to Trudeau's personal papers, revealed that he had attempted to organize a separatist coup in Quebec in 1942 while Canada was at war with the Axis powers, though his planning did not go as far as the FLQ's and his preference was for a right-wing state, since he also expressed admiration for the Vichy collaborationist government then in power in France at that time.

In fairness, Trudeau's politics had changed dramatically by the time he was elected to the House of Commons in the 1960s—he's justly credited for liberalizing Canada's laws on divorce and abortion, as well as famously declaring that "there's no place for the state in the bedrooms of the nation" when he led the charge to decriminalize homosexual acts between consenting adults (Wright 2016, 114–123). Even so, on December 30, 1977, Trudeau threatened to invoke the War Measures Act *again* if Quebec attempted to unilaterally declare its independence (Bélanger 2000). In doing so, Trudeau illustrated why the use of emergency measures (and, to the extent they widen the ability of police to use coercive methods of interrogation, potentially up to and including torture) is attractive to policymakers: even if they don't deliver rewards in the area of increased intelligence about their adversaries, they can help frame the boundaries of a debate and intimidate other political actors to remain within those lines. In the case of Quebec, it helped to channel separatist agitation to the Parti Québécois, which ultimately won power in Quebec in 1976, and away from those who chose to contest the streets instead, like the FLQ.

In regimes that are less open to public debate and criticism than the United States and Canada, the torture of political opponents can sometimes serve other purposes.

"There are seventeen feminists in Saudi prison, who have been there since May, who are being tortured," said Mona Eltahawy (2018), an Egyptian women's rights activist and columnist. "One has been waterboarded. They have been subjected to electric shocks, they've been flogged, they've been threatened with sexual harassment."

Eltahawy (2018) doesn't believe the choice of torture method used by the Saudis wasn't accidental. "What do you associate the word 'waterboarding' with? It's terrorism, right? What does that mean? That the Crown Prince of Saudi Arabia, that the Saudi regime, associates feminism with terrorism," she said. "Chew on that."

Based on Eltahawy's comments, it would appear that torturing the women in its custody serves two purposes for the Saudi government other than information gathering. First, it can inflict extrajudicial punishment on those holding a point of view (in this case, feminism) that the regime disagrees with, both to cause them pain and to potentially deter others from sharing their position and beliefs. Second, by subtly conflating feminist activists with "terrorists," the Saudi government dehumanizes them, helps to split them from their families and other support networks and makes it easier to gain societal consent to take even sterner methods if it wishes against women who are no longer daughters, sisters, mothers, or wives, but "terrorists."

On a deeper level, by showing what it is prepared to do to those who transgress the established limits of "debate" on a particular issue, the Saudis can try to herd activists onto a path where they can be more easily controlled or managed, as Trudeau did with the Quebec separatists through his use of the War Measures Act.

What Alternatives to Torture Exist?

Assuming one's objective is to extract information from a subject, the alternatives to torture are not only well known but well known to be more effective than physical or mental coercion. As shown in Chapter 1, Hanns Joachim Scharff managed to break 480 out of 500 captured American pilots just by interrogating them in an office or when taking them for a walk in the woods or the officer's club and following a five-point strategy: "(1) Employ a friendly approach . . . (2) Do not press for information . . . (3) [Maintain] the illusion of knowing it all . . . (4) [Deploy] the use of confirmations/disconfirmations . . . (5) Ignore new information . . ." (Granhag et al. 2016, 137–138).

The FBI (Federal Bureau of Investigation) has successfully followed a similar set of protocols for years. Because the Bureau's primary interest is securing statements that will later be admissible for trial, Section 7–1 of its *Legal Handbook for Special Agents* reminds personnel that "the most important limitations on the admissibility of accused's incriminating statements are the requirements that they be voluntary; that they be obtained without the government resorting to outrageous behavior; and that they be obtained without violating the accused's right to remain silent or to have a lawyer present" (Federal Bureau of Investigation, 2003). Not surprisingly, Section 7–2.1 of the *Handbook* provides, "It is the policy of the FBI that no attempt be made to obtain a statement by force, threats, or promises. Whether an accused or suspect will cooperate is left entirely to the individual" (Federal Bureau of Investigation 2003).

A similar set of rules applies to persons arrested abroad with the cooperation of foreign police agencies, with the proviso that the *Miranda* warning may be delayed if the local officials contend it would violate the law in their jurisdiction to give it, as set forth in Section 7–15 of the *Handbook* (Federal Bureau of Investigation 1987).

The Bureau is unwilling, at least on paper, to bend these rules even in the case of suspected terrorists nabbed in the United States. In 2010 the Bureau reemphasized that agents were required to advise such persons of their "*Miranda* rights and seek a waiver of those rights before any further interrogation occurs, absent exceptional circumstances" (Caproni 2010, 2).

That said, the Bureau's broad definition of "exceptional circumstances" grants a lot of leeway to its interrogators if they wish to delay notification of a detainee's right to remain silent in a terror case.

In light of the magnitude and complexity of the threat often posed by terrorist organizations, particularly international terrorist organizations, and the nature of their attacks, the circumstances surrounding an arrest of an operational terrorist may warrant significantly more extensive public safety interrogation without *Miranda* warnings than would be permissible in an ordinary criminal case. Depending on the facts, such interrogation might include, for example, questions about possible impending or coordinated terrorist attacks; the location, nature, and threat posed by weapons that might pose an imminent danger to the public; and the identities, locations, and activities or intentions of accomplices who may be plotting additional imminent attacks. (Caproni 2010, 3)

While agents are admonished to seek the approval of their Special Agent in Charge (and through them, the FBI's headquarters and the Department of Justice; Caproni 2010, 3) before delaying a *Miranda* notification, reading between the lines of the memo gives the strong indication that headquarters will not second-guess the decisions of agents in this regard unless they're clearly unreasonable, since "the agents on the scene who are interacting with the arrestee are in the best position to assess what questions are necessary to secure their safety and the safety of the public, and how long the post-arrest interview can practically be delayed while interrogation strategy is being discussed" (Caproni 2010, 3–4).

While giving what amounts to a wink and a nudge to agents who are inclined not to interrupt a chatty suspect with an advisement about their rights that is constitutionally required is troubling, from a harm reduction perspective it is far preferable to the bureau using physical or mental coercive tactics on the prisoner. If the warning is unreasonably delayed, the prisoner has at least a theoretical remedy to have the statements they made before they were *Mirandized* suppressed at any later trial. If, on the other hand, the prisoner is tortured, it is very unlikely that the government will ever put them on trial in a civilian courtroom, since evidence obtained under torture would likely be found inadmissible and cause the case to collapse—which is why the United States has proceeded under some form of the "military commissions" system for trials of high-level al-Qaeda and Taliban detainees captured in the aughts and in its custody at Guantanamo Bay, Cuba.

That said, in 2012 the Bureau was sharply criticized for adopting some portions of the CIA's *KUBARK* manual, including the isolation of prisoners suspected of terrorism as an interrogation tactic, by the American Civil Liberties Union (Chaffee 2012). The FBI and other law enforcement agencies have also been slammed for using the Reid technique, "a common law enforcement interview method that has been known to produce false confessions" (Baumann 2013).

In a law enforcement context, it specifically does that in the following ways:

A Reid interrogation involves nine steps. The first seven steps require the investigator to: (1) confidently state the suspect's guilt; (2) develop a theme designed to elicit a confession; (3) prevent the suspect from engaging in 'unnecessary denials' (4) turn the suspect's denials into reasons why the suspect should tell the truth (5) regain the suspect's attention to the theme when the suspect has psychologically withdrawn; (6) continue to develop the theme to prevent the suspect from drifting into a passive mood; and (7) provide the suspect with an alternative question that requires the suspect to choose between two explanations for why he committed a crime. The eighth step occurs after the suspect has finally admitted to some or all of his participation in a crime, and it calls for the suspect to orally detail the crime. The ninth and final step requires the interrogator to preserve the oral confession by converting it into a written document. (Jordan 2016, 146)

Note the focus of the Reid technique is not to get at the truth, but to get the suspect to confess regardless of their level of involvement in a crime. If interrogators use it without sufficient checks in an intelligence context, they run the risk of getting a similar set of bad results as their comrades who used torture.

As the Senate Intelligence Committee's Report on Torture found, "Throughout the period during which KSM [Khalid Sheikh Mohammed, believed to be the mastermind behind the 9/11 attacks] was subjected to the CIA's enhanced interrogation techniques, KSM provided inaccurate information, much of which he would later acknowledge was fabricated and recant" (U.S. Congress 2012, 177). While the Committee credits the FBI for getting Abu Zubaydah to identify KSM as the main planner behind the 9/11 plot, among other things (U.S. Congress 2012, 38), because the Bureau didn't use torture, later disclosures regarding the FBI's favoring the Reid technique are disturbing. It does neither the truth nor public safety any good if someone who interrogators erroneously believe is involved with al-Qaeda can be manipulated via the Reid technique into "admitting" this.

Ironically, the best argument against prejudging the outcome of an interrogation comes from Don Rumsfeld, who enthusiastically supported the use of torture on al-Qaeda and Taliban detainees when he was the secretary of state. "As we know, there are known knowns; there are things we know we know. We also know there are known unknowns; that is to say we know there are some things we do not know. But there are also unknown unknowns—the ones we don't know we don't know" (Graham 2014).

Using the Reid technique reduces the chance that one will discover these "unknown unknowns," as the entire process is directed toward forcing the detainee's story to fit the interrogator's mental picture of the situation, rather than amending the interrogator's vision to fit the facts. It may be that the bureau has sufficient safeguards to lessen the chance of this happening or it may be that the United States has simply been luckier since 9/11 than it was in the months and weeks leading up to the attack.

Even so, based on the information available to us, abstaining from physical or mental torture and utilizing the tactics pioneered by Scharff and others appear to maximize the chances of success, at least if success is defined as the extraction of information from a reluctant subject.

Should Torture Be Abolished?

Given that torture is an inefficient (and often ineffective) means of extracting information yet inflicts significant trauma on the subject (and often on the perpetrators), is abolishing its use on a worldwide basis practical—and, if so, would doing so be desirable?

Except for Zimbabwe, Bhutan, Suriname, Tanzania, Oman, Iran, Myanmar, Malaysia, Papua New Guinea, and North Korea, every country on earth has signed the CAT (Office of the High Commissioner for Human Rights 2019; OHCR). Of the signatories, only Angola, India, and Sudan have failed to ratify the agreement (OHCR 2019), so the official answer to the first question by most nations would be yes.

Unofficially, of course, a number of countries have signed on to the CAT in public only to attempt to evade it in private—to say nothing of the public efforts of the United States to limit its exposure under the CAT as much as it can, supposedly to protect its spies, soldiers, and other personnel abroad, notwithstanding the fact that domestic American law criminalizes torture under the War Crimes Act of 1996.

Given the popularity of its use by governments around the world throughout most of recorded history, torture is probably best classified as a *malum prohibitum*, rather than a *malum in se* act. "The distinction between malum in se and malum prohibitum offenses is best characterized as follows: a malum in se offense is 'naturally evil as adjudged by the sense of a civilized community,' whereas a malum prohibitum offense is wrong only because a statute makes it so" (Ireland 2000).

If countries wish to normalize the practice of torture, they are free to denounce their commitments under the CAT and, if applicable, the regional commitments they may have made, which were discussed at the start of this chapter. However, pursuing a policy that proscribes torture (via the CAT and related agreements) while simultaneously seeking to evade those commitments for political advantage simply sows the seeds of contempt and cynicism toward all international commitments.

The situation regarding the International Criminal Court's (ICC's) investigation of the UK for alleged war crimes committed in Iraq between 2003 and 2009 is a prime example. After initially closing out its investigation in 2006, the ICC reopened it in 2014 after receiving new information and eventually determined that "the information available provides a reasonable basis to believe that in the period from 20 March 2003 through 28 July 2009 the UK servicemen committed the following war crimes against at least 61 victims in their custody in the context of armed conflicts in Iraq: wilful killing/murder (article 8(2)(a)(i)) or article 8(2)(c)(i)); torture and inhuman/cruel treatment (article 8(2)(a)(ii) or article 8(2)(c)(i)); outrages upon personal dignity (article 8(2)(b)(xxi) or article 8(2)(c)(ii)); rape and other forms of sexual violence (article 8(2)(b)(xxii) or article 8(2)(e)(vi))" (Office of the Prosecutor 2018, 50).

While Iraq was not a party to the Rome Statute, because the UK was, the ICC has jurisdiction over British nationals who allegedly committed war crimes (including torture) on Iraqi territory (Office of the Prosecutor 2018, 49).

On the surface, given the criticism the ICC has received recently for focusing most of its work on the developing world (Hatcher-Moore 2017), moving forward with prosecution of the British nationals would seem like an easy decision for the court. However, the Office of the Prosecutor (2018, 54) apparently feels otherwise, noting that it "expects to finalise its admissibility assessment of any potential case(s) arising from the situation in Iraq/UK in the near future, with a view to reaching a final determination within the best possible timeframe."

Of course, even if the ICC filed charges and brought some of the British defendants accused of torture to court in 2019—which is far from assured—the case(s) would be brought anywhere from a decade to a decade and a half or more after the alleged events took place, with all of the expected negative impacts on the availability and memories of witnesses and the likely loss of key evidence. Still, even a flawed prosecution would be better than the ICC taking no action at all, at least from the perspective of enforcement of the CAT.

Conclusion

Given that torture has been repeatedly shown to be a suboptimal solution at best and wholly ineffective at worst, there are strong arguments in favor of removing it from the toolbox of governmental policy options. Unfortunately, so long as governments view the use of force against critics and adversaries as one of their core prerogatives, high-sounding rhetoric is likely to be more common than substantive action to enforce the ban all but a handful of countries have publicly committed themselves to.

References

"African (Banjul) Charter on Human and Peoples' Rights." Organization of African Unity, Conclusion Date: June 27, 1981, https://au.int/sites/default/files/treaties/36390-treaty-0011_-_african_charter_on_human_and_peoples_rights_e.pdf (accessed November 24, 2019)

"ASEAN Human Rights Declaration." Association of Southeast Asian Nations, Conclusion Date: November 18, 2012, https://www.asean.org/storage/images/ASEAN_RTK_2014/6_AHRD_Booklet.pdf (accessed January 4, 2019).

Association for the Prevention of Torture, Center for Justice and International Law. "Torture in International

Law: A Guide to Jurisprudence," Center for Justice and International Law Geneva, APT/CEJIL 2008, https://www .apt.ch/content/files_res/jurisprudenceguide.pdf (accessed October 18, 2018).

Baumann, Nick. "You'll Never Guess Where This FBI Agent Left a Secret Interrogation Manual," *Mother Jones*, December 20, 2013, https://www.motherjones.com/ politics/2013/12/fbi-copyrighted-interrogation-manual-unredacted-secrets/ (accessed January 27, 2019).

Bélanger, Claude. "Readings in Quebec History: October Crisis," August 23, 2000a, http://faculty.marianopolis .edu/c.belanger/quebechistory/readings/october.htm (accessed January 27, 2019).

Bélanger, Claude. "Chronology of the October Crisis, 1970, and Its Aftermath," August 23, 2000b, http://faculty .marianopolis.edu/c.belanger/quebechistory/chronos/ october.htm (accessed January 27, 2019).

Biderman, Albert D. "Communist Attempts to Elicit False Confessions from Air Force Prisoners of War," *Bulletin of the New York Academy of Medicine*, 33 (9): 616–625 (1957).

Canadian Broadcasting Corporation. "The October Crisis," 2001, https://www.cbc.ca/history/EPISCONTENT SE1EP16CH1PA4LE.html (accessed January 27, 2019).

Canadian Broadcasting Corporation. "The October Crisis: October 1970: The FLQ, the Kidnappings and the Response," October 4, 2010, https://www.cbc.ca/news/ canada/the-october-crisis-1.973762.

Canadian Broadcasting Corporation. "'Just Watch Me,' Pierre Trudeau and the October Crisis," June 21, 2018, https://www.cbc.ca/archives/just-watch-me-pierre-trudeau-and-the-october-crisis-1.4676740.

Caproni, Valerie. "Custodial Interrogation for Public Safety and Intelligence-Gathering Purposes of Operational Terrorists Arrested inside the United States," Federal

Bureau of Investigation, October 21, 2010, https://vault
.fbi.gov/policy-custodial-interrogation-for-public-safety/
custodial-interrogation/view (accessed January 27, 2019).

Central Intelligence Agency. *KUBARK Counterintelligence
Interrogation* (Langley: Central Intelligence Agency, 1963).

Chaffee, Devon. "FBI Interrogation Primer Encourages
Prisoner Isolation," *American Civil Liberties Union*, August
2, 2012, https://www.aclu.org/blog/national-security/
torture/fbi-interrogation-primer-encourages-prisoner-
isolation (accessed January 27, 2019).

"Convention against Torture." United Nations Human
Rights Office of the High Commissioner, Conclusion
Date: December 10, 1984, https://www.ohchr.org/en/
professionalinterest/pages/cat.aspx.

Coogan, Tim Pat. *The IRA* (New York: Palgrave, 2002).

"Cooperation in Asia," *The New York Times*, August 9, 1967,
p. 38.

Davis, Kevin. "The Chicago Police Legacy of Extracting False
Confessions Is Costing the City Millions," *ABA Journal*,
July 1, 2018, http://www.abajournal.com/magazine/article/
chicago_police_false_confessions (accessed January 20, 2019).

Dawit Isaak v Republic of Eritrea. Decision of the
African Commission on Human and Peoples Rights
on the Preliminary Objection, Communication
428/12, April 27, 2018, http://www.achpr.org/files/
sessions/19th-eo/comunications/428.12/decision_on_
communication_428_12_eng.pdf.

Donadio, Rachel. "Italy Convicts 23 Americans for
C.I.A. Renditions," *The New York Times*, November 4,
2009, https://www.nytimes.com/2009/11/05/world/
europe/05italy.html (accessed October 14, 2018).

Eghigian, Mars, Jr. *After Capone: The Life and World of Chicago
Mob Boss Frank "The Enforcer" Nitti* (Nashville: Cumberland
House Publishing, 2006).

Eltahawy, Mona, Twitter Post, 1:28 P.M., January 21, 2019. https://twitter.com/monaeltahawy/status/108746 2077478961154

Federal Bureau of Investigation. *Legal Handbook for Special Agents*, 1987, 2003, https://vault.fbi.gov/Legal%20 Handbook%20for%20FBI%20Special%20Agents/Legal%20 Handbook%20for%20FBI%20Special%20Agents%20 Part%201%20of%201/view (accessed January 27, 2019).

"The FLQ Situation." 1970–10–15, RG2, Privy Council Office, Series A-5-a, Volume 6359, Access Code: 90, http:// central.bac-lac.gc.ca/.redirect?app=cabcon&id=137& lang=eng (accessed January 26, 2019).

Friedman, Matthew, Ames C. Grawert, and James Cullen. "Crime Trends: 1990–2016," Brennan Center for Justice at New York University School of Law, 2017, https://www .brennancenter.org/sites/default/files/publications/Crime%20 Trends%201990-2016.pdf (accessed January 20, 2019).

Front de libération du Québec. "FLQ Manifesto 1970," http://faculty.marianopolis.edu/c.belanger/quebechistory/ docs/october/documents/FLQManifesto.pdf (accessed January 26, 2019). Damien Claude Bélanger, ed.

Glass, Andrew. "Bush Reads 'The Pet Goat' to Schoolchildren, Sept. 11, 2001," *Politico*, September 11, 2015, https://www .politico.com/story/2015/09/bush-reads-the-pet-goat-to-schoolchildren-sept-11-2001-213544 (accessed January 21, 2019).

Graham, David A. "Rumsfeld's Knowns and Unknowns: The Intellectual History of a Quip," *The Atlantic*, March 27, 2014, https://www.theatlantic.com/politics/archive/2014/03/ rumsfelds-knowns-and-unknowns-the-intellectual-history-of-a-quip/359719/ (accessed January 28, 2019).

Granhag, Par Anders, Steven Kleinman, and Simon Oleszkiewicz. "The Scharff Technique: On How to Effectively Elicit Intelligence from Human Sources,"

International Journal of Intelligence and Counterintelligence,
29 (1): 132–150 (January 2016).

Ha, Tu Thanh. "Jacques Cinq-Mars Was a Tough, Rule-Bending Montreal Police Captain," *The Globe and Mail,*
December 1, 2016, updated April 10, 2017, https://
www.theglobeandmail.com/news/national/jacques-cinq-mars-was-a-tough-rule-bending-montreal-police-captain/
article33130058/ (accessed January 27, 2019).

Hatcher-Moore, Jessica. "Is the World's Highest Court Fit for
Purpose?" *The Guardian*, April 5, 2017, https://www
.theguardian.com/global-development-professionals-network/2017/apr/05/international-criminal-court-fit-purpose (accessed February 1, 2019).

"Human Rights in Southeast Asia: Briefing Materials for the
ASEAN-Australia Summit," Human Rights Watch, 2018,
https://www.hrw.org/sites/default/files/supporting_resources/
asean_australia0318.pdf (accessed January 4, 2019).

"Inter-American Convention to Prevent and Punish Torture."
Organization of American States, Conclusion Date:
December 9, 1985, https://www.oas.org/juridico/english/
treaties/a-51.html (accessed November 9, 2019).

Ireland, Faith E. (Dissent). *State v. Anderson*, 141 Wash. 2d
357 (2000).

"Italian President Pardons CIA Kidnappers." *Telesur*, December
24, 2015, https://www.telesurtv.net/english/news/Italian-President-Pardons-CIA-Kidnappers-20151224-0001.html
(accessed October 14, 2018).

Jordan, Quincy A. M. "The Odd Couple: Reid Interviews and
Miranda Custody," *Arkansas Law Review*, 69 (1): 143–172
(2016).

Lazreg, Marnia, and Eric Weitz. *Torture and the Twilight of
Empire: From Algiers to Baghdad* (Princeton: Princeton
University Press, 2008).

Leader, Elizabeth. "Does the ASEAN Human Rights
Declaration Even Matter?" Asia Unbound, Council on

Foreign Relations, September 28, 2012, https://www.cfr
.org/blog/does-asean-human-rights-declaration-even-matter
(accessed January 4, 2019).

McAuley, James. "France's Macron Admits to Military's
Systematic Use of Torture in Algeria," *The Washington
Post*, September 13, 2018, https://www.washingtonpost
.com/world/europe/frances-macron-admits-to-militarys-
systematic-use-of-torture-in-algeria-war/2018/09/13/
6b0e85cc-b729-11e8-94eb-3bd52dfe917b_story.html
(accessed October 18, 2018).

McCain, John. "John McCain, Prisoner of War: A First-
Person Account," *U.S. News and World Report*, January 28,
2008, https://www.usnews.com/news/articles/2008/01/28/
john-mccain-prisoner-of-war-a-first-person-account

Military Commissions Act of 2006, Pub. L. 109–366, 120
Stat. 2633, (109th Congress).

Naidu, M. V. "Democracy versus Terrorism: Flq Terrorism
in Quebec: A Case Study." Peace Research 27 (4): 1–15
(1995). http://www.jstor.org/stable/23607375.

Nemni, Max, and Monique Nemni. *Young Trudeau: 1919–1944
Son of Quebec, Father of Canada*, William Johnson, trans.
(Toronto: McClelland & Stewart, 2006).

Nowicki, Dan. "John McCain POW Recordings Revive
Historic, Painful Episode," *The Arizona Republic*, August
13, 2016, https://www.azcentral.com/story/news/
politics/azdc/2016/08/13/john-mccain-pow-recordings-
revive-historic-painful-episode/88547416/ (accessed
January 29, 2019).

Office of the High Commissioner for Human Rights,
United Nations. "Status of Ratification: Convention
against Torture and Other Cruel, Inhuman or Degrading
Treatment or Punishment," January 31, 2019, http://
indicators.ohchr.org/ (accessed January 31, 2019).

Office of the Military Government for Germany.
"Nuremberg Military Tribunals: Indictments," 1946,

https://www.loc.gov/rr/frd/Military_Law/pdf/NT_Indict ments.pdf (accessed October 10, 2018).

Office of the Prosecutor. "Report on Preliminary Examination Activities 2018," International Criminal Court, December 5, 2018, https://www.icc-cpi.int/itemsDocuments/181205-rep-otp-PE-ENG.pdf (accessed February 1, 2019).

Peritz, Ingrid. "October Crisis Hit Unknowns the Hardest," *The Globe and Mail*, October 16, 2000, updated April 7, 2018, https://www.theglobeandmail.com/news/national/october-crisis-hit-unknowns-the-hardest/article1042856/ (accessed January 26, 2019).

Persico, Joseph E. "The World: Early Warnings; What Did He Know and When?" *The New York Times*, April 18, 2004, https://www.nytimes.com/2004/04/18/weekinreview/the-world-early-warnings-what-did-he-know-and-when.html (accessed January 21, 2019).

Reidy, Aisling. *The Prohibition of Torture: A Guide to the Implementation of Article 3 of the European Convention on Human Rights* (Strasbourg: Council of Europe, 2003).

"Robben Island Guidelines for the Prohibition and Prevention of Torture in Africa." African Commission on Human and Peoples' Rights, Conclusion Date: October 23, 2002, https://apt.ch/content/files_res/RobbenIsland2_ENG.pdf

Rochester, Stuart I. *The Battle behind Bars: Navy and Marine POWs in The Vietnam War* (Washington, D.C.: Naval History and Heritage Command, United States Navy, 2010), https://www.history.navy.mil/content/dam/nhhc/research/publications/publication-508-pdf/BatBehindBars_508.pdf (accessed January 29, 2019).

Shapira, Ian. "'Foul Traitor' New JFK Assassination Records Reveal KGB Defector's 3 Year Interrogation," *The Washington Post*, August 16, 2017, https://www.washingtonpost.com/news/retropolis/wp/2017/08/16/foul-traitor-new-jfk-assassination-records-reveal-kgb-defectors-three-year-interrogation/ (accessed January 21, 2019).

Smith, Denis. "War Measures Act," *The Canadian Encyclopedia*, Richard Foot and Eli Yarhi, updaters, July 25, 2013, updated July 25, 2018, https://www.the canadianencyclopedia.ca/en/article/war-measures-act (accessed January 26, 2019).

Sobol, Rosemary, Jeremy Gorner, and David Heinzmann. "Disgraced Ex-Chicago Police Cmdr. Jon Burge, Accused of Presiding over Decades of Brutality and Torture, Has Died," *Chicago Tribune*, September 19, 2018, https://www.chicagotribune.com/news/local/breaking/ct-met-jon-burge-dead-20180919-story.html (accessed January 20, 2019).

Stein, Jeff. "When Torture Backfires: What the Vietcong Learned and the CIA Didn't," *Newsweek*, December 15, 2014, https://www.newsweek.com/cia-torture-report-vietcong-vietnam-war-292041 (accessed January 29, 2019).

Stevenson, William. *A Man Called Intrepid*, 8th ed. (New York: Ballentine Books, 1978).

Tetley, William. "The October Crisis: Appendix D," *Canada's Human Rights History*, 2000, https://historyofrights.ca/wp-content/uploads/documents/FLQ_appendixd.pdf (accessed January 27, 2019).

Tetley, William. "The October Crisis: Appendix E," *Canada's Human Rights History*, https://historyofrights.ca/wp-content/uploads/documents/FLQ_appendixe.pdf (accessed January 27, 2019).

"Treaty of Amity and Cooperation in Southeast Asia." Association of Southeast Asian Nations, Conclusion Date: February 24, 1976, https://asean.org/treaty-amity-cooperation-southeast-asia-indonesia-24-february-1976/.

United Nations. "Report of the Committee against Torture," General Assembly, Seventy-Third Session, Supplement No. 44 A/73/44, 2018.

"Universal Declaration of Human Rights." United Nations Human Rights Office of the High Commissioner, Conclusion Date: December 10, 1948, http://undocs.org/A/RES/217(III).

University of Chicago Crime Lab. "Gun Violence in Chicago, 2016," 2016, https://urbanlabs.uchicago.edu/projects/gun-violence-in-chicago-2016 (accessed November 24, 2019).

U.S. Congress. Congressional Record, 101st Cong., 2nd Sess., 1990 Vol. 136, Pt. 25, 36198–36199.

U.S. Congress. Senate, Committee on Government Operations, Permanent Subcommittee on Investigations. *Communist Interrogation, Indoctrination and Exploitation of American Military and Civilian Prisoners*, 84th Cong., 2d Sess., June 19, 20, 26, and 27, 1956.

U.S. Congress. Senate, Committee on Government Operations, Permanent Subcommittee on Investigations, Subcommittee on Korean War Atrocities. *Korean War Atrocities*, S. Res 40, 83rd Cong. 2d Sess., 1954, S. Rep. 848, https://www.loc.gov/rr/frd/Military_Law/pdf/KW-atrocities-Report.pdf.

U.S. Congress. Senate Select Committee on Intelligence. Committee Study of the Central Intelligence Agency's Detention and Interrogation Program. *Findings and Conclusions*, Executive Summary (2012).

Vargo, Marc E. *Women of the Resistance: Eight Who Defied the Third Reich* (Jefferson, NC: McFarland & Company, 2012).

Wright, Robert. *Trudeaumania: The Rise to Power of Pierre Elliott Trudeau* (Toronto: HarperCollins, 2016).

3 Perspectives

This chapter differs from the others in two key respects. First, it provides a set of perspectives on the issue of torture from individuals—including several torture survivors—whose points of view sometimes differ from the author's. Second, it provides additional material for readers to consider asthey form their own views about some of the questions posed by this book, including "Is torture ever justified?" "Is it ever effective?" "If so, under what circumstances is it appropriate?" and "What is the human cost?"

Fekade Ancho's piece explains how he survived both mental and physical torture at the hands of his government, which was made worse by his status as a polio survivor, while Andrea Barron discusses how the Washington, D.C.–based Torture Abolition and Survivors Support Coalition (TASSC) helps survivors like Ancho. Marjorie Cohn, former president of the National Lawyers Guild, outlines the legal objections to torture.

Sabrina Crews discusses how the Center for Victims of Torture (CVT) began its work in 1985 as the first facility concentrating on the treatment of torture survivors in the United States, while Jonathan Horowitz reviews the CIA's torture

---

Nadia Murad Basee Taha, an Iraqi Yazdi, addresses a U.S. State Department gathering in February 2019. Murad was kidnapped by ISIS in 2014 and was raped and tortured for three months before she escaped. She is a winner of both the Nobel Peace Prize and the Sakharov Prize (which is awarded by the European Parliament). (Ron Przysucha/U.S. Department of StateRon Przysucha)

program during the George W. Bush presidency. Elif Isitman explores how terrorist groups like Daesh/the Islamic State in Iraq and the Levant (ISIL/ISIS) and Boko Haram have used sexual and other forms of torture as a weapon of war. Similarly, Marissa Quenqua talks about how so-called conversion therapy, which purports to forcibly change a person's sexual orientation, amounts to torture when applied against queer children and teenagers in the United States and elsewhere. Finally, Rebecca Smith shares her own story as a survivor of two years of state torture in the Florida prison system.

Seeking Freedom and Justice: A Survivor's Story
Fekade Ancho

I am a torture survivor from Ethiopia; here is my short story. I was born in Addis Ababa, the capital city of Ethiopia, fifty-three years ago. When I was a small child, I unfortunately contracted polio, leaving me partially paralyzed for the rest of my life.

However, thanks to my family and my society, I received treatment that enabled me to walk with some support. After that, I was able to go to school and then attend the Asmara and Addis Ababa universities, where I completed degrees in the fields of philosophy and accounting.

However, as a polio victim, I faced discrimination and stigma against people with disabilities. This discrimination became more serious after I graduated and started looking for a job. I was not hired for many jobs even though I was extremely qualified, mainly because of my disability.

Finally, I got a good job in accounting at Ethiopian Airlines. But the deputy managers were not sure if they would hire me. Finally, they hired me to work in positions far below my ability. Moreover, I suffered tremendous harassment and discrimination at various levels throughout my work history.

At one point, I made a decision to learn about my rights and duties to overcome *any* challenge *I might face*. First, I defended myself, and then I started defending the rights and benefits of workers at Ethiopian Airlines. I became an activist for myself and for others whose rights were being violated. Airline employees knew I would do a good job representing them in the company union. They elected me as executive and financial officer of our basic trade union for three terms—a total of nine years.

I faced serious and life-threatening challenges, especially during my last three-year term. That is when the Ethiopian government demanded that everyone in the airline, especially people holding high positions like myself, promote the government agenda. Government propaganda was incorporated into the vision, mission, and strategy of Ethiopian Airlines. Top management carried out mass terminations of employees and replaced them with members and supporters of the ruling coalition—the Ethiopian People's Revolutionary Democratic Front (EPRDF). This party has controlled the country since 1991 and demanded total obedience from everyone in society, particularly employees in major economic sectors such as Ethiopian Airlines. Anyone who was not a party member was treated like a second-class citizen.

As union leaders, we refused to allow the airline to fire the employees who did not belong to the ruling party. We remained in constant resistance to defend union members who were being replaced by EPRDF members and their supporters.

The government response to us was powerful. Higher officials started to attack us immediately. While some union leaders retreated, some others and I continued to resist. It was at this time that I suffered serious mental and physical torture: a kind of "double discrimination." These officials discriminated against me because I was physically disabled from polio and because I did not belong to the ruling political party.

This is how the government punished me for standing up for union workers at Ethiopian Airlines. They opened a campaign against me to force me to resign from the union. They constantly fined me and lowered my performance reports. They concentrated on my physical disability weakness to isolate and marginalize me from the workers. I was constantly singled out by top management and accused of challenging their vision and strategies. There were a few other disabled employees at the airline. But they did not defend workers like I did, so management left them alone.

I was arrested and interrogated by the company's security director and agents, who accused me of not following the government agenda. The worst time was when they beat me and forced me to take off my clothes and tried to make me go into the corridor naked in front of all my colleagues. When I refused, they beat me again and again and humiliated me with insults, until I finally stood naked in front of my coworkers. This humiliation and insults were a terrible kind of mental torture.

Then they forced me to resign from the company. But just before my resignation, they offered me a higher position at Ethiopian Airlines as well as a driver who would pick me up from home and take me to work every day. But I would then have been under government control and would have had to quietly accept the management's decision to replace union employees with EPRDF party members. I rejected this bribe.

After I resigned, the company security director told me that I was privy to confidential information about the company. He warned me that I would remain under constant surveillance and that I would be severely punished if I disclosed any of this information.

I became totally desperate and hopeless and, for the first time, my wife and I discussed leaving the country. Finally, we left Ethiopia in 2016 and arrived in Washington, D.C. That is where I found TASSC. I have become active in TASSC's advocacy program and had the opportunity to visit many offices in the U.S. Congress. I told people what happened to me and why Congress should speak out against torture and human rights abuses in Ethiopia and other countries.

I applied for asylum in September 2016 and am still waiting for an interview with the asylum office. Meanwhile, I am working as an administrative assistant helping people with their tax-related paperwork. I look forward to remaining in the United States. I am proud that America has given hope to oppressed people all over the world by telling them they are entitled to universal human rights, including the right of peaceful assembly, right to free expression, and of course the right not to be jailed, tortured, raped, or even killed for criticizing their government.

Fekade Ancho Arore is a torture survivor from Ethiopia who was an accountant and union leader at Ethiopian Airlines. He contracted polio at a young age but was determined to excel in life. Fekade graduated from Addis Ababa University and was hired by Ethiopian Airlines. As a union leader, he strongly protested when management replaced union members with supporters of Ethiopia's ruling party. Fekade was tortured for his activities and fled to the United States in 2016, where he has been involved with the TASSC.

Torture Survivors as Policy Advocates
Andrea Barron

Torture treatment centers and other U.S. organizations that work with survivors of torture provide a range of services to survivors, including case management, medical care, psychological counseling, forensic evaluations, and pro bono legal assistance. The National Consortium of Torture Treatment Programs and some treatment centers also advocate for policies that benefit survivors, asylum seekers, and refugees, such as opposing President Donald Trump's ban on admitting Syrian refugees. But the TASSC, located in Washington, D.C., is the only torture treatment center where survivors themselves have become active advocates.

The organization's advocacy mission goes back to its founder, Sister Dianna Ortiz, who is both a torture survivor and an advocate. She was an Ursuline nun brutally raped and tortured by the Guatemalan military in 1989 while teaching poor Mayan children in Guatemala. After being freed, Sister Dianna and other human rights activists pressured the Clinton administration to release information on the horrendous human rights abuses committed by the Guatemalan military.

TASSC's location in the nation's capital makes it uniquely suited for advocacy. However, torture survivors living outside Washington, either as part of an organization or independently, can also use the power of their compelling stories to make policymakers more aware of torture carried out by governments in their countries. By interacting directly with policymakers and their staff, survivors can play a critical role in emphasizing the need for the United States to be a leader on global human rights and to protect refugees and asylum seekers.

Survivors from TASSC provide an inspiring model of what can be accomplished. They are involved in crafting, implementing, and evaluating advocacy priorities. They have testified before the Subcommittee on Africa and Global Human Rights in the U.S. House of Representatives; the Tom Lantos Human Rights Commission in the House; and the African Affairs Office in the State Department's Bureau of Democracy, Human Rights and Labor. Thirteen African survivors gave their personal testimonies to California congresswoman Karen Bass, chair of the House Africa Subcommittee.

These survivor advocates come from all over the world, with the majority from Africa, especially Ethiopia, Cameroon, and Eritrea. They also are from the Democratic Republic of Congo, Rwanda, Sudan, Congo-Brazzaville, Burundi, Bangladesh, Balochistan (in southwest Pakistan), Egypt, Syria, and other countries. Most survivors were forced to flee their countries because they "dared" to publicly challenge their repressive governments. They were tortured and raped by government agents for participating in peaceful demonstrations; publishing critical newspaper articles and blogs; exposing corruption; working with international organizations; refusing to join the ruling party; or just for being related to a political activist. An estimated 5–10 percent of survivors were persecuted because they are lesbian, gay, bisexual, or transgender.

In 2018, over seventy survivors from fourteen countries visited more than sixty offices in the House of Representatives and the Senate. Fifty-two of these congressional meetings took place during TASSC's annual June Survivors Week, which is held every year around June 26, designated by the United Nations as International Day in Support of Victims of Torture. Survivors told their personal stories, at times going into detail about what happened to them and the abuses security forces committed against others.

Many survivors do not want to be identified publicly, frightened that their governments are monitoring their activities and could retaliate by targeting their families back home. But through focus groups and surveys, they spoke of their advocacy experience with a sense of pride. And they expressed enthusiasm about learning more about the democratic process and how they could influence U.S. policy toward their countries. Wrote one survivor:

> I was amazed that I could visit an office of a Congressperson even though I was not a citizen, and everyone would listen to my story, treat me with respect and even take notes on what I said. This never would happen in my country.

Public advocacy also presented some challenges to participants. "Talking about torture was difficult," said one. "It reminded me of the beatings and the dark, crowded prison cells where I was interrogated. But I wanted to tell my story in Congress, and it became easier each time I did it."

In 2017 and 2018, a major focus of the advocacy program was on supporting passage of House Resolution 128 on

Ethiopia, introduced by Republican congressman Chris Smith from New Jersey. This bipartisan Resolution condemned torture, the killing of peaceful protestors by Ethiopian security forces, and the arrest of journalists, students, and political leaders who protested against brutal government policies. Survivor Guya Deki testified before the Africa Subcommittee about how he was tortured and left to die in a forest because he refused to allow the government to control his organization, the National Association of the Physically Handicapped; Guya had contracted polio as a child and uses a wheelchair.

Guya and dozens of other Ethiopians visited Congress to persuade representatives to cosponsor House Resolution 128, which passed the House on April 10, 2018. Twelve human rights organizations and Ethiopia diaspora groups collaborated to achieve this significant victory, which helped bring to power a new reformist prime minister in Ethiopia who has renounced torture, freed thousands of political prisoners, and begun the process of democratization. Fekade Ancho, a former lead accountant of Ethiopian Airlines, was one of the most active survivor advocates. Fekade said,

> Watching House Resolution 128 pass gave me great confidence in the American people—I saw how much they believe in freedom, democracy, human rights and justice. I am so grateful to the Congress Members who supported us, and that I was involved in the campaign to pass this Resolution.

Congressional staff in both Democratic and Republican offices responded positively to their meetings with survivors. This quote from Zach Cafritz, deputy chief of staff for Democratic congressman Don Beyer from Virginia, typifies reactions from staff:

> Hearing the searing, first hand testimony of the TASSC survivors was incredibly powerful. It is critical that

humanitarian policymaking be informed whenever possible by the stories of victims and survivors so that we do not lose sight of the people who must remain at the core of our work.

Public forums provide other opportunities for survivor activism. The Truth Speakers program brings survivors' voices to universities, churches, synagogues, and human rights groups. Volunteers are trained to deliver impactful testimonies to spread awareness about torture and encourage audiences to take action on behalf of those still being targeted. An Eritrean survivor, for instance, told college students how he was detained and beaten simply for asking why Eritrea does not have a constitution and why it forces everyone into indefinite military service. A survivor from Bangladesh spoke to a religious congregation about being attacked by extremist fundamentalist mobs because he was a Christian.

Nanythe Talani, an investigative journalist from Congo-Brazzaville, is a Truth Speaker and also participated in an event on Torture and the Press held shortly after the murder of Saudi journalist Jamal Khashoggi. Nanythe expressed the views of many journalists when she asked, "How can you do your job when you are constantly worried about being jailed, raped, or even killed by people who can walk away without any consequences. This is what I was facing in Congo. Even here in the U.S. I always lock my bedroom door if I am alone because I'm worried about being attacked."

We know the grim statistics: according to Amnesty International, over 140 states—three-fourths of all countries in the world—still practice torture. But everyone repulsed by these statistics can also be encouraged by the commitment and courage of the survivors, who are willing to relive their own pain to end the scourge of torture.

Andrea Barron is the Advocacy and Outreach Program Manager at TASSC. You may learn more about TASSC at www.tassc.org.

Torture Is Never Legal
Marjorie Cohn

Torture entered the national discourse after the September 11, 2001, terrorist attacks, when the George W. Bush administration instituted a program of torture and abuse of prisoners in U.S. custody. In a 2014 report, the Senate Select Intelligence Committee (2014, 10; SSCI) documented the use of waterboarding and other "enhanced interrogation techniques"—a euphemism for torture and cruel treatment—on terrorism suspects. Torture is always illegal; it violates both U.S. and international law.

Bush's administration admitted waterboarding three people. But waterboarding was utilized much more frequently, according to Steven Bradbury, a lawyer in the Department of Justice's Office of Legal Counsel (Bradbury 2005, 43).

The Senate Committee report describes the waterboarding of al-Qaeda suspect Abu al-Rahim al-Nashiri (SSCI 2014, 66–73). U.S. Navy Reserve Dr. Sondra Crosby said al-Nashiri was "one of the most severely traumatized individuals I have ever seen" (In re Al-Nashiri 2018).

- After water was poured into his nose and mouth, al-Nashi began to choke and aspirate. Then the rag was lowered, which suffocated him with the water in his lungs, throat and sinuses. The process was repeated several times. (In re Al-Nashiri 2018)
- A broomstick was wedged behind al-Nashiri's knees and his body forced backward, which pulled his knee joints apart. He was placed in a coffin between interrogations, and locked in a small box. (Savage 2017)
- Agents created in al-Nashiri "learned helplessness" to make him passive and depressed. (In re Al-Nashiri 2018) Agents racked a pistol and a revved-up power drill near al-Nashiri's head. They raked a stiff brush across his scrotum, anus, and mouth. (Savage 2017)

- Majid Khan was subjected to "rectal feeding," which is rape. Its purpose is to exert "total control" over the subject. Agents forced a concoction of pureed hummus, pasta, sauce, nuts and raisins into his rectum. This torture technique was also used on Al-Nashiri and Khalid Shaykh Mohammad. (SSCI 2014, 73, 82, 100, 115)
- Agents tied a rolled towel around Abu Zubayda's neck and swung him into a plywood wall so the towel became an object of fear. (SSCI 2014, 40–41)

Waterboarding has long been considered torture. After World War II, the U.S. government tried, convicted, and hung Japanese military leaders for the war crime of torture based on waterboarding.

Indeed, the United States has always prohibited torture—in its Constitution, legislation, executive orders, court decisions, and treaties. When the president ratifies a treaty, with the advice and consent of the Senate, it becomes part of U.S. law under the Supremacy Clause of the Constitution.

The United States has ratified three treaties that prohibit torture: the Convention against Torture and Other Cruel, Inhuman or Degrading Treatment or Punishment; the Geneva Conventions; and the International Covenant on Civil and Political Rights. The War Crimes Act makes torture a felony punishable by death or imprisonment.

Torture is forbidden under all circumstances. The Convention against Torture states unequivocally, "No exceptional circumstances whatsoever, whether a state of war or a threat of war, internal political instability or any other public emergency, may be invoked as a justification for torture" (Convention against Torture 1984, art. 2(2)).

The Geneva Conventions list torture as a grave breach, which constitutes a war crime. And the International Covenant on Civil and Political Rights (1966, art. 7) states, "No one shall be subjected to torture or to cruel, inhuman or degrading treatment or punishment."

When the United States ratified the Convention against Torture and the Geneva Conventions, it promised to prosecute or extradite those who commit or assist in the commission of torture. Under the doctrine of "command responsibility," commanders are legally accountable for torture if they knew or should have known their subordinates would use torture, and they did not take steps to stop or prevent it. Moreover, the Take Care Clause of the Constitution requires that the president "take care that the laws be faithfully executed."

Nevertheless, Barack Obama refused to hold the Bush officials legally accountable for torture. Before his first inauguration, Obama stated, "We need to look forward as opposed to looking backwards" (Johnston and Savage 2009). After the Senate report became public, Obama admitted, "We tortured some folks" (Lewis 2014).

Obama's grant of impunity to torturers sent a dangerous message to future administrations that they can torture and get away with it.

Eric Holder, Obama's attorney general, investigated only two of the most egregious cases of torture. One involved the death of Manadel al-Jamadi at the notorious Abu Ghraib prison in Baghdad, Iraq. CIA agents suspended al-Jamadi from the ceiling by his wrists bound behind his back. Military police officer Tony Diaz, who witnessed al-Jamadi's torture, reported that blood gushed from his mouth like "a faucet had turned on" as he was lowered to the ground. Al-Jamadi's death was listed as homicide after a military autopsy (Cohn 2012).

But Holder declined to prosecute those responsible for the torture and killing of al-Jamadi. And no officials from the Bush administration have faced justice for their crimes. The Principals Committee, which included Vice President Dick Cheney, Secretary of State Condoleezza Rice, Defense Secretary Donald Rumsfeld, CIA director George Tenet, Secretary of State Colin Powell, and Attorney General John Ashcroft, approved the torture of prisoners (ACLU 2008).

Bush's Justice Department lawyers, including Bradbury, John Yoo, and Jay Bybee, wrote memos purporting to justify torture. Their infamous "torture memos" contain twisted legal analysis that defines torture more narrowly than the law provides for. These legal mercenaries advised Bush officials how they could torture and get away with it (Cohn 2008).

Besides being illegal, torture does not yield accurate information. The Senate Committee's report cites several examples in which "the use of the CIA's enhanced interrogation techniques was not an effective means of obtaining accurate information or gaining detainee cooperation." The report states, "Multiple CIA detainees fabricated information, resulting in faulty intelligence . . . on critical intelligence issues including the terrorist threats which the CIA identified as its highest priorities" (SSCI 2014, 2).

Moreover, torture actually makes us less safe. The gruesome photos of torture and abuse leaked from Abu Ghraib prison and reports of torture at Guantanamo Bay have served as effective recruiting tools for those who wish to harm the United States.

References

ACLU. "Letter to Senate Judiciary Leadership Urging the Questioning into the National Security Council's Role in Torture," June 9, 2008.

Bradbury, Steven G. "Memorandum for John A. Rizzo, Senior Deputy General Counsel, CIA," May 10, 2005, https://fas .org/irp/agency/doj/olc/techniques.pdf.

Cohn, Marjorie. "Testimony before the House Judiciary Committee's Subcommittee on Constitution, Civil Rights and Civil Liberties," May 6, 2008, https://marjoriecohn .com/congressional-testimony-of-marjorie-cohn-on-torture-policy/.

Cohn, Marjorie, ed. *The United States and Torture: Interrogation, Incarceration, and Abuse* (New York and London: NYU Press, 2011).

Cohn, Marjorie. "No Accountability for Torturers," September 3, 2012, https://marjoriecohn.com/no-accountability-for-torturers/.

"Convention against Torture and Other Cruel, Inhuman or Degrading Treatment or Punishment," G.A. Res. 39/46, 1984, https://www.ohchr.org/en/professionalinterest/pages/cat.aspx.

"International Covenant on Civil and Political Rights," G.A. Res. 2200A (XXI), 1966, https://www.ohchr.org/en/professionalinterest/pages/ccpr.aspx.

Johnston, David, and Charlie Savage. "Obama Reluctant to Look into Bush Programs," *The New York Times*, January 11, 2009.

Lewis, Paul. "Obama Admits CIA 'Tortured Some Folks' but Stands by Brennan over Spying," *Guardian*, August 1, 2014, https://www.theguardian.com/world/2014/aug/01/obama-cia-torture-some-folks-brennan-spying.

Savage, Charlie. "C.I.A. Torture Left Scars on Guantánamo Prisoner's Psyche for Years," *The New York Times*, March 17, 2017, https://www.nytimes.com/2017/03/17/us/politics/guantanamo-bay-abd-al-rahim-al-nashiri.html.

Senate Select Committee on Intelligence. "Committee Study of the Central Intelligence Agency's Detention and Interrogation Program: Executive Summary," 2014, https://fas.org/irp/congress/2014_rpt/ssci-rdi.pdf.

Marjorie Cohn is professor emerita at the Thomas Jefferson School of Law, former president of the National Lawyers Guild, and editor/contributor to The United States and Torture: Interrogation, Incarceration, and Abuse. *She testified before Congress about the George W. Bush administration's interrogation policy.*

These Are the Facts about Torture
Sabrina Crews

"Dad, what are you doing for human rights?" Rudy Perpich Jr., a college student in the mid-1980s, asked his father Rudy Perpich, then governor of Minnesota. Inspired by his son's challenge, the governor assembled a task force of human rights experts and arrived at an unconventional proposal: opening a center for the specialized rehabilitative care of survivors of torture. The Center for Victims of Torture was thus founded in Minnesota in 1985, as the first organized program for care and rehabilitation of torture survivors in the United States and the third in the world.

We have been learning about torture ever since. Today, CVT is an international nongovernmental organization with locations in Africa, the Middle East, and the United States. We help heal survivors who have experienced physical and mental pain and suffering intentionally inflicted upon them by someone in a position of power. In our efforts to end torture worldwide, and to combat arguments in favor of this widespread scourge, our thirty-plus years of experience and research have allowed us to arrive at the following facts:

Torture Is Illegal

On December 10, 1948, in Paris, a coalition of forty-eight UN member states led by former First Lady Eleanor Roosevelt signed the Universal Declaration of Human Rights. The thirty articles in the Declaration outlined basic human rights that apply to everyone, everywhere. Article 5 of the Declaration prohibits torture and cruel, inhuman, or degrading treatment or punishment. In 1987, the United States adopted the UN Convention against Torture and Other Cruel, Inhuman or Degrading Treatment or Punishment. Torture is illegal under domestic and international law. It is a violation of human rights.

Torture Is Immoral

A 2016 Pew Research study found that 48 percent of Americans supported the use of torture related to anti-terrorism efforts. At CVT, we've heard the firsthand accounts of more than 33,000 survivors of torture. These individuals endured unimaginable cruelty. From them, we know that torture often has more to do with destroying communities, wielding control, and creating a climate of fear than gathering information. Its use is, regardless of culture and circumstances, unambiguously and morally wrong.

Torture Makes Us Less Safe

A 2016 *Foreign Affairs* article partly authored by CVT's former executive director Douglas Johnson explains how the CIA's post-9/11 Enhanced Interrogation program was a national security misstep, stating, "It incited extremism in the Middle East, hindered cooperation with U.S. allies, exposed American officials to legal repercussions, undermined U.S. diplomacy, and offered a convenient justification for other governments to commit human rights abuses." Torture makes our country weaker.

Ending Torture Has Bipartisan Support

American politicians have historically decried the use of torture. It was President Ronald Reagan who signed the 1988 UN Convention against Torture. President Barack Obama signed an executive order in 2009 disallowing CIA torture. In 2015, Republican senator John McCain and Democratic senator Dianne Feinstein persuaded Congress to sign components of that executive order into law.

The "Ticking Bomb" Scenario Is Fiction

Many Americans learn about torture from the media. In movies, television, and video games, it is often portrayed as the key to conquering evil. There is usually a villain, such as a terrorist or a spy, and a "ticking time-bomb" scenario, where the only way to glean vital information and save the day is through the use of torture. There is no evidence to suggest that such a situation has occurred anywhere in the world. Many of our clients have told us that they would have said anything, true or false, just to get their torture to stop. The information torture yields is never guaranteed to be reliable.

Torture Is Psychological as Well as Physical

Torture targets an individual's identity and humanity through pain and suffering that is not only physical but psychological. Psychological methods include sleep deprivation; sensory overload, which involves assaulting the senses with bright lights and loud noises; and sensory deprivation, which involves isolation and removing stimuli from the senses for extended periods of time.

Torture Is Used to Control Communities and Families

Torture erodes the fabric of societies by inciting fear and revoking rights. In the face of extreme violence, civilians retreat, activists fall silent. People are afraid to engage in active citizenship. Families and communities lose trust in their governing bodies, and future generations inherit their suspicions. Being raised to believe that social activism and reform result in arrests and torture makes an individual feel reticent to speak out. But many CVT clients did speak out. They were lawyers, teachers, journalists, and community leaders. They were mothers and daughters, fathers and sons. In several cases, they were targeted for raising their voices.

Even Children Are Tortured

Jana was only ten when she was kidnapped. In Syria, her home country, a strange man abducted her and threw her in a crowded, underground jail with other children to blackmail her father to come out of hiding. Her father did, and he was killed. When Jana fled with her mother to Jordan and found CVT, she was severely traumatized. Twenty-nine percent of CVT Jordan's clients are children like Jana. According to staff, working with children is very different from working with adults. It's something that affects everyone in the organization, from psychosocial counselors to drivers. It's also part of how systematic the abuses have been in the home countries of CVT Jordan's clients. In cases of widespread oppression, no one is safe.

As Many as 1.3 Million Refugee Torture Survivors Live in the United States

Currently, the world is confronting its worst displacement crisis in history. Many individuals fleeing war and violent conflict have experienced torture—in their home countries, during their flight, or sometimes in both cases. CVT's research team determined that nearly half of the refugees in the United States are torture survivors. From this alarming statistic, the organization has concluded that the current refugee crisis is also a torture crisis.

Rehabilitative Care Is Critical to Rebuilding Lives

Torture inflicts long-lasting wounds. Physical reminders include headaches, scars, chronic pain, and respiratory problems. The psychological damage is sometimes even worse. Sleeplessness, PTSD, depression, and anxiety prevent survivors from living productive lives. With the help of CVT's direct healing care, advocacy efforts, and rigorous research, monitoring, and evaluation methods, our clients can and do get better. We will continue to advocate on their behalf and to work tirelessly toward a future free from torture.

References

Friedersdorf, Conor. "The 'Ticking Time-Bomb' Defense of Torture Is Evasive and Irrelevant." *The Atlantic*, 2014, https://www.theatlantic.com/politics/archive/2014/12/the-ticking-time-bomb-defense-of-torture-is-embarrassing/383 797/ (accessed December 22, 2018).

Goering, Curt. "Why Torture Is Wrong," Center for Victims of Torture, 2017, https://www.cvt.org/blog/healing-and-human-rights/why-torture-wrong-0 (accessed December 21. 2018).

Higson Smith, Craig. "US Home to Far More Refugee Torture Survivors Than Previously Believed," Center for Victims of Torture, 2015, https://www.cvt.org/sites/default/files/SurvivorNumberMetaAnalysis_Sept2015_0 .pdf (accessed December 21, 2018).

"Jana's Story," Center for Victims of Torture, Survivor Stories, 2015, https://www.cvt.org/what-we-do/survivor-stories (accessed December 21, 2018).

Johnson, Douglas A. Mora, and Averell Alberto Schmidt. "The Strategic Costs of Torture," *Foreign Affairs*, 2016, https://www.foreignaffairs.com/articles/united-states/strategic-costs-torture (accessed December 21, 2018).

"Reclaiming Hope, Dignity and Respect: Syrian and Iraqi Torture Survivors in Jordan," Center for Victims of Torture, 2015, http://www.cvt.org/sites/default/files/attachments/u11/downloads/ReclaimingHope_01042016 .pdf (accessed on December 21, 2018).

"Ten Facts about Torture," Center for Victims of Torture, 2017, https://www.cvt.org/blog/healing-and-human-rights/ten-facts-about-torture (accessed December 21, 2018).

Tyson, Alec. "Americans Divided in Views of Use of Torture in U.S. Anti-Terror Efforts," Pew Research, 2017,

http://www.pewresearch.org/fact-tank/2017/01/26/
americans-divided-in-views-of-use-of-torture-in-u-s-anti-
terror-efforts (accessed on December 21, 2018).

Wood, Stanton. "An Open Letter to Dramatic Artists Who
Write About Torture: Video Games, Films and More,"
Center for Victims of Torture, 2016, https://www.cvt
.org/blog/healing-and-human-rights/open-letter-dramatic-
artists-who-write-about-torture-video-games-films (accessed
December 21, 2018).

*Sabrina Crews is a Minneapolis-based writer focused on women's
rights and human rights. She previously managed the CVT speakers' bureau, in which she trained a dynamic team of speakers to
educate the public about torture and enhanced interrogation. Now
she serves as the organization's communications writer, generating
content for CVT's website, newsletter, blog, and advertising campaigns. Her work has also appeared in the* Nonprofit Quarterly
and Minneapolis Star Tribune.

The CIA's Global Counterterrorism Torture Program, 2001–2009
Jonathan Horowitz

After September 11, 2001, the United States propelled itself
into several wars, but it also put in place an international network of secret detention and torture sites (known as "black
sites"). The director of the CIA's Counterterrorist Center told
Congress in a 2002 hearing, "After 9/11 the gloves come off"
(Black 2002). This included the use of thirteen methods of torture and other ill-treatment that the government euphemisti-
cally called "enhanced interrogation techniques," or EITs. The
techniques were (1) dietary manipulation, (2) nudity, (3) attention grasp, (4) walling (slamming someone against a wall), (5)
facial hold, (6) facial slap or insult slap, (7) abdominal slap, (8)

cramped confinement, (9) wall standing, (10) stress positions, (11) water dousing, (12) sleep deprivation (for more than forty-eight hours), and (13) the waterboard (SSCI report 2014, 421).

The CIA's post–September 11, 2001, torture program had a number of significant features. One of the most notable was the program's transnational nature. To keep detainees beyond the reach of U.S. courts, government officials set up secret detention sites in foreign countries—such as Afghanistan, Poland, Romania, and Thailand—where CIA agents and contractors could apply their EITs. In what one former CIA official described as a convenient way to get other countries to do the agency's "dirty work" (60 Minutes 2005), the United States also outsourced torture by flying people to other governments, including Egypt, Morocco, Syria, and Jordan. This was known as "rendition." Over fifty governments participated in the U.S. torture and rendition program to some degree or another (Open Society Justice Initiative 2013, 6).

The United States classified the program at the highest levels. Keeping it secret turned out to be impossible, however. Setting up a global torture network requires infinite operational requirements that leave behind infinite clues. Take for example the complex task of moving people from one black site to the next. To do this, the CIA had to contract private aircraft to fly detainees and their interrogators in criss-crossing paths around the world. This made the flights detectable in flight logs and under the watchful eyes of aviation enthusiasts who monitored the comings and goings of planes. These and other clues eventually added up and helped expose the program, allowing anti-torture advocates to successfully hold Macedonia, Romania, Poland, and a few others accountable for the roles they played in the program. Additional accountability initiatives remain underway, but those most responsible have not yet faced justice.

A second feature of the CIA's torture and rendition program was its false patina of science and law. The program's brutality hid behind a psychological theory that detainees would become passive and depressed in response to harsh interrogation techniques, and would thus cooperate and provide information. But a report by the U.S. Senate assessing the CIA's activities after September 11 revealed that neither of the two CIA-contracted psychologists who created the interrogation program had interrogation experience; specialized knowledge of al-Qaeda; a background in terrorism; or relevant regional, cultural, or linguistic expertise (SSCI report 2014, 21). The president of the American Psychological Association wrote a scathing letter expressing outrage and sadness that "two psychologists allegedly devised and engaged in brutal interrogation methods" (Kaslow 2014). The organization Physicians for Human Rights labeled the work "junk science" (Physicians for Human Rights 2015).

Another problem with the program was its assumption that interrogators would use it only on people who had useful intelligence to give up. Contrary to this, the Senate report revealed that at least 26 of 119 of the known detainees held in CIA custody were wrongfully held (SSCI 2014, 15–17). (The CIA contests this number as being too high, but it nonetheless admits that it frequently moved too slowly to release detainees.)

Alongside the program's so-called scientific foundations, the government developed legal justifications that rested on equally precarious theories. One government lawyer, Jay S. Bybee, wrote an influential memorandum arguing that several EITs, including the waterboard, which brings detainees to the brink of death by forcing water down their throats and noses, would not inflict enough pain to constitute torture and, therefore, the interrogators should not be held criminally liable (Bybee 2002b). Other lawyers argued that September 11 was an extraordinary situation, that many of the laws protecting the rights of detainees were "quaint" and even "obsolete," and that the government could not protect its citizens from another attack and respect the human rights of the people it detained all at the same time.

The worst of the torture program's tenuous legal foundations broke under the weight of criticism from within the government and from outside. Some of the memos were eventually rescinded, and many top military leaders opposed the CIA interrogation methods when lawyers approved those same methods for U.S. military personnel. Years later, a Department of Justice investigation concluded that the Bybee memo was "seriously deficient" of applicable professional standards. One former official characterized the memo as "insane." Another person interviewed for the investigation found the memo "riddled with error" and concluded that key portions were "plainly wrong" (Department of Justice Office of Professional Responsibility 2009, 160).

The impact that the CIA's interrogation techniques had on people was unquestionably disturbing. During waterboarding, one detainee vomited and had "involuntary spasms of the torso and extremities" (SSCI 2014, 41). At one point, he became unresponsive and required medical intervention (SSCI 2014, 44). Multiple detainees exhibited psychological and behavioral issues, including paranoia, insomnia, and attempts at self-harm and self-mutilation (SSCI 2014, 4). At least five detainees experienced disturbing hallucinations due to sleep deprivation of up to 180 hours while being forced to stand or while in stress positions, sometimes with their hands shackled above their heads (SSCI 2014, 3). Loud white noise was also used to keep detainees awake. In November 2002, a detainee named Gul Rahman died in CIA custody in Afghanistan because a CIA officer had ordered him to remove all his clothes, aside from a sweatshirt, after he was uncooperative during an interrogation. The CIA left Rahman shackled to the wall of his cell, sitting on a bare concrete floor without pants. The next day, Rahman was dead, apparently having frozen to death (SSCI 2014, 54–55).

And once the government left the door to torture ajar, interrogators pushed it open wide. The use of unauthorized techniques by CIA officers included placing a pistol near a detainee's head, operating a cordless drill near his body, and using improvised stress positions that, according to the Senate investigation, "caused cuts and bruises resulting in the intervention of a medical officer" (SSCI 2014, 69–70).

The CIA's program—which ended in 2009—was not the first time the United States engaged in torture; and it is doubtful it will be its last. Blind faith in American exceptionalism feeds the notion that the United States is able to do torture "right" despite history repeatedly demonstrating that torture is unconditionally wrong. This exceptionalism—that America's values and its security interests are uniquely suited to allow the United States to do what it chastises other countries for doing—exposes not much more than a trail of double standards. The United States prosecuted Japanese interrogators for waterboarding U.S. service members during World War II. Yet, after September 11, 2001, the government said it should be immune from engaging in similar cruelty. Former U.S. senator John McCain suffered through the agony of solitary confinement as a prisoner of war in Vietnam (Gawande 2009), and yet the CIA placed detainees in cells alone for lengthy periods of isolation. To buck this trend there needs to be greater public awareness of the historical, legal, and scientific justifications for banning torture. It is also important that all the people who ordered, supervised, designed, and carried out the CIA's torture program are held accountable. It is disappointing that this has not yet happened. Some people were even rewarded for their role in the program. Unless this grave situation changes, the United States is bound to repeat its past mistakes.

References

Black, Cofer. "Testimony to Joint Investigation into September 11th: Fifth Public Hearing 26 September 2002—Joint House/Senate Intelligence Committee Hearing," 2002, https://fas.org/irp/congress/2002_hr/092602black.html.

Bybee, Jay S. "Memorandum for John Rizzo Acting General Counsel of the Central Intelligence Agency: Interrogation of al Qaeda Operative (Bybee I)," August 1, 2002a, https://www.hsdl.org/?abstract&did=37518.

Bybee, Jay S. "Memorandum for Alberto R. Gonzales Counsel to the President Re: Standards of Conduct for Interrogation under 18 U.S. C. §§ 2340–2340A (Bybee II)," August 1, 2002b, https://www.justice.gov/olc/file/886061/download.

Department of Justice Office of Professional Responsibility. "Investigation into the Office of Legal Counsel's Memoranda Concerning Issues Relating to the Central Intelligence Agency's Use of 'Enhanced Interrogation Techniques' on Suspected Terrorists," 2009, http://cdm16064.contentdm.oclc.org/cdm/ref/collection/p266901coll4/id/2317.

Gawande, Atul. "Hellhole: The United States Holds Tens of Thousands of Inmates in Long-Term Solitary Confinement. Is This Torture?" *The New Yorker*, March 30, 2009, https://www.newyorker.com/magazine/2009/03/30/hellhole/.

Kaslow, Nadine J. "Letter to the Editor: Response to Article about Psychologists' Participation in CIA Interrogation," *The New York Times*, December 16, 2014, https://www.apa.org/news/press/response/cia-interrogation.aspx.

Méndez, Juan E. "Interim Report of the Special Rapporteur on Torture and Other Cruel, Inhuman or Degrading Treatment or Punishment," 2016, http://antitorture.org/wp-content/uploads/2016/09/Report_A-71-298_English.pdf.

Open Society Justice Initiative. "Globalizing Torture: CIA Secret Detention and Extraordinary Rendition," 2013, https://www.opensocietyfoundations.org/reports/globalizing-torture-cia-secret-detention-and-extraordinary-rendition.

Physicians for Human Rights. "Lawsuit Filed against CIA Torture Psychologists: Physicians for Human Rights Welcomes ACLU's Case, Demands Federal Investigation,"

Press Release, October 13, 2015, https://phr.org/news/
lawsuit-filed-against-cia-torture-psychologists/#top.

Senate Select Committee on Intelligence. "Committee
Study of the Central Intelligence Agency's Detention and
Interrogation Program: Executive Summary," 2014, https://
fas.org/irp/congress/2014_rpt/ssci-rdi.pdf.

60 Minutes. "CIA Flying Suspects to Torture?" CBS,
March 4, 2005, https://www.cbsnews.com/news/
cia-flying-suspects-to-torture-04-03-2005/.

*Jonathan Horowitz has worked for over fifteen years on human
rights issues, much of that time focusing on situations of armed
conflict and terrorism.*

Human Trafficking and Terrorist Groups
Elif Isitman

The link between human trafficking and terrorist groups can
be examined through two case study groups: Islamic State and
Boko Haram. Both groups are notorious for practices of forced
marriage, sexual violence, and abuse of women and girls, although group characteristics and the means through which
they conduct their practices appear to differ.

Islamic State in Iraq and Greater Syria

The Islamic State in Iraq and Greater Syria (ISIS) is a predomi-
nantly Sunni jihadist group. Its self-proclaimed leader and ca-
liph is Abu Bakr al-Baghdadi, a former prisoner of the U.S.-led
Camp Bucca in Iraq. ISIS seeks to establish a caliphate: a single, transnational Islamic State based on Sharia law (Laub and
Masters 2014). The militant group, characterized by the use
of brutal violence and force to gain ground, has been held accountable by the United Nations for large-scale human rights
abuses and war crimes. Amnesty International reports that the
group has been engaged in ethnic cleansing on a historic scale.

Kidnapping Yazidi Women and Girls, Mount Sinjar

In August 2014, ISIS invaded the northwestern Sinjar region in Iraq, home to Yazidi communities. The Yazidis are a minority in Syria and Iraq. They adhere to polytheistic religious views and thus are viewed as infidels and are labeled "devil worshippers" by Muslim extremists. Hundreds of Yazidi men were killed, and many were forced to convert to Islam. At least 2,500 women and children were abducted by ISIS fighters. Younger women and girls were separated from their parents and older relatives, were sold, were given as gifts, or were forced to marry ISIS fighters and supporters (Amnesty International 2015). The women and girls have been subjected to torture, rape, and sexual violence.

Up to 300 of those abducted have managed to escape captivity in Iraq and parts of Syria. However, the majority of them are still being held captive. They are frequently moved from place to place in order to escape detection (Amnesty International 2014). According to estimates from the University of Bristol's Gender and Violence Research Center (2014), around 4,600 women are still missing.

Victim Testimonies of Escaped Yazidi Women and Girls

Yazidi women have undergone abhorrent treatment under ISIS control, from systematic rape to sexual slavery to forced marriage. Many of them have attempted suicide, with some of them ending their lives. ISIS fighters regularly threaten to kill or harm victims' relatives if the women attempt to kill themselves (Amnesty International 2014).

Twenty victims (eleven women and nine girls, including two who were twelve years old) who have escaped ISIS tell harrowing tales of rape. Almost all reported being sold or given as gifts and forced into marriage (Human Rights Watch 2015).

ISIS held about 150 girls and women in their *maqarr* (headquarters) in the northern Iraqi city of Mosul. Various news reports have documented how terrorists conducted live slave markets, and ISIS has released videos in which their fighters brag about buying and trading sex slaves. ISIS has made widespread use of social media both in recruiting foreign fighters and in spreading propaganda in general (Barret 2014).

Following the large-scale kidnapping of Yazidi women and children, the militant group released a pamphlet on how to conduct "sexual jihad," or how to capture, treat, keep, and sexually abuse female slaves. Researchers speaking with news reporters describe the women as being "treated like cattle" (Damon 2015).

The ISIS pamphlet explains that it is permissible to take non-Muslims captive and particularly points out Jews and Christians as targets. "Unbelief" in Islam is enough to make someone a slave, the pamphlet sets out. According to the ISIS rules, it is permissible to rape a female slave immediately after taking her captive if she is a virgin. If she is not, however, "her uterus must be purified first." Moreover, the pamphlet endorses and encourages child sexual abuse, saying that intercourse with female slaves is allowed who have not yet reached puberty, as long as they are "fit for intercourse." It also allows fighters to buy, sell, and give female slaves as a gift because women are "merely property." There have even been reports of some fighters attempting to sell female sex slaves on social media (Warrick 2016).

The hostage taking and sexual slavery of women are not limited to Yazidis. In 2015, the *Washington Post* reported that twenty-six-year-old Kayla Mueller, an American humanitarian worker, was used as a sex slave by the leader of the Islamic State, Abu Bakr al-Baghdadi (Goldman and Miller 2015).

New Form of Human Trafficking by ISIS

The U.S. government has obtained documents produced by ISIS that sanction the removal of organs from infidels to save the life of a Muslim. The January 31, 2015, document, in the form of a *fatwa* (religious ruling), states: "The apostate's life and organs don't have to be respected and may be taken with impunity." There is no objection to removing the captive's organ, even if this results in the death of the captive. Although accusations of organ trafficking have been levied against ISIS by Iraq, there is no proof that the organization has yet been involved in this activity. The fatwa does, however, "provide religious sanction for doing so" (Strobel et al. 2015).

Boko Haram

Boko Haram, an Islamic extremist group based in northeastern Nigeria, is also active in Chad, Niger, and northern Cameroon. The group, founded in 2002, is led by Abubakar Shekau and has alleged links to al-Qaeda. In March 2015, Abubakar Shekau announced the group's allegiance to ISIS. The aim of the group is similar to that of ISIS—to establish a "caliphate" (Islamic State) in Nigeria. The group is notorious for being opposed to Western-style modern education. Members of the group believe it lures students away from following Islamic teaching as a way of life. This embodies the group's name: "Boko Haram" means "Western education is forbidden." The group believes that the Nigerian government, by fostering schools, has interfered with traditional Islamic education (Okpaga et al. 2012).

Boko Haram has been targeting Western-style schools since 2010 and has killed or abducted hundreds of students in the process. Girls are kidnapped rather than killed and used as cooks or sex slaves. In line with radical Islam, Boko Haram does not believe girls and women should be educated (Onuoha 2010).

Boko Haram and the Chibok Girls, 2014

One of the most prominent mass abductions by Boko Haram took place on the night of April 14–15, 2014. Members of the militant group, posing as guards, kidnapped 276 female students from the Government Secondary School in the town of Chibok in Borno State, northeastern Nigeria. More than 50 girls managed to escape during transit, but 219 of them have been living in captivity ever since (Amnesty International 2015). They are believed to have been forced to convert to Islam and forced into marriage with members of Boko Haram. The bride price for the girls is 2,000 naira each, the equivalent of US$12.50. Many of the girls have been taken across the border to neighboring countries such as Chad and Cameroon.

On May 5, 2014, in a recorded message, Boko Haram's leader claimed responsibility for the Chibok kidnapping, proclaiming that "Allah instructed me to sell them. . . . I will carry out his instructions" and that "slavery is allowed in my religion, and I shall capture people and make them slaves." The group believes that girls as young as nine years old are suitable for marriage and thus sexual intercourse.

Chibok is a village dominated by Christians, and Boko Haram acknowledged that many of the kidnapped girls are not Muslims. "The girls that have not accepted Islam, they are now gathered in numbers, and we treat them the way the Prophet Muhammed treated the infidels he seized," Abubakar Shekau is quoted as saying in his video. Later, the terrorist group released a video showing about half of the kidnapped girls dressed in a *hijab* and a long Islamic chador.

Since the abduction, the Nigerian government has made a number of attempts to rescue the girls. In May 2015, the Nigerian military reportedly had reclaimed most of the areas previously controlled by Boko Haram, including many of the camps in the Sambisa forest, where the Chibok girls allegedly had been held. Although many women were freed, none of the Chibok girls has yet been found. They may have been either killed or transported elsewhere.

Victim Testimonies of Boko Haram Escapees

No victim testimonies are available for the kidnapped Chibok girls, as none of them has managed to escape. However, Amnesty International has collected victim testimonies from other escapees.

Aside from committing other forms of war crimes, such as conducting mass killings and enlisting child soldiers, Boko Haram has been conducting various forms of sexual violence against populations in Nigeria. From victim testimonies and reports, forced marriages seem to be the primary way in which Boko Haram militants conduct sexual violence against female detainees.

The militant group has abducted women and girls during raids on towns in northeastern Nigeria and has kept them under control in camps (Amnesty International 2015). Women and girls who have managed to escape Boko Haram reported that many of them were forced to marry members of the militant group.

Young women in captivity were reportedly separated from older women. In Boko Haram camps, women who were considered infidels were told to convert to Boko Haram's interpretation of Islam, after which they received religious instruction classes and were forced into marriage with one of the fighters. Women speaking to Amnesty International testify that, in captivity, they were given food once a day and that many had suffered from a lack of safe drinking water. In many instances, women who drank the water given to them had contracted severe illnesses or died.

People who have lived for extended periods of time in Boko Haram camps or in territories controlled by the militants have told Amnesty International that sexual violence and rape of abducted women is strictly forbidden under Boko Haram's version of Sharia law. However, women have reported that militants raped them secretly at night or in the bush. Others were subjected to forced marriage and rape by their "husbands" afterward. Victims report that many militants do not use condoms or other form of protection, so they fear unwanted pregnancies and contraction of sexually transmitted diseases.

Terrorism and Human Trafficking

The systematic abduction, sexual exploitation, sale, forced marriage, forced child soldiers, trafficking in organs, and human rights abuses of women and children by terrorist organizations have created a new vehicle for human trafficking, which has grown on a scale not seen since the abolition of slavery in the previous centuries. Combating this form of human trafficking will require eradication of patriarchal and extremist religious ideology as well as the terrorist groups involved in this modern-day slavery.

References

Amnesty International. *Escape from Hell—Torture and Sexual Slavery in Islamic State Captivity in Iraq.* (London: Amnesty International, 2014).

Amnesty International. *"Our Job Is to Shoot, Slaughter and Kill"—Boko Haram's Reign of Terror in North-East Nigeria.* (London: Amnesty International, 2015).

Barret, R., and J. Myers. "Foreign Fighters in Syria." Carnegie Council for Ethics in International Affairs, 2014, pp. 1–17, http://soufangroup.com/wp-content/uploads/2014/06/TSG-Foreign-Fighters-in-Syria.pdf (accessed November 6, 2016).

Damon, A. "A Yazidi Captive's Tale: Sold by ISIS as a Sex Slave," CNN, April 14, 2015, http://edition.cnn.com/2015/04/14/middleeast/yazidi-sex-slaves-isis-damon/index.html.

Goldman, Adam, and Greg Miller. "Islamic State Leader Used U.S. Hostage as Sex Slave," *The Washington Post*, August 15, 2015, p. 1.

Human Rights Watch. "Iraq: ISIS Escapees Describe Systematic Rape," April 14, 2015, https://www.hrw.org/news/2015/04/14/iraq-isis-escapees-describe-systematic-rape (accessed January 15, 2016).

Laub, Z., and J. Masters. "Islamic State in Iraq and Greater Syria," Council on Foreign Relations, 2014, pp. 1–4, http://www.cfr.org/iraq/islamic-state/p14811.

Okpaga, A., U. S. Chijioke, and O. I. Eme. "Activities of Boko Haram and Insecurity Question in Nigeria," *Arabian Journal of Business and Management Review*, 1 (9) (2012).

Onuoha, F. C. "The Islamist Challenge: Nigeria's Boko Haram Crisis Explained," *African Security Review*, 2 (19): 54–67 (2010).

Strobel, Warren, Jonathan Landay, and Phil Stewart. "Report: ISIS Sanctions Harvesting of Human Organs." *The World Post*, December 24, 2015, http://www.huffingtonpost.com/entry/isis-sanctions-harvesting-organs_567cc1a1e4b06fa6888016ed (accessed October 15, 2016).

Warrick, J. "ISIS Fighters Seem to Be Trying to Sell Sex Slaves Online," *The Washington Post*, May 28, 2016, https://www.washingtonpost.com/world/national-security/isis-fighters-appear-to-be-trying-to-sell-their-sex-slaves-on-the-internet/2016/05/28/b3d1edea-24fe-11e6-9e7f-57890b612299_story.html (accessed November 15, 2016).

Elif Isitman received her MSc in International Crimes and Criminology and an MA in journalism from VU University in Amsterdam. Her MSc dissertation concerned the trafficking of women and girls in post-conflict areas, using Bosnia and Herzegovina and Kosovo as case studies.

Following her studies, she interned and worked at the Bureau of the Dutch National Rapporteur on Trafficking in Human Beings and Sexual Violence against Children, where she conducted research into child pornography and corresponding perpetrator profiles. She is currently working as a journalist and editor at the Dutch weekly magazine Elsevier *in Amsterdam.*

My True Direction
Marissa Quenqua

When I was thirteen I was in love with my best friend. What started as me showing her "what it was like to kiss a boy" quickly turned into kissing all the time, spending every moment we could together. We secretly kissed in her backyard, in her pool under an inflatable raft. We snuck out at night to go "night swimming." We kept a marble notebook of letters to each other. I broke up with the boy I was going out with because I didn't feel anything romantic toward him. I thought she and I were going to be together forever.

I knew for sure I was attracted to girls starting in eighth grade because I began noticing them in the hallways in middle school. I am femme and love clothing, but I'd notice a cute skirt on a girl and then keep staring. I knew I wasn't just envious of what she was wearing, I was looking at her legs. In the locker room in gym class, I felt embarrassed when other girls got changed in front of me. Like I shouldn't be allowed in there. Once my girlfriend and I said I love you, I felt like I had to tell my mom. It was the biggest secret I'd ever kept, and when you're in love at that age everything seems incredibly intense and important. My family isn't religious, and I knew my mother wouldn't reject me. I felt safe to come out because I knew my housing wasn't at risk. She'd always accepted me for who I was. I have mild cerebral palsy, I was used to being different. When I realized I was gay I thought, "Of course I am. Everything about me has to be different. This is just one more thing." When I told my mom I was in love with my best friend, she said: "Of course you love her. She's your best friend." No. In love. I cried in her lap and asked her to tell me it was okay. That she wouldn't want me to be any different. She held me and told me she loved me exactly for who I was. I was very lucky.

The first lesbian film I'd ever seen with a happy ending was *But I'm a Cheerleader* (1999). I was used to gay characters ending up dead in the end or ostracized or humiliated. In this film, a young feminine popular girl named Megan is suspected of being gay by her family and friends. She has pictures of girls in bikinis hanging in her locker instead of male heartthrobs, she kisses her boyfriend like it's a chore, she admits to having thoughts about other girls but thinks everyone else does, too. Her parents send her to a rehabilitation center called True Directions, run by RuPaul (out of drag). They hold an intervention at Megan's house where he hilariously points out the music she listens to (Melissa Etheridge), the pillows she owns with flowers blooming *à la* Georgia O'Keefe. Her boyfriend says, "You don't even want to kiss me." Megan is overwhelmed and agrees to go to True Directions. The facility is decked out in bright pink and blue, outlining traditionally "male" and "female" activities. The boys chop wood and the girls change diapers. RuPaul is a self-proclaimed "ex gay," even though he is constantly checking out a member of the male staff. True Directions is an obvious parody of conversion therapy. It's a film by queers for queers. It's clear that none of these young kids are going to be "converted," that it isn't possible. In fact, it's here that Megan realizes that she is gay, and becomes more comfortable with that truth. The whole concept of "turning gay kids straight" seems ridiculous and harmful in this universe. The best one can do at True Directions is pretend the treatment is working while planning escape. Megan meets and falls in love with Graham (Clea Duvall) during treatment and the two run off together. I identified with Megan at fourteen because she's feminine and liked girls. I didn't think the two could coexist. Not all depictions of conversion therapy are this humorous.

According to the National Center for Lesbian Rights (NCLR), a 2009 report by the American Psychological Association states: "The techniques therapists have used to try to change sexual orientation and gender identity include inducing nausea, vomiting, or paralysis while showing the patient homoerotic images; providing electric shocks; having the individual snap an elastic band around the wrist when aroused by same-sex erotic images or thoughts; using shame to create aversion to same-sex attractions; orgasmic reconditioning; and satiation therapy. All of the nation's leading professional medical and mental health associations have rejected conversion therapy as unnecessary, ineffective, and dangerous" (NCLR).

I recently watched *Boy Erased* (2018), a film based on the memoir by Garrard Conley. Conley was raised in a fundamentalist Arkansas family, the son of a conservative Baptist preacher. In the film, Jared (the character based on Conley) is enrolled in a program called Love in Action. He is asked to create a list of family members who might be gay, or sinners in another manner, such as alcoholics or gamblers, in an effort to assign blame for his "affliction." The printed curriculum for Love in Action is littered with grammatical errors and questionable exercises. Students are asked to express anger toward their family members and beaten with bibles. They are "ranked" by masculinity and femininity. Jared quickly realizes not only that this therapy is going to fail but that it's actively harmful. He is still attracted to men even though he's complying with the program. He meets another boy in treatment who tells him to "play the part," as in, pretend the treatment is working so they'll release you. A student who was beaten with bibles after failing an exercise is forced to attend his own staged "funeral." He takes his own life in response to the program. Jared confides in his mother, who gets him out of Love in Action. He moves to New York, becomes a successful writer and accepts himself for who he is. Victor Sykes, the character who runs Love in Action is based on the ex-minister John J. Smid. Smid married a woman and fathered children before divorcing. He married his husband in 2014. He said, "I've never met a man who experienced a change from homosexual to heterosexual" (Besen 2011).

As a gay person I am horrified at the thought that young people were forced into these programs. Thinking about myself as a teenager, and I came out really early, going through a program like that would have been incredibly psychologically damaging to me. I was struggling to accept myself at that age, not just for being gay but for everything. You're desperate to fit in and compare yourself to your peers constantly. Am I pretty enough? Do people like me? What does everyone think about me? Am I going to get into a good college? Will I achieve my dreams? What are my dreams? Add sexual orientation into the mix and it's so much more complicated. I could have easily been brainwashed into a conversion program if my family rejected me and forced me into it. The only reason why I was able to come out to my mother at thirteen, and then to my father at sixteen, and take a girl to my prom at seventeen, was constant unwavering love and acceptance. I am thirty-four now and I've been happily married to a woman for six years. We are planning to have a baby. I knew who I was at thirteen. It never changed. I was right. Believe in yourself, you know who you are.

References

Besen, Wayne. "Former 'Ex-Gay' Activist Admits Gay People Don't Change," *Falls Church News Press*, October 12, 2011, https://fcnp.com/2011/10/12/former-ex-gay-activist-admits-gay-people-dont-change/.

Brinton, Sam. "I Was Tortured in Gay Conversion Therapy. And It's Still Legal in 41 States," *The New York Times*, January 24, 2018, https://www.nytimes.com/2018/01/24/opinion/gay-conversion-therapy-torture.html.

NCLR. "Born Perfect: The Facts about Conversion Therapy," NCLR, n.d., http://www.nclrights.org/bornperfect-the-facts-about-conversion-therapy/.

Marissa Quenqua is a freelance writer living in Brooklyn. Her work has been featured by Freerange Nonfiction, SMITH Maga-zine: *Home of the Six-Word Memoir project, and she's written several romance novels under a pseudonym for the publisher En-amored Ink. Marissa is currently at work on a memoir about invisible otherness and is a writing mentor for young girls through the nonprofit organization Girls Write Now.*

Systematically Stripped of Dignity
Rebecca Smith

The word "torture" brings up several different images or concepts, to any number of different people. The sound of nails on a chalkboard, sitting through an insufferably boring

PowerPoint presentation, being forced to attend a family func-tion from start to finish. By the word's very definition, it is something intended to cause anguish and/or pain, done so to "punish, coerce, or afford sadistic pleasure." For many, tor-ture may also bring to mind high school history lessons about myriad devices used to illicit heretical confessions or punish crimes against God and state. I would venture to say that, for the majority of folks, the idea that real, actual torture still takes place in the world—in the United States, the back yards of what is supposedly the most civilized and prosperous country on the planet—would be a shocking if not downright foolish-sounding proposition.

Well. Shocking or foolish as it may *sound,* the sick reality is that it does happen. Every day. In every state of this nation. And I lived through two years of it.

The Third Geneva Convention states that prisoners in cap-tivity must be subject to "no physical or mental torture, nor any other form of coercion." Of course, this applies only to prisoners taken during times of conflict, but all in all, it's not a bad guideline for how to treat any prisoner, I'd say.

They are, after all, still living and breathing human beings. During the two years I spent housed in a minimum-security state prison located in north-central Florida, I came to see that the concept of torture, whether called by that name or labeled as an acceptable and appropriate punishment by the state, is very much alive and kicking.

Solitary confinement, for instance. A prisoner can be sen-tenced to solitary confinement for any number of infractions, ranging from disrespect toward a guard, to being caught with dangerous contraband, and the sentence may last anywhere from a few days to several *months* at a time. The only difference is the amount of time they receive. A small, usually two-person cell (although whether or not one ends up with a roommate is purely the luck of the draw), you're locked in 24 hours a day, 5 days a week. On the other two days, you're let out for *maybe* 30 minutes, long enough to take a quick freezing cold shower, in a stall located approximately 30 feet from your cell, the walk to which you are handcuffed and shackled for. And when you're done with your half-hour respite, you're re-secured, and walked that 30 feet back to your cell. My offense? I was on a road crew picking up trash and happened to have picked up several cigarette butts that day. One of my fellow inmates told the guard supervising us that she had heard me state I was going to sneak them back onto the compound to sell the leftover tobacco. Didn't really matter that I'd not said that at all, or that no one else on a crew of twenty women had heard me say it. I was sentenced to 30 days in solitary confinement. You aren't allowed books, you rarely actually get any mail that's sent to you, no phone calls or contact with family members or other loved ones. Your meals are shoved through a hole in a door three times a day.

By and large, the methods employed were small. Things that would, on their own, amount to nothing more than minor annoyances were employed en masse and systematically, ensuring that inmates were reminded during every waking moment that they were not in any sort of control over their own lives and well-being. This could range from a "random" locker search, during which all of an inmate's possessions—including items purchased with money sent to the inmate, and even mail and books they had received—were torn out of the tiny space we were given to cram our lives into, strewn about, scrutinized, and oftentimes destroyed or confiscated with absolutely no rhyme or reason given (Well, none other than "Because I said so."). 0300 fire drills were commonplace. Every inmate would be marched outside to a designated area, lined up, counted, and named—sometimes more than once if the drill wasn't carried out to the standard of whatever officer was in charge that night. These drills were performed at least once a month if not more. In the midst of one, during which we stood outside for an hour in our flimsy state-issued pajamas or basketball shorts, we were informed in a mocking tone that although the drills were in fact a state safety requirement and mandated monthly, there was no rule anywhere stating that they *had* to be performed during the wee hours of the morning. That is simply when the officers always decided to pull the alarm. And did I mention that daily wake-up time, Monday through Friday, was 0430? Typically, by the time the drill had been done, redone, and completed to the satisfaction of the commanding officer, it was time to begin getting ready for the work day. (More than once, the entire compound ran behind for the day because multiple repeats of the drill spilled over into designated feeding time, meaning that work crews were then late reporting to the gate for work. This may come as a shock, but inmates were penalized when this happened also.)

The most prevalent form of torture in my personal prison experience was, hands down, constant and persistent verbal abuse. It was worse than being denied pain medication after getting second degree burns in a kitchen accident, worse than having a 1,200 pound horse crush my foot and barely receiving ibuprofen to manage the injury. Guards are instructed during their training not to refer to inmates by name unless absolutely necessary, just "inmate," as a means of dehumanizing and demoralizing individuals. This was the most common method of stripping the women of individuality and humanity, but others included purposely mispronouncing names when they were used, disparaging remarks about an inmate's personal appearance (as if she could do something about looking like total crap while incarcerated), even insulting comments about an inmate's family and/or children if a guard happened to see these people during visitation. Although on paper their only job was to make sure we followed the rules and didn't kill each other, they often made it their personal mission to remind each and every one of us that no matter what law we had broken we were all worthless pieces of human garbage, not fit to lick the dirt from the bottom of their boots.

The torture, in this instance, was not physical. It involved no grotesque medieval devices—no bed of nails, nor Iron Maidens. It wasn't water boarding, or sticks shoved under fingernails, no starvation or red-hot pincers applied to exposed flesh. Not to say that any and all of those things are not horrific; however, flesh wounds eventually scar over and heal. Psychological damage, however, tends to fester beneath the surface, eating away at the very substance that makes a human just that. Those invisible scars may heal, but typically only after great labor and at great cost to the person upon whom those wounds were inflicted. That particular brand of horror is permanent.

I've been out of prison, at home with my family, for a little over two years now. I work, I spend time with my loved ones, I do all of the things most normal adults do in life. But there are nights I still awaken, heart racing and sweat beaded on my forehead, from an all too real nightmare of being locked inside of a prison with people far more treacherous than any other fellow inmate I ever encountered —the very people whose supposed charge was to look after my well-being during my stay. People who instead took it upon themselves to ensure that, in the end, any vestiges of humanity, self-esteem and self-worth, and individuality were systematically stripped from me through the employment of what can be called nothing else but modern-day torture.

Rebecca Smith is working and attempting to rebuild her life and her credit score, as well as saving money to go back to school to pursue a Master of Arts degree in substance abuse counseling. She also volunteers with community organizations dedicated to helping convicted felons readjust to life after prison and finding the assistance they need to become productive members of society—housing, job placement, financial assistance, and mental health care.

4 Profiles

While torture is a worldwide phenomenon that spans most of recorded history, at least in Western Europe and North America, it is possible to identify several individuals (and one organization) whose actions have affected its spread, for good or for ill.

They include a pope, a child soldier, a whistleblower, current and former intelligence officers from both the United States and the Soviet Union, several lawyers, a scientist, a military contractor, and—depending on one's political views—multiple terrorists or freedom fighters.

Some of the names may be familiar. Others may not be. However, each of their stories is an important ingredient in understanding how torture reached its current level of prevalence across the world.

Gerry Adams

Born on October 6, 1948, in Belfast, Northern Ireland, Adams came of age during the civil rights movement in the six counties of Ireland under British administration in the late 1960s. As Tim Pat Coogan, Ireland's foremost historian of that period, puts it,

> Gerry Adams carried his weapons with him as he left his job in the famous Belfast pub, the Duke of York, on a fine

---

Gina Haspel, Acting Director of the CIA, went from supervising a "black" (or secret) site in Thailand where Agency personnel tortured detainees prior to her arrival, to head of the Agency within less than two decades. (Alex Edelman/CNP/MediaPunch Inc./Alamy)

August day in 1969. The regulars, many of them British TV and print journalists, were sorry to learn of his departure. He had been the most popular barman in the pub. Nor would they have seen much to indicate it from what he was holding as he headed towards the rioting and petrol bombing which had erupted between the Catholic Falls Road area and the Protestant Shankill Road. Gerry Adams was going to war with a dozen large empty stout bottles. (Coogan 2002, 619)

As a Catholic from Belfast, Adams was soon in the thick of the fight against the Royal Ulster Constabulary and later the British Army. While his opponents had access to firearms and other modern weapons, Adams and his comrades relied upon "the 'Tipperary rifle', a hurling stick . . . [and] the 'kidney paver', that stock-in-trade of the Belfast rioter, a cobble-stone" (Coogan 2002, 626).

Several months after the British imposed internment without trial on the Six Counties in 1971, Adams was arrested and detained (McDonald 2018). At that time, "he was interrogated and systematically beaten up. Other methods were also employed" (Coogan 2002, 628). As Adams described it to Coogan (2002, 628), "You faced the wall for hours at a time, supporting yourself only with your finger tips. You'd be waiting all day for something to happen. Sometimes they came up behind you and dropped a tray with a crash. It would scare the living daylights out of you. Once they showed me a blood stained hatchet."

In Adams's description, we can recognize the classic tools of torture as recommended by the CIA in its KUBARK manual, from the use of stress positions to threats of violence (which torturers often find is more effective than actual violence when it comes to gaining information).

To counter this, Adams came up with a technique the IRA would later incorporate into its 1977 Green Book, or manual for its volunteers—that of "mind over matter" (Coogan 2002,

628). "By way of example he indicated the room we were talking in. I had thought it rather spartan but he judged it a good place to be interrogated in: 'You see that curtain for example. It's made of tweed. You could think about how the tweed was made, where the materials came from, how they dyed it, what sort of people worked at making tweed, what their lives were like and so on'" (Coogan 2002, 628).

The IRA's Green Book has this to say about the subject. "While being tortured in a brutal, physical manner it is important that the volunteer should consolidate his position, he should realize that it's seven days if he keeps silent, perhaps seventeen years if he speaks. It's no easy thing to dismiss physical torture as a small meaningless thing. It is by no means small and by no means meaningless to the receiver. . . . People who were brutalized found that by directing their powers of concentration away from their interrogators and directing it to images formed in their own mind they could in effect overcome the physical pain" (Coogan 2002, 569).

Adams was released later in 1972 both to negotiate a truce with the British (which, for a period of time, granted quasi-political status to imprisoned members of the Irish Republican Army) and to clandestinely meet with Northern Ireland secretary of state William Whitelaw about the possibilities of a British withdrawal from the Six Counties (Coogan 2002, 628–629).

"During his exchange with Whitelaw concerning their pact, Adams agreed that in the event of certain eventualities, 'all bets were off.' The truce only held for a matter of days and the next time Adams heard that phrase he was lying naked on the floor of a cell in the Springfield Road Barracks being kicked by a Special Branch interrogator who punctuated his kicks with the words 'All bets are off now, Gerry.' He still has kidney problems from that episode" (Coogan 2002, 629).

Adams was convicted twice in 1975 for trying to escape from the Maze prison in Northern Ireland while interned there (McDonald 2018). While he has been repeatedly accused of being a member of the IRA by the British, he has never been convicted of that association.

Through his work with Sinn Fein ("Ourselves Alone"), which the British have long claimed is the political wing of the IRA, Adams became the conduit for information from the imprisoned Republicans who launched a hunger strike in 1981 at the Maze to reach the outside world. He survived an assassination attempt in 1984 (British Broadcasting Corporation 2006) and continued his political work on both sides of the Irish border and in the UK. He received a backhanded endorsement of his effectiveness in 1988, when the British banned broadcasters in the UK from airing tapes of his speeches. "It meant that instead of hearing Gerry Adams, viewers and listeners would hear an actor's voice reading a transcript of the Sinn Fein leader's words" (Welch 2005) a situation which lasted until 1994.

Despite—or because of—this history, Adams successfully brought Sinn Fein (and, through it, the IRA) to the negotiating table with the British and the Republic of Ireland, a process that ultimately led to the Good Friday Agreement in 1998, which brought an end to the armed-struggle phase of the troubles. While power-sharing between the Catholic and Protestant communities has been on and off since then, the Provisional IRA put its weapons beyond use in the early 2000s and have since maintained the ceasefire set by the Agreement.

Adams retired as leader of Sinn Fein on February 10, 2018. In July of that year, his house was subjected to a bomb attack, though no one was hurt (Watts 2018). Northern Irish police suspected the New IRA, a splinter group from the Provisional IRA that opposed the Good Friday ceasefire, of involvement, but Adams and his colleagues blamed "vigilantes" on the "fringe" of anti-ceasefire groups (Morris 2018).

Philip Agee

Born on July 19, 1935, in Tacoma Park, Florida (*The Independent* 2008), Philip Burnett Franklin Agee would go on to do more damage to the operations of the Central Intelligence Agency than any whistleblower before him—and, in all likelihood, more than Chelsea Manning and Edward Snowden would do long after his death.

In some ways, the Agency had only itself to blame. Agee was not turned by any Soviet or Chinese agent, or by money or blackmail, but by what the CIA had taught its counterpart agencies in American client states, as commentators pointed out much later.

"He was the first person to publish what many Americans had preferred to ignore during the Cold War, that the CIA supported 'dirty tricks,' including assassinations, to keep pro-Soviet movements out of power in Latin America" (*The Independent* 2008). "[Agee] described how, while based in the CIA's station in Montevideo, Uruguay, he visited police headquarters to find they were torturing a prisoner he had tipped them off about merely as a possible leftist. When he complained, the police simply turned up the volume of a radio-broadcast football match to drown out the screams" (*The Independent* 2008).

Agee's road from conservative Catholic to radical critic of American intelligence was a long one. As he told it, back in April 1956, just as he was finishing up his undergraduate work at the University of Notre Dame, "I hadn't signed up for any [corporate] interviews but I've just had my first, and probably only, job interview. To my surprise a man from the CIA came out from Washington to see me about going into a secret junior executive training program" (Agee 1975, 13).

Ironically, Agee initially turned him down, as he preferred to pursue a law degree at the University of Miami. He soon had second thoughts.

"I suppose it was the lack of a sense of purpose or maybe I couldn't adjust to secular learning after four years of Jesuits and four at Notre Dame" (Agee 1975, 16). He soon found that purpose at the Agency, or so he told himself at the time,

"I'll be a warrior against communist subversive erosion of freedom and personal liberties around the world—a patriot dedicated to the preservation of my country and our way of life" (Agee 1975, 19).

Agee became not only an agent but one who was assigned to the Agency's Clandestine Service division, which works undercover (and usually overseas). (Agee 1975, 44). After three years of training at the CIA's then-secret facility at Camp Peary, Virginia, and elsewhere, Agee "worked under cover for eight years in Ecuador, Uruguay and Mexico" (Shane 2008).

On those assignments, he soon saw the disconnect between the Agency's stated high ideals and the reality of the CIA's work in the field.

Recalling the torture victim referenced earlier, Agee wrote, "I wondered out loud if the victim could be Bonaudi, whose name I had given to Otero for preventative detention. Tomorrow, I'll ask Otero and if it was Bonaudi I'm not sure what I'll do" (Agee 1975, 455–456).

Ultimately, after leaving the Agency following a 12-year career (Shane 2008), Agee decided what to do. In his 1975 memoir *Inside the Company: CIA Diary*, Agee not only disclosed his training and other experiences with the CIA but identified several hundred agents and front organizations that served the Agency.

As their own review of the work put it, "The book will affect the CIA as a severe body blow does any living organism: some parts obviously will be affected more than others, but the health of the whole is bound to suffer" (Central Intelligence Agency 1975, 36). Calling Agee the CIA's "first real defector in the classic sense of the word" (Central Intelligence Agency 1975, 35), the Agency's reviewer declared, "Though it is unlikely that he could be successfully prosecuted in a cold or at least cooling war, in a hotter context Agee would fall into the area which the Constitution, speaking of enemies in time of war, defines as 'giving them aid and comfort'" (Central Intelligence Agency 1975, 35).

However, as even the Agency reviewer pointed out,

Agee's knowledge of local personalities and history is impressive. I have no great quarrel with his reporting and analysis of events, though I remain uneasy as to the extent of the bias introduced into his recollections from 1970–1974 by his research in institutions in Mexico City, Havana, Paris and London, as well as by his strong, but not ultimately clear, attitudes and feelings about his own past or the world about him. Nor do I fault his concern (shared by the U.S. Government) for the unequal distribution of income in Latin America, a point he returns to frequently. I can even stay with him as he claims that U.S. policies do not always deal fully with injustices. (Central Intelligence Agency 1975, 36)

Others within the agency were less kind. George H.W. Bush, who took over as the director of the CIA the same year *Inside the Company* was published, continued to refer to Agee as a "traitor to our country" as late as 1997 (Shane 2008). His wife, Barbara Bush, accused Agee, through his disclosures, of being partly responsible for the death of Richard Welch, the CIA station chief in Greece who was murdered in 1975. Agee successfully sued Barbara Bush for libel, and she removed the claim from later editions of her biography (Shane 2008).

However, Agee was to spend most of the next three decades in exile. The U.S. State Department suspended his passport in 1979, a decision the U.S. Supreme Court—in a 7–2 ruling—upheld in 1981 (Greenhouse 1981). A year later, Congress passed the Intelligence Identities Protection Act, which made blowing the cover of a CIA agent a crime, as Agee had done in his book (Shane 2008). The existence of the law has likely discouraged reprints of *Inside the Company*, given the disclosures made throughout the book, but paperback versions from 1975 are still available through used booksellers, though it can take a bit of digging to find one.

Agee continued to work to expose what he considered to be CIA abuses until his death in Havana, Cuba, on January 7, 2008, at the age of 72 (Shane 2008).

Amnesty International

On May 28, 1961, British lawyer Peter Berenson published "The Forgotten Prisoners" in the *Observer*, where he announced the formation of "Appeal for Amnesty, 1961." The campaign—then described as "an initiative by a group of lawyers, writers and publishers in London, who share the underlying conviction expressed by Voltaire: 'I detest your views, but am prepared to die for your right to express them'" (Berenson 1961)—grew into what we now know today as Amnesty International, which is still based in London.

Because the organization focused its efforts on what it described as "prisoners of conscience"—which Berenson defined as "any person who is physically restrained (by imprisonment or otherwise) from expressing (in any form of words or symbols) an opinion which he honestly holds and which does not advocate or condone personal violence" (Berenson 1961)—it was controversial in some quarters.

For example, after being released following twenty-seven years in prison for opposing the apartheid regime in South Africa, Nelson Mandela (1995, 612) pointed out, "Even during the bleakest years on Robben Island, Amnesty International would not campaign for us on the grounds that we had pursued an armed struggle, and their organization would not represent anyone who had embraced violence."

Even with that limitation, Amnesty International quickly became the main nongovernmental organization documenting the use of torture around the world during the 1960s and 1970s. As Aase Lionæs (1977), chairman of the Norwegian Nobel Committee, pointed out in awarding one of two Nobel Prizes for Peace in 1977 (the other went to the Northern Ireland Peace Movement), in sixteen years of operation Amnesty

International had 100,000 members and 2,000 affiliated groups in thirty-three countries. At that time, "to avoid involvement in internal political strife an Amnesty group never 'adopts' prisoners from its own country. Nor does Amnesty organise demonstrations in support of its demands. Despite this, it succeeds in making its views known. This is due not least to the revealing reports published regularly by Amnesty on prison conditions and torture in various countries" (Lionaes 1977).

In a pre-Internet era, Amnesty International pressured governments to release prisoners of conscience through letter-writing campaigns. According to the organization, its first success was the release of Ukrainian archbishop Josyf Slipyi from Soviet custody in 1963 (Amnesty International 2017). Thanks to advances in technology, supporters of Amnesty International can engage in electronic letter-writing and petition campaigns from the group's website.

In 1972, Amnesty International formally broadened its focus to include the elimination of torture, adding the ending of the death penalty to its mission as well in 1980 (Amnesty International 2017). By the end of the twentieth century, Amnesty International was also advocating for reproductive freedom and attempting to hold corporations accountable for human rights violations, as well as its traditional work (Amnesty International 2017).

Amnesty International produced the first history of the use of torture in Greece after the military regime there fell in the early 1970s (which is extensively discussed in Chapter 1) and successfully lobbied for the enactment of the Convention against Torture at the UN and elsewhere. It has also pressured the United States to fully document its past use of torture in Iraq and Afghanistan and at CIA black sites around the world as well as condemning the practices of detention and family separation of asylum seekers that were expanded under the Trump administration in 2017 and 2018 (Amnesty International 2018b).

Besides its own efforts, Amnesty International served as an organizational incubator for Freedom from Torture, which "began more than 30 years ago growing out of Amnesty International's Medical Group" (Freedom from Torture 2017a) and which has provided direct services to torture survivors in the UK, going from 1 location and 88 clients in 1985 to 5 clinical centers and 1,034 clients by the end of 2017 (Freedom from Torture 2017, 6). That year, Freedom from Torture (2017b, 7) raised over £9 million pounds from nearly 30,000 donors.

Amnesty International has been criticized both for expanding its mission to the point where it has—to some—lost its focus and for what some see as a loosening of the prohibition against violence needed to qualify as a prisoner of conscience (Tusa 2010). In 2010, Gita Sahgal—who once headed Amnesty International's gender unit—resigned in protest of what she believed were excessively close relations between Amnesty International and certain persons and groups sympathetic to the Taliban and other Islamist organizations engaged in armed struggle (Townsend 2010).

Similarly, Amnesty International has campaigned for the closure of the detention facility at the U.S. Naval Base at Guantanamo Bay, Cuba, and the release of all detainees or their transfer to civilian courts for criminal trials since the facility opened (Amnesty International 2018a), despite the fact that several of the prisoners—like Khalid Sheikh Mohammed, considered by most historians to have been the main planner behind the 9/11 attacks on New York, Washington, D.C., and Pennsylvania—have admitted to engaging in armed struggle against civilian targets. In contrast, Mandela's Umkhonto we Sizwe (Spear of the Nation) organization focused on sabotage of the infrastructure of the apartheid regime and tried *not* to take life, much less target unprotected civilian targets as al-Qaeda would do in the late 1990s and thereafter (Laing 2011).

To Amnesty International, both positions can be harmonized insofar as the organization has long advocated for prisoners who did not receive (or who are not receiving) a fair trial before an impartial court. While Mandela was not considered a prisoner of conscience, Amnesty International did advocate for an improvement of his conditions of imprisonment on Robben Island at the time (Amnesty International 2014). Furthermore, "if Nelson Mandela's case was to arise today, we would call for him to be released on the grounds that he had not been given a fair trial—an area we have worked on since 1964. Unjust systems cannot deliver just verdicts or sentences, and the apartheid system founded on racism did not give Nelson Mandela a fair trial, nor could it have done" (Amnesty International 2014).

By 2017, Amnesty International had grown its membership to over 7 million people in over 150 countries and seventeen areas of focus in the United States, from armed conflict to sexual and reproductive rights, as well as continuing its efforts to end torture and the death penalty. Its annual report on the state of human rights provides journalists and the public with an accessible and comprehensive survey of human rights abuses around the world that don't always make the news.

Cesare Beccaria

Cesare Beccaria was an Italian criminologist who is best known for his 1764 seminal work "An Essay on Crimes and Punishments" (also known as "On Crimes and Punishments"), which recast torture as a manifest abuse of the sovereign's authority rather than an acceptable tool in the sovereign's arsenal.

When Beccaria was born on March 15, 1738, his province of Lombardy was under the rule of the Archduchess of Austria Maria Theresa and the Catholic Church's Holy Office of the Inquisition remained active (Hostettler 2011, xii). Even after the rule of the latter group of torturers ran its course (Hostettler 2011, xii), "the new liberal despotism drew back from touching the cruel penal laws and the constant use of torture, which remained as they were. Following secret allegations torture was still the accepted means of providing proof of guilt. It is true that torture could only be applied in regard to capital crimes but almost all crimes fell within that category" (Hostettler 2011, xiii).

Worse, during this period, "secret adjudications were endemic in France, Italy, Russia and many other countries. In these places punishments were determined, often behind closed doors, at the whim of magistrates and judges who often bought their way onto the Bench for which many of them were demonstrably unsuited" (Hostettler 2011, ix). In short, "the presumption of innocence and equality before the law were concepts unknown and an accused person was regarded as guilty unless he could prove his innocence" (Hostettler 2011, ix).

After he received his law degree in 1758 from the University of Pavia (Bessler 2014, 4) and eventually became the marquis of Gualdrasco and Villareggio, it would have been expected for Beccaria to come to terms with the legal system as it then was (and under which his family and privileged social class was benefiting from). Instead, with "Crimes and Punishments," he attacked the political legitimacy that made the use of torture acceptable at its root.

"It is confounding all relations to expect that a man should be both the accuser and accused; and that pain should be the test of truth, as if truth resided in the muscles and fibres of a wretch in torture," Beccaria declared. "By this method, the robust will escape and the feeble be condemned" (Beccaria and Ingraham 1819, 60).

But Beccaria recognized not just the ineffectiveness of torture—at least when it came to exposing the guilty rather than just those susceptible to physical abuse—but its impact on the public judicial system.

"What is the political intention of punishments?" he wrote. "To terrify and be an example to others. Is this intention answered by thus privately torturing the guilty and the innocent? It is doubtless of importance that no crime should remain unpunished; but it is useless to make a public example of the author of a crime hid in darkness. A crime already committed, and for which there can be no remedy, can only be punished by a political society with an intention that no hopes of impunity should induce others to commit the same" (Beccaria and Ingraham 1819, 60).

Beccaria was also an early opponent of capital punishment. "By what right do men kill other men? Certainly not the right from which the laws themselves derive because they represent the general will, which is the aggregate of particular wills; and who ever wished to leave to other men the option of killing him?" (Maestro 1973, 464). Aside from what he saw as the death penalty's lack of legitimacy, Beccaria attacked it on utility grounds. "It is not the terrible but momentary spectacle of the death of a wretch, but the long and painful example of a man deprived of liberty for the rest of his life which is the strongest deterrent" (Maestro 1973, 464).

As a result of his work, "Beccaria's native Lombardy, Portugal, Austria, Russia and France all abolished torture and reformed their criminal justice systems as a direct result of the potency of his onslaught. And in Tuscany the Grand Duke Leopold introduced sweeping reforms of the penal system along the lines advocated by Beccaria" (Hostettler 2011 xi).

It wasn't long before Beccaria's work and influence crossed the Atlantic. "The first four U.S. Presidents—George Washington, John Adams, Thomas Jefferson and James Madison— were inspired by Beccaria's treatise and, in some cases, read it in the original Italian. On Crimes and Punishments helped to catalyze the American Revolution, and Beccaria's anti-death penalty views materially shaped American thought on capital punishment, torture and cruelty. America's foundational legal documents—the Declaration of Independence, the U.S. Constitution, and the U.S. Bill of Rights—were themselves shaped by Beccaria's treatise and its insistence that laws be in writing and be enforced in a less arbitrary manner" (Bessler 2016, 1). Indeed, John Adams and his co-counsel for the British soldiers charged in the aftermath of the Boston Massacre each quoted Beccaria at the soldiers' trial (Bessler 2016, 98).

After his presidency, Jefferson wrote in his autobiography that "Beccaria and other writers on crimes and punishments had satisfied the reasonable world of the unrightfulness and inefficacy of the punishment of crimes by death" (Bessler 2014).

While he abhorred torture and capital punishment, Beccaria also strongly opposed what today we would call gun control. "It certainly makes the situation of the assaulted worse, and of the assailants better, and rather encourages than prevents murder, as it requires less courage to attack unarmed than armed persons" (Beccaria and Ingraham 146). According to the Thomas Jefferson Foundation, that quote is one of those most often wrongfully attributed to Jefferson, perhaps because he had copied it in his papers for reference.

While Beccaria wrote several other works, including *A Discourse on Public Economy and Commerce* (1769), none became as famous as "On Crimes and Punishments." Even so, Beccaria is considered to be one of the pioneers of modern criminology (Monachesi 1955, 441) and is ranked with Adam Smith of Scotland and Anne-Robert-Jacques Turgot of France when it comes to important economists of the eighteenth century (Groenewegen 2002, 4). Beccaria died on November 28, 1794.

Jay Bybee

Born on October 27, 1953, in Oakland, California, Bybee grew up in Clark County, Nevada, before going on a Mormon mission to Santiago, Chile, from 1973 through 1975. He earned a bachelor's degree in economics from Brigham Young University (BYU) in 1977 and a juris doctorate from BYU in

1980 (*The Washington Post* 2010). After clerking for a judge at the Fourth Circuit Court of Appeal and a stint in private practice, Bybee joined the Office of Legal Policy at the Department of Justice (DOJ) in 1984 (*The Washington Post* 2010). He also worked as an appellate lawyer within DOJ before becoming a White House attorney under President George H.W. Bush (*The Washington Post* 2010). After President Bill Clinton took office in 1993, Bybee, a conservative Republican, spent most of the next decade teaching at the Louisiana State College of Law and the William S. Boyd School of Law at the University of Nevada, Las Vegas, where he was one of the founding faculty at the latter institution.

In October 2001, he was appointed to be the assistant attorney general in charge of the Office of Legal Counsel, which "provides legal advice to the President and all executive branch agencies. The Office drafts legal opinions of the Attorney General and provides its own written opinions and other advice in response to requests from the Counsel to the President, the various agencies of the Executive Branch, and other components of the Department of Justice" (Department of Justice 2019).

It was in this capacity that Bybee would enter history. As the *Salt Lake Tribune* would describe it eight years later,

> BYU law school graduate Jay S. Bybee was the assistant attorney general directing the Department of Justice's Office of Legal Counsel. At the instigation of [David] Addington and [John] Yoo, Bybee issued official legal opinions that redefined the crime of torture to make it all but impossible to commit. Barbarity was not torture unless it created pain equal to death or organ failure. A newly-declassified Bybee memorandum lists 10 previously top-secret interrogation techniques approved for use by the CIA, including waterboarding. Incredibly, Bybee seems to have been unaware that the United States had prosecuted waterboarding as a war crime after World War II. (Irvine 2009)

While much of the work on these memos was apparently done by his colleague John Yoo, by endorsing the memos with his signature, Bybee ensured his name would be associated with them and the George W. Bush administration's torture apparatus forevermore. Probably the most infamous is the August 2, 2002, memo to Alberto Gonzales, the then counsel to President Bush and future attorney general, where Bybee literally wrote a defense strategy in case American torturers were ever prosecuted under the War Crimes Act of 1996. As he put it, "We conclude below that Section 2340A proscribes acts inflicting, and that are specifically intended to inflict, severe pain or suffering, whether mental or physical. Those acts must be of an extreme nature to rise to the level of torture within the meaning of Section 2340A and the Convention [against Torture]. We further conclude that certain acts may be cruel, inhuman, or degrading, but still not produce pain and suffering of the requisite intensity to fall within Section 2340A's proscription against torture. We conclude by examining possible defenses that would negate any claim that certain interrogation methods violate the statute" (Bybee 2002).

Bybee was attempting to cloak the reservations attached to the United States' ratification of the Convention against Torture, which, among other things, "narrowed the standard for psychological torture by requiring that 'prolonged mental harm' be caused by just four specific acts[:] '(1) the intentional infliction or threatened infliction of severe physical pain or suffering; (2) the administration or application, or threatened administration or application, of mind altering substances or other procedures calculated to disrupt profoundly the senses or the personality; (3) the threat of imminent death; or (4) the threat that other person will imminently be subjected to death, severe physical pain or suffering, or the administration . . . of mind altering substances'" (McCoy 2012, 31–32), with the force of law, or at least the force of law as interpreted by the OLC. Indeed, he arguably went beyond the reservations to craft an argument to effectively nullify not only America's obligations under the Convention but the provisions of the Act.

While Bret Kavanaugh was staff secretary to President George W. Bush, he pushed for both Bybee and Yoo to be nominated for the Ninth Circuit (Sacks 2018). Although Yoo declined, Bybee was confirmed with bipartisan support about a year before the torture memos came to light. While he and Yoo were sharply criticized by a more-than-200-page report by the Office of Professional Responsibility at the U.S. Department of Justice regarding their violation of several ethical canons in providing the legal advice they offered to the administration, the DOJ's decision to overrule the report and merely state the duo of lawyers showed poor judgment meant that Bybee, like Yoo, would never be punished for his work on the memos, at least as of this writing.

Bybee continues to serve as a judge on the Ninth Circuit Court of Appeals.

Felix Dzerzhinsky

Born on September 11, 1877, near what is now Minsk in Belarus, Dzerzhinsky spent his youth and young adulthood in a running battle against both the Czar's security services (who arrested him six times) and Siberian exile (which he frequently escaped from) before being freed in 1917, when the Provisional Government replaced the Czar's regime in Russia (Encyclopedia Britannica 1998). Or, as another scholar put it,

> The simplest way to summarise Dzerzhinsky's career from this time to the revolution is to look at it as a twenty year period of only intermittent activity, broken up by six arrests, three escapes and long sojourns in prison and exile— around eleven years in jail and Siberia: late 1897 to August 1899; February 1900 to August 1902; July 1905 to October 1905; December 1906 to June 1907; April 1908 to November 1909; September 1912 to March 1917. His experiences here are again similar to those of Stalin, and

can be summed up in three themes: the close proximity of death, the omnipresence of violence, and *the necessity of conspiracy.* This infused both chekism and Stalinism with three of their chief characteristics: *impatience, the readiness to fall back on violence as a first (rather than a last) resort and paranoia.* (Lauchlan 2013, 13; emphasis added)

Toward the end of 1917, not only was Dzerzhinsky a free man, but the new Bolshevik government in Russia (which had overthrown the Provisional Government in the October Revolution and which was led by Vladimir Lenin) was asking him to set up the first security service for the first Marxist state in human history. At the time, Lenin's new regime was threatened not only by partisans of the deposed Czar, some of whom would ultimately organize as the White Army to fight the Bolsheviks in the Russian Civil War, but also by the armies of Russia's former allies in World War I, which were unfriendly to the new government and which occupied Russian soil.

In response, Dzerzhinsky created the All-Russian Extraordinary Commission, which was abbreviated as VChK in Russian and quickly became known as the Cheka. "The chekist system improvised by Dzerzhinsky was a governmental ethos which seemed to predate, anticipate and even create Stalinism. It was proto-Stalinist because it combined tyranny with populism and social engineering. The Cheka used coercion to build orphanages and organize famine relief, to secure food supplies, uproot corruption in government and make sure the trains ran on time. Dzerzhinsky was behind the first show trials, he had a hand in the theory of the intensification of the class struggle and the mummification of Lenin" (Lauchlan 2013, 5).

Shortly after he was appointed, Dzerzhinsky declared, "We stand for organized terror—this should be frankly stated—terror being absolutely indispensable in current revolutionary conditions" (Peters 1985, 128). His words were no idle boast. Following an unsuccessful attempt on Lenin's life in August 1918, Dzerzhinsky inaugurated what would be known as the

"Red Terror," where "over 800 socialists were arrested and shot without trial" (Simpkin 1997).

After the Bolsheviks crushed their opponents and won the Russian Civil War, the Cheka became the GPU and then the OGPU, with Dzerzhinsky at its head, whatever its name. During this time and by his orders, "suspects might be arrested late at night, verbally and physically abused, rushed into a prison, threatened with death (and even led to a place of execution several times, only to be returned to prison) and were tried by no regular procedure, with no defence permitted" (Peters 1985, 128).

Despite the untold numbers of people who were imprisoned, tortured, and murdered under his orders, the paradoxical thing about Dzerzhinsky is that he was seen by his peers and by later historians as having a strong moral character. "He was incorruptible, selfless, and intrepid—a soul of deep poetic sensibility, constantly stirred to compassion for the weak and the suffering. At the same time his devotion to the cause was so intense that it made him a fanatic who would shrink from no act of terror as long he was convinced that it was necessary for the cause. Living in permanent tension between his lofty idealism and the butchery which was his daily job, high-strung, his life-force burning itself out like a flame, he was regarded by his comrades as the strange 'saint of the revolution' of the Savonarola breed" (Lauchlan 2013, 6).

While Dzerzhinsky died on July 20, 1926, in some ways, his life's work had a greater effect on Russia than that of either Lenin or Josef Stalin. Russia continues to celebrate "Cheka Day" on December 20 each year to commemorate the secret police he founded, though it's now officially referred to as "Security Agency Worker's Day" thanks to former president Boris Yeltsin, who made it an official holiday in 1995 (Luhn 2015). As one Russian commentator put it when Dzerhinsky's creation turned hundred in 2017, "The numerous reforms of the security agencies and even the transition from socialism to capitalism had little effect on the ideas of the heads and officers of the special services about their purpose and social status. The ideas of 'Chekism', the superiority of state and official necessity over law and justice turned out to be tenacious—but if earlier they were justified by the interests of the party, now they are often used for personal purposes" (Aptekar 2017).

Lynndie England

Born on November 8, 1982, in Ashland, Kentucky, England grew up in West Virginia. Although she was diagnosed with "selective mutism" (Brockes 2009), which is described "as a childhood anxiety disorder characterized by a child or adolescent's inability to speak in one or more social settings (e.g., at school, in public places, with adults) despite being able to speak comfortably in other settings (e.g., at home with family)" (Selective Mutism Association 2019), as well as an additional learning disability, she graduated from high school and worked as a cashier and at a chicken-processing facility before joining the Army Reserve (Brockes 2009).

After her military police unit was activated for service, England was deployed to Iraq, where she and her colleagues put the advice John Yoo, Jay Bybee, and others gave the government regarding detainee treatment into practice.

> The circumstances in which England and her fellow soldiers of the 372nd Military Police Company found themselves in October 2003 are well known by now. They were posted to Iraq from Kuwait earlier that year and first stationed at Al Hillah, 60 miles south of Baghdad. In the autumn of 2003, they were moved to Abu Ghraib, the prison where inmate numbers had swelled from 700 in the summer to 3,000, and then to 7,000 without anything like the necessary gain in staff. Janis Karpinski, the commanding officer in charge of the prison and 14 others in Iraq, described the situation as "understaffed, overwhelmed and harried." It would be the testimony of

England, Graner and the five other soldiers identified in the photos that when they arrived at the prison, the abusive practices—keeping inmates naked, making them wear female underwear and crawl on the floor—were already established in some form as part of pre-interrogation "softening up" techniques approved by military intelligence officers. (Brockes 2009)

Unfortunately for England, who was engaged to (and pregnant with the child of) Charles Graner—one of the other soldiers involved in the abuse—it was the photos he took of her that got out to the world (Brockes 2009). "In the most notorious photo, she holds a leash with a naked man crawling out of his cell on the end of it. In another, she makes the thumbs up sign behind a human pyramid. In another, she grins at a naked prisoner as he is forced to simulate masturbation" (Brockes 2009).

A May 2004 report by Major General Antonio Taguba found that "US Soldiers have committed egregious acts of abuse to detainees in violation of the UCMJ [Uniform Code of Military Justice] and international law at Abu Ghraib" (Taguba 2004, 6).

According to Taguba (2004, 16–17), these included the following:

a. (S) Punching, slapping, and kicking detainees; jumping on their naked feet;

b. (S) Videotaping and photographing naked male and female detainees;

c. (S) Forcibly arranging detainees in various sexually explicit positions for photographing;

d. (S) Forcing detainees to remove their clothing and keeping them naked for several days at a time;

e. (S) Forcing naked male detainees to wear women's underwear;

f.   (S) Forcing groups of male detainees to masturbate themselves while being photographed and videotaped;

g.   (S) Arranging naked male detainees in a pile and then jumping on them;

h.   (S) Positioning a naked detainee on a[n] MRE Box, with a sandbag on his head, and attaching wires to his fingers, toes, and penis to simulate electric torture;

i.   (S) Writing "I am a Rapest" [sic] on the leg of a detainee alleged to have forcibly raped a 15-year old fellow detainee, and then photographing him naked;

j.   (S) Placing a dog chain or strap around a naked detainee's neck and having a female Soldier pose for a picture;

k.   (S) A male MP guard having sex with a female detainee;

l.   (S) Using military working dogs (without muzzles) to intimidate and frighten detainees, and in at least one case biting and severely injuring a detainee;

m.   (S) Taking photographs of dead Iraqi detainees.

While Taguba ultimately recommended that fourteen officers and noncommissioned officers (NCOs) and civilian contractors be reprimanded and nine officers and NCOs be relieved of their commands (Taguba 2004, 3–5), with some military personnel subjected to disciplinary actions under the UCMJ, only one officer—Lieutenant Colonel. Steven Jordan—was ever court-martialed over the scandal, and Jordan's conviction was thrown out in early 2008 and replaced with a reprimand ("US Army Rejects Court Martial of Abu Ghraib Commander" 2008).

Instead, the military focused on enlisted personnel like England, who ended up being sentenced to three years under a plea bargain for her acts at Abu Ghraib, though she would eventually serve only half that sentence (Brockes 2009). Graner, deemed the "ringleader" of the abuse by some observers—and the soldier who posed with his hand in a "thumbs up" signal in front of a dead Iraqi detainee—received a ten-year sentence, of which he served six-and-a-half years before being released

(Johnson 2011). As for Taguba, he was pressured to retire in 2007 after he refused to back the claims of former secretary of defense Donald Rumsfeld that the latter was ignorant of what had happened at Abu Ghraib (Hersh 2007). A 2008 report from members of the Senate Armed Services Committee declared that Rumsfeld bore ultimate responsibility for the abuses at Abu Ghraib, a conclusion the former secretary of defense rejected (Scott and Mazzetti 2008, A14).

After her release from custody in March 2007, England authorized Gary S. Winkler to write her biography *Tortured: Lynndie England, Abu Ghraib and the Photographs That Shocked the World*, which appeared in 2009. In the intervening years, England has rejected calls to apologize for her actions, declaring in 2012 that "they weren't innocent. They're trying to kill us, and you want me to apologize to them? It's like saying sorry to the enemy" (Ralph 2012). England also claimed, in reference to those she had tortured, that "their lives are better. They got the better end of the deal" (Ralph 2012).

In reality, most of those incarcerated at Abu Ghraib at the time England was there "were civilians, many of whom had been picked up in random military sweeps and at highway checkpoints. They fell into three loosely defined categories: common criminals; security detainees suspected of 'crimes against the coalition'; and a small number of suspected 'high-value' leaders of the insurgency against the coalition forces" (Hersh 2004).

In 2006, the United States turned over Abu Ghraib to the government of Iraq, which ran it from 2009 through 2014 as Baghdad Central Prison. The facility was closed in 2014, and the remaining prisoners were relocated due to security concerns caused by the Islamic State, or Daesh, insurgency then raging in Iraq and Syria (British Broadcasting Corporation 2014).

Gina Haspel

Born on October 1, 1956, in Ashland, Kentucky, Haspel would go on to be a living example of the consequences of President Obama's decision to draw a line under abuses committed by the CIA during the Bush administration at the agency's black sites and elsewhere.

Haspel initially attended the University of Kentucky in Louisville in 1974 before transferring to the University of Louisville in 1977, where she earned a BS degree "with honors" (Haspel 2018, 2) in languages and journalism (Youssef 2018). "Upon leaving college, she traveled to Massachusetts to work as a contractor for the U.S. Army's Tenth Special Forces Group, which was then based there, working in the library and foreign language lab. There, she ran into a young officer named Michael Vickers, who would eventually become the undersecretary of Defense for Intelligence, and he encouraged her to apply to the CIA, according to an agency biography" (Youssef 2018).

After she joined the Agency in January 1985, her résumé became a state secret. Even now, all that is publicly known of what she did for the CIA before 9/11 is that she apparently was either seconded to the U.S. State Department or given diplomatic cover at a foreign post, that she "participated in humanitarian work during the Gulf War and has served as chief of station in the capital of a 'major U.S. ally'" (Youssef 2018). In the context of the CIA, a chief of station is the highest-ranking Agency representative in the country. The Agency goes to considerable lengths to protect the identities of its chiefs, as shown by its dogged (if ineffectual) pursuit of former agent Philip Agee, who exposed around "250 officers, front companies and foreign agents working for the [CIA]" (Shane 2008) in his 1975 book *Inside the Company: CIA Diary.*

In 1999, she received the Agency's George H.W. Bush Award for Excellence in Counterterrorism, apparently for "pull[ing] together a capture operation involving two terrorists with suspected connections to an embassy bombing" (Youssef 2018).

Shortly thereafter, she became the deputy group chief of the CIA's Counterterrorism Center. Ironically, her first day on the job was September 11, 2001 (Youssef 2018). Over the next few years, she would go on to supervise the CIA's black site in

Thailand, which caused the American Civil Liberties Union (ACLU) to later describe her as being "up to her eyeballs in torture" (Hamilton 2018). Her former CIA colleague, John Kiriakou—who would end up serving five years in federal prison (NBC News 2012) after he confirmed that the CIA tortured Abu Zubaydah via waterboarding (Stelter 2009)—declared that "many of the rest of us who knew and worked with Haspel at the CIA called her 'Bloody Gina'" (Kiriakou 2018) and that "the CIA will not let me repeat her résumé or the widely reported specifics of how her work fit into the agency's torture program, calling such details 'currently and properly classified'. But I can say that Haspel was a protege of and chief of staff for Jose Rodriguez, the CIA's notorious former deputy director for operations and former director of the Counterterrorism Center. And that Rodriguez eventually assigned Haspel to order the destruction of videotaped evidence of the torture of Abu [Zubaydah]. The Justice Department investigated, but no one was ever charged in connection with the incident" (Kiriakou 2018).

While Haspel was originally thought to have been running the black site at the time Zubaydah was waterboarded, this turned out not to have been the case (Engelberg 2018). However, "she did oversee CIA personnel who were involved in the interrogation of other suspects, current and former officials have said. Her defenders have said she was carrying out lawful orders during those times" (Youssef 2018).

In addition, Haspel admits she was the one who wrote the cabled order to the Thailand base in 2005 to destroy "92 videotapes of interrogations said to include the use of techniques widely described as torture" (Taddonio 2018), including the interrogation of Zubaydah.

From 2005 through 2008, she served as chief of staff of the CIA's Directorate of Operations, which oversees the Agency's clandestine operations (Gazis 2018). Like Jay Bybee, John Yoo, and so many others involved with the Bush administration's torture program, Haspel not only was not sanctioned for her actions, but continually promoted by the Agency, ultimately becoming chief of station for the CIA's Europe division in 2014 (Gazis 2018).

In 2017, the Trump administration made Haspel the first female case officer to serve as the deputy director of the CIA (Toosi 2017). Shortly thereafter, after Mike Pompeo left the Agency to serve as secretary of state, Haspel was nominated to succeed him as CIA director.

On May 10, 2018, former vice president Dick Cheney publicly called for the United States to resume the use of waterboarding and other "interrogation programs," which later deemed to be torture, despite the fact that those methods have been banned under U.S. law since 2015 (Gstalter 2018).

He also praised the nomination of Haspel, declaring, "I think she's done a great job in terms of the career she's built, and the people I know at the agency are very enthusiastic about having one of their own, so to speak, in the driver's seat at the CIA" (Gstalter 2018).

After promising not to resume the CIA's "detention and interrogation program" (Beavers 2018), Haspel was confirmed by the U.S. Senate in a 54–45 vote on May 17, 2018, as the first woman to lead the CIA in its history (Taddonio 2018). All of the Republicans present (and six Democrats) backed Haspel, while the rest of the Democrats and the two independents in the chamber voted against her. In contrast, her immediate predecessor—Pompeo—had been confirmed by a vote of 66–32 in January 2017.

Donald O. Hebb

Donald O. Hebb was born on July 22, 1904, in Chester, Nova Scotia. While his mother and father were both doctors, his mother was only the third woman in history to receive her MD from Dalhousie University (Brown 2006, 128). While he had been homeschooled by his mother until he was eight,

Hebb advanced from second to ninth grade within four years (Brown 2006, 129).

Rebelling against parental pressure to follow his father into the sciences, Hebb earned a bachelor of arts degree in English and philosophy at Dalhousie in 1925 and obtained a teaching credential shortly thereafter (Brown 2006, 129). He moved to Montreal in 1927 and soon began graduate work in psychology at McGill University while he was principal of Rushbrooke School in Verdun, which was then a suburb of Montreal (Brown 2006, 129).

Rushbrooke was the site of Hebb's first experiment with human subjects. "As a teacher and principal, Hebb found that students of all intellectual abilities were failing in school. He decided to change the school procedures to facilitate education and persuade the children that schoolwork was a privilege. He gave the students interesting things to do in class and no homework. Students were not punished for inattention and those who disrupted the class were sent outside to play. He described this experiment in a teacher's journal (Hebb 1930) and continued with it for four years" (Brown 2007, 5). While physically incapacitated by tuberculosis, he wrote his master's thesis on the "nature of [brain] synaptic activity during conditioning" (Brown 2007, 5).

While he began his PhD work at McGill, after the Verdun authorities ended his Rushbrooke experiment and his wife died in a car accident, Hebb decided to transfer to the University of Chicago and later to Harvard (Brown 2007, 5–6). He returned to Montreal in 1937 to work at the Montreal Neurological Institute, where his research on patients who had received lobotomies led to the development of two new tests to measure intelligence (Brown 2007, 6–7). Following stints at Queens University and Yale's primate research center in Florida, Hebb wrote his first book, *The Organization of Behavior*, in 1949, after his return to McGill, this time as a professor (Brown 2007, 8–11).

As the Cold War raged, Hebb and McGill began what many would see as their most controversial research. "In the early

1950s, Hebb embarked on a research project examining the effects of restricted environments on adult human volunteers, research that was caught up in intelligence concerns" (McCoy, 2006; Brown, 2007; Klein, 2007; McCoy, 2007). During that period, psychologists, many influenced by notable behaviorist B. H. Skinner, turned their attention to examine how psychological methods could be used to modify human behavior. Within the context of the Cold War, this field of research resonated both with intelligence officials and with the American public. Communist trials, prisoners' false confessions, and the fear of secretly turning citizens against their own country, epitomized in the 1959 classic novel *The Manchurian Candidate*, quickly established "'mind control' as a topic of public fascination" (Raz 2013, 380).

While theories about mind control may have been part of the cultural *zeitgeist* at that moment in history, Hebb had a closer relationship to the subject than others. "Hebb had an official role that tied him to security interests, serving as chair of the Human Resources Research Advisory Committee for the Canadian Defence Research Board (DRB). The DRB was established in 1947 to meet the Canadian military's research needs. Closely tied to academia, the DRB funded research programs in Canadian universities and relied on the consultancy of university professors" (Raz 2013, 381). In that capacity, "Hebb met with senior Central Intelligence Agency (CIA) researcher Cyril Haskins; Omond Solandt, chairman of the Canadian DRB; and additional leading Canadian scientists. This meeting would become known as the birth of sensory deprivation research" (Raz 2013, 381).

After a 1951 meeting between members of British and Canadian intelligence as well as the CIA, in Montreal, the Canadian Research Board gave Hebb a grant "to explore 'sensory isolation' as a means for 'intervention in the individual mind'" (McCoy 2012, 20). Through the use of paid volunteers, who were McGill students, Hebb learned he could induce virtual psychosis in 24 to 48 hours just by depriving the subjects of sensory stimuli (McCoy 2012, 20).

In addition, he found that sensory deprivation enabled him to change the views of his research subjects. "As part of the research protocol, subjects were asked about their attitudes toward controversial topics, such as the evolutionary theory or the existence of psychic phenomena before the experiment. They then underwent sensory deprivation and were subsequently played recordings of arguments against the views they had previously voiced. Repeat testing indicated that sensory deprivation rendered individuals susceptible to attempts to induce attitude change (Hebb, Heron, & Bexton, 1952). Hebb and his team had found an extremely powerful tool" (Raz 2013, 381).

Hebb's findings were classified and not published—and then, only in a sanitized form—until 1954 (Raz 2013, 381). Four years later, "Harvard University held a symposium on sensory deprivation, funded indirectly by the intelligence community" (Raz 2013, 382). Hebb's work would strongly influence the CIA's KUBARK counterintelligence interrogation manual (Raz 2013, 382) and, long after his death, the actions of CIA interrogators in Afghanistan and Iraq and at the agency's black sites around the world during the early 2000s.

Aside from his work used by torturers, Hebb is best known for developing the theory of Hebbian plasticity as applied to neurons in the brain, which holds, "When an axon of cell A is near enough to excite a cell B and repeatedly or persistently takes part in firing it, some growth process or metabolic change takes place in one or both cells such that A's efficiency, as one of the cells firing B, is increased" (Hebb 1949, 62). Referred to as Hebb's Rule, the concept has important implications for the design of artificial neural networks and machine learning.

Hebb died on August 20, 1985. Each year, the American Psychological Association's Society for Behavioral Neuroscience

and Comparative Psychology gives the D.O. Hebb Distinguished Scientific Contributions Award in his memory.

Innocent IV

Born sometime around 1195 to a noble family in Genoa, Sini-
baldo Fieschi would ultimately become—according to some
observers—"the greatest lawyer that ever sat on the chair of
St. Peter" (Muldoon 1979, x). After his uncle, the bishop of
Parma, appointed him as a church canon (or priest) in his cathe-
dral, Fieschi would go on to earn his law degree at the University
of Bologna and teach there for a period of time (Reis 1972, 21).

He ascended to the papacy as Pope Innocent IV on June 25,
1243, and while his reign is best known for a series of conflicts
with the Holy Roman Empire, he made two key legal contributions relevant to this story.

Innocent IV was the first pope to definitively articulate the
idea of a corporation as a *persona ficta*, "a fiction of the law,
and in general advocated the authoritarian interpretation of
corporation structure" (Reis 1972, 32). While Innocent IV
was primarily interested in creating a vehicle that would allow
ecclesiastical organizations to have a legal existence separate
from that of their members—among other things, "the doctrine was stated as the reason why an ecclesiastic *collegium* or
universitas or *capitulum* could not be excommunicated or be
guilty of a delict" (Dewey 1926, 665)—his thinking helped
advance the end of the Middle Ages in Europe. "The later
political interpretation of this doctrine would have a great impact on the medieval world. If the personality of the corporation was a legal fiction, it was the gift of the prince. Needless
to say, this doctrine became an apt lever for those forces which
were transforming the medieval nation into the modern state"
(Reis 1972, 32).

In our own day, Innocent IV's doctrine of *persona ficta* would
eventually lead to the concept of a corporation as a means of
limiting the liability of its owners both for financial reverses

and as to torts arising out of the corporation's actions and those of its employees. It is one of history's ironies that Innocent IV would do so much to help large organizations avoid the consequences of the actions of their servants, given for what he's most famous for, as set forth here.

Innocent IV has the distinction—or the dishonor, depending on your point of view—of being the first pope to explicitly authorize the use of torture by church Inquisitors. In 1252, he issued "Ad Extirpanda," a papal bull that declared that

> the Podestà [Mayor] or the Rector [City official] should be allowed, without damage to their [the heretics'] bodies or lives, to force all the heretics whom he has held captive—as if they are really thieves and murderers of souls, and robbers of the Sacraments of God and of the Christian faith—to confess their errors unambiguously and to accuse other heretics who they know, and to proscribe their goods, and to accuse fellow believers, and those who receive them and their defenders—just as robbers and thieves of temporal things are forced to accuse their accomplices and to confess the evils which they have committed. Indeed any home in which some heretical man or heretical woman has been found should be razed to the ground without any possibility of re-building. (Léglu et al. 2014, 70)

Stripped of Papal prolixity, "this bull authorized and controlled the use of preventive torture, which was intended for the extraction of a confession by the ecclesiastical tribunals. The accused were to confess their errors and reveal their accomplices just as in the case of felony in the temporal order. The peculiar nature of this organization was that, while it operated under papal directives, it was manned for the most part by laymen and was controlled by the Podestà" (Reis 1972, 49–50). In other words, the laity would be the ones to get their hands dirty strapping recalcitrant Cathars and Albigensians to racks, not the clergy, at least under Innocent IV.

Besides clearing the way for the use of torture by Inquisitors, "Ad Extirpanda" is credited (or blamed, again depending on your point of view) for standardizing the procedures of the inquisition in Italy (Reis 1972, 50–51). It also allowed Innocent IV's successors to approve the Spanish Inquisition, which lasted from 1478 until 1834, and the Roman Inquisition, which began as an anti-Protestant crusade in 1542 and which is now known as the Congregation for the Doctrine of the Faith (Stanley 1998). The Spanish Inquisition's use of torture has been well documented, while the Roman Inquisition is probably best known for banning the works of Nicolaus Copernicus and trying Galileo Galilei as a heretic.

While the Vatican's records on the Roman Inquisition are still gradually being released—its archives were closed to scholars until 1998, and the first volume of documents in Latin with commentary, covering "science and natural philosophy from 1542 to 1600," were only published in 2012 (Archdiocese of Baltimore 2012)—it is generally believed that the Roman Inquisition abandoned the use of torture before the twentieth century.

As the modern Roman Catholic Catechism notes,

> In times past, cruel practices were commonly used by legitimate governments to maintain law and order, often without protest from the Pastors of the Church, who themselves adopted in their own tribunals the prescriptions of Roman law concerning torture. Regrettable as these facts are, the Church always taught the duty of clemency and mercy. She forbade clerics to shed blood. In recent times it has become evident that these cruel practices were neither necessary for public order, nor in conformity with the legitimate rights of the human person. On the contrary, these practices led to ones even more degrading. It is necessary to work for their abolition. We must pray for the victims and their tormentors. (Vatican 2298)

Based on that Catechism, in 2014, the United States Conference of Catholic Bishops applauded the partial release of the U.S. Senate's report on the use of torture by the CIA, declaring, "The acts of torture described in the Senate Intelligence Committee's report violated the God-given human dignity inherent in all people and were unequivocally wrong" (Desmond 2014).

Innocent IV died on December 7, 1254, about two years after "Ad Extirpanda" was issued.

Omar Khadr

Born on September 19, 1986, in Toronto, Canada, to Egyptian- and Palestinian-Canadian parents, by the time Khadr was a teenager he would have more direct and personal experience with American interrogation techniques in the Bush era than most men twice his age.

Shortly after his birth, Khadr's family moved to Pakistan, where his father, Ahmed, was deeply involved in relief work for Afghan civilians and Pakistanis impacted by the Soviet Union's invasion of Afghanistan in 1979 and subsequent war with the *mujahideen* Islamist insurgency, particularly with Human Concern International (HCI), a Canadian charity.

During the 1980s, the United States, through the Central Intelligence Agency and its Pakistani counterpart, the PSI, funded several *mujahideen* groups as a means of waging a proxy war with the Soviet Union and force it to devote military and other resources to maintaining its position in Afghanistan (Singh 2007, 61). After the Soviet forces withdrew in 1989 and the *mujahideen* turned their guns on each other, Ahmed Khadr continued his dual life of direct services to refugees in Afghanistan and Pakistan and fundraising trips to Canada to keep his relief work going (Shephard 2008, 34).

A short article published in October 1989 in the *Toronto Star*, again profiling [Ahmed] Khadr's involvement with

H.C.I. began "Ahmed Khadr is a fighter in a forgotten war, whose living casualties make up almost half the world's refugee population. The Afghan children have the highest mortality rate in the world, he says. Almost one in three dies. The never-ebbing human tide had long since engulfed the meager resources Khadr has at hand. 'Still we continue,' he said[.] 'What else can we do?'" (Shephard 2008, 34)

However, it wasn't just refugees in Afghanistan and financial backers in Canada that Ahmed Khadr reportedly knew during this time of his life. According to some observers, during this period, "[Ahmed] Khadr had contact with [Osama] Bin Laden from at least 1988. Canadian intelligence agents claim that in 1995 he funneled money through Human Concern to finance the al-Qaida bombing of the Egyptian embassy in Pakistan that was orchestrated by [Ayman] Al Zawahiri" (NBC News 2005). Furthermore, after the attack on the Egyptian embassy "Ahmed Khadr was arrested in Pakistan in 1995 but was released in 1996 following what Canada's National Post described as 'an extraordinary intervention' by Prime Minister Jean Chretien during a state visit to Islamabad" (NBC News 2005).

On July 27, 2002, American soldiers and their Afghan allies tried to search a house in the village of Ab Khail near Khost, Afghanistan, when a firefight broke out (Baldauf 2002). When the guns fell silent four hours later, Sergeant First Class Christopher J. Speer was dead and Omar Khadr—then 15 years old—was badly wounded, as well as the prime suspect, in American eyes, of being the fighter who threw the grenade that killed Speer (Krauss 2002).

On paper, this shouldn't have mattered, as the United States signed the United Nations' Optional Protocol on the Rights of the Child on the Involvement of Children in Armed Conflict in 2000 and ratified it in 2002 and was therefore obligated to cooperate "in the rehabilitation and social reintegration of persons who are victims of acts contrary to this Protocol," which, as a child under the age of 18, Khadr clearly was (United Nations, May 2000). Accordingly, one would have expected the Pentagon to treat him differently than combatants who were over 18.

Instead, the United States claimed that instead of rehabilitation "the Protocol *obligates* the United States to prosecute Khadr" (Human Rights Watch 2008, 3), supposedly because "'prosecuting Khadr would constitute a 'feasible measure to prevent' and a 'legal measure necessary to prohibit and criminalize' acts committed under Article 4 of the Optional Protocol" (Human Rights Watch April 2008).

Due to ongoing legal challenges to the various attempts of the Bush administration to conduct trials at the U.S. Naval Base at Guantanamo, Cuba, under rules not explicitly sanctioned by the Geneva Convention, it took until November 2005 for the United States to charge Khadr with murder (Freeman and Sallot 2005). Khadr was subjected to sleep deprivation and social isolation for extended periods during his time at Guantanamo. "Documents released in 2008 related to the case revealed that Canadian authorities knew that while Khadr was at Guantanamo he was subjected to 'the frequent flyer program,' where detainees were moved from location to location every three hours, denying him uninterrupted sleep for three weeks. This was apparently followed by three-week periods of isolation where he was denied any human contact" (Carvin 2017).

Moreover, "according to [his] affidavit, Khadr says interrogators dropped him, shackled him for hours, spit on him and threatened him with rape during his detention at Bagram and Guantanamo Bay" (Teotonio 2008). Although Khadr told Canadian consular officials what was going on when they visited him at Guantanamo, it did him little good.

"'I showed them my injuries,' recalled Khadr in an affidavit filed with a U.S. military war crimes court. 'I said that I told the Americans whatever they wanted me to say because they would torture me. The Canadians called me a liar and I began to sob. They screamed at me and told me that they could not do anything for me,' said Khadr, recalling one of six visits in 2003 and 2004 by Canadians to the U.S. naval base in Guantanamo Bay, Cuba, which is being used as a prison for terrorism suspects" (Teotonio 2008).

In 2010—after more than eight years behind bars—Khadr entered a guilty plea to the murder of Speer and several other charges. At the time, sources said under the terms of his plea agreement, Khadr was to spend another year in Guantanamo and a further seven in Canadian custody (Cable News Network 2010). However, Khadr was not returned to Canada until September 2012 (Shephard 2012). Three years later, an Alberta court released him on strict bail conditions ("The Bail Conditions Omar Khadr Must Now Live by" 2015).

Meanwhile, in 2013, Khadr filed a $20 million lawsuit against the Canadian government for cooperating with the United States regarding his detention, which he said led to his coerced guilty plea (Shephard 2013). Four years later, the Canadian government settled Khadr's lawsuit by paying him $10.5 million and publicly apologizing to him (Tasker 2017). On March 25, 2019, Court of Queen's Bench Chief Justice Mary Moreau deemed Khadr's sentence served and released him unconditionally (Weber 2019).

Pieter (Peter) H. Kooijmans

Born on July 6, 1933, in Heemstede, the Netherlands, less than seven years before Nazi forces would storm across his country's neutral border and torture its people for almost a decade, Pieter Kooijmans would go on to dedicate his life to helping to create a body of international law aimed at ensuring the atrocities Adolf Hitler's legions inflicted on his country would not happen again.

After completing his undergraduate work in economics and a master's degree in law at the Free University of Amsterdam,

Kooijmans went on to earn his PhD in international law in 1964 (PDC 2013). In 1966, while a professor at the Free University, he served on the Vietnam Committee, which helped organize a major demonstration against the Vietnam War in Amsterdam in May 1967 (PDC 2013). In the early 1970s, he attempted to secure a reduction in the size of the Dutch army and the transfer of some of the missions of the Royal Dutch Air Force to other NATO countries (PDC 2013). From 1973 through 1977, he served as secretary of state for foreign affairs for the Netherlands (Van Leeuwen 2013).

In 1984, Kooijmans chaired the United Nations' Commission on Human Rights (United Nations 1984, 1330) when it drafted the Convention against Torture, which the UN General Assembly adopted unanimously without a vote on December 10, 1984 (United Nations 1984, 813). The Convention's smooth passage through the General Assembly appears shocking in retrospect, given the divisions between U.N. members on issues ranging from the apartheid regime in South Africa to tensions in the Middle East. Moreover, this was during the last (and in some ways, the hottest) years of the Cold War between the United States and the Union of Soviet Socialist Republics—and this was just a year after the Soviet Union shot down Korean Air Lines Flight 007, which its pilots mistook for a military aircraft, causing New York and New Jersey to later deny the use of *their* airspace to Soviet aircraft.

> The United States, which opposed the legislation, offered the Soviet Union landing rights at a military base so its foreign minister, Andrei A. Gromyko, could fly in for the General Assembly meeting. But the Soviets refused. When the United Nations committee met to review the situation, the Soviet delegate, Igor I. Yakovlev, said the ban on landing "raises the question of whether the United Nations should be in the United States. A furious Mr. [Charles M.] Lichenstein [the United States' alternate

delegate to the U.N.] replied that if member states felt "they are not being treated with the hostly consideration that is their due," they should consider "removing themselves and this organization from the soil of the United States." "'We will put no impediment in your way,' he continued, 'The members of the U.S. mission to the United Nations will be down at the dockside waving you a fond farewell as you sail off into the sunset.'" (Lewis 2002)

Somehow, Kooijmans transcended these ideological and national differences and not only got the Convention against Torture approved, but without even the need for a contested vote (and thus without even one member state voting no). Appropriately, he then became the first Special Rapporteur for Torture at the United Nations in 1985, a post he held until 1993. In 1986, he began to argue that rape should be considered a form of torture, a position the United Nations ultimately accepted ("Report by the Special Rapporteur, Mr. P Kooijmans, Appointed Pursuant to Commission on Human Rights Resolution" 1986, 29).

His time as Special Rapporteur coincided with the breakup of the former Republic of Yugoslavia, and after his visit there in 1992, he reported back to the United Nations,

It is no surprise that in the war-stricken areas of Bosnia and Herzegovina torture is a daily phenomenon. During an armed conflict human life as such is held in low esteem and under such conditions basic human rights violations such as arbitrary detention, torture, deliberate killings and disappearances usually go hand in hand. Disrespect for human rights seems to have reached its apex, however, in Bosnia and Herzegovina. The delegation received horrendous information about people being clubbed to death and others who died from injuries suffered during torture, in particular in detention camps in the Serbian-controlled areas. Rape of women belonging to other ethnic groups was alleged to be practised systematically. ("Report by the Special Rapporteur, Mr. P Kooijmans, Appointed Pursuant to Commission on Human Rights Resolution" 1992, 124)

He went on to sound an early warning about a future conflict that would burst into flames by the end of the decade, when NATO would attack Serbia to force it to withdraw from Kosovo.

Of particular concern is the situation in Kosovo, which forms part of the Republic of Serbia. In 1990 the previously autonomous status of this province was abolished and the Serbian Government took over the administration. Since that time the participation of Albanians, who constitute about 90 per cent of the province's population, in public, economic and social life has become practically become non-existent. Since that time the Special Rapporteur has regularly received communications about torture and serious mistreatment of Albanians. Such mistreatment is not only practised during detention. Mention was made of punitive expeditions by large police forces against towns and villages to search for arms. During these expeditions, the people are beaten and otherwise mistreated. . . . The situation in Kosovo is highly volatile and demands the closest possible attention from the international community. ("Report by the Special Rapporteur, Mr. P Kooijmans, Appointed Pursuant to Commission on Human Rights Resolution" 1992, 124–125)

After a stint as the foreign minister of the Netherlands, Kooijmans was appointed to the International Court of Justice, where—ironically—he got to rule on Serbia's application for a restraining order to stop Belgium, the Netherlands, the United

States, and other NATO countries from attacking it in the campaign to free Kosovo from Serbian control.

He remained on the International Court of Justice until 2006. Kooijmans died on February 13, 2013.

Chelsea Manning

Chelsea Manning, who would go on to become the most famous transgender whistleblower in American history when it came to exposing the military's involvement in war crimes, was born on December 17, 1987, in Oklahoma City, Oklahoma. Due to her parents' struggle with alcoholism, she was mostly raised by her sister Casey until she was a teenager (Lewis 2013).

When her family moved to Crescent, Oklahoma, when she was a child, she had "few, if any, friends and spent nearly all of [her] time building Lego blocks or playing on the computer" (Lewis 2013). Her interest in both computers and system design would grow to play a major part in her life as she grew older.

After her parents' divorce, Manning lived in Wales with her mother until she was 17 and then returned to the United States (Lewis 2013). While then presenting as male, she joined the U.S. Army at 19 in 2007 and was inducted at the Fort Meade military base outside Baltimore, where she would face a court martial several years later (Lewis 2013).

Assigned to Iraq as an intelligence analyst, Manning leaked several hundred thousand documents to the online site WikiLeaks, which eventually repackaged and released them as the Iraq War Logs. Unfortunately, she also admitted her involvement to fellow hacker Adrian Lamo, who, despite claiming in an electronic chat with Manning that he was "a journalist and a minister. You can pick either, and treat this as a confession or an interview (never to be published) & enjoy a modicum of legal protection" (Hansen 2011), informed on her to the United States Army, who subsequently arrested her on May 29, 2010.

Manning was transferred to the U.S. Marine base at Quantico, Virginia in July 2010, where she was held "in conditions that aroused widespread condemnation, including being held in solitary confinement for 23 hours a day and being made to strip naked at night" (Pilkington 2012). In February 2012, the U.N. Special Rapporteur on Torture formally informed the United States that such conditions, particularly the solitary confinement aspect, could "amount to a breach of article 7 of the International Covenant on Civil and Political Rights, and to an act defined in article 1 or article 16 of the Convention against Torture" (Méndez 2012, 74). Indeed, when Manning was finally brought to trial in 2013, the military judge hearing the case awarded her an additional 112 days of custody credit because of the abuse she suffered at Quantico (Tate and Nakashima 2013).

Manning was ultimately acquitted of the most serious charge against her—that of "aiding the enemy"—but convicted of seventeen other violations, in July 2013, in a verdict condemned by human rights groups around the world (Pilkington 2013).

Originally sentenced to thirty-five years in prison (Tate 2013) in August 2013, years of advocacy by her supporters ultimately persuaded President Barack Obama to commute her sentence on January 17, 2017, just before he left office (Pilkington et al. 2017). She was released on May 17, 2017.

Manning, who began her gender transition while in military custody, has worked as an activist for digital privacy since she was freed. At one of her first public speaking appearances in San Francisco after her release, she told the crowd, "I think it's really important to remember, especially at a time like this, that institutions which matter, and which make decisions about us . . . can, and regularly do, fail. Whenever systems fail, you do have power" (DiEdoardo 2017, 9).

On March 8, 2019, U.S. district judge Claude Hilton had Manning arrested after she refused to testify before a federal grand jury that was believed to be investigating WikiLeaks (British

Broadcasting Corporation 2019). Manning told the court she has already disclosed all she knows about WikiLeaks during her 2013 court martial (British Broadcasting Corporation 2019). In a prepared statement, Manning said, "I will not participate in a secret process that I morally object to, particularly one that has been historically used to entrap and persecute activists for protected political speech" (Manning 2019).

About a month later, on April 11, 2019, British authorities arrested WikiLeaks co-founder Julian Assange at the Ecuadorean Embassy in London after Ecuador withdrew its protection. Shortly thereafter, the United States unsealed an indictment accusing Assange of engaging in computer-hacking offenses with Manning related to the Iraq War Logs (Savage et al. 2019). As of April 2019, Manning is not a co-defendant in that case.

On April 22, 2019, a three-judge panel of the Fourth Circuit Court of Appeals denied Manning's appeal of Hilton's contempt order and refused to order her release on bail, while the case continues (Barakat 2019).

After the Fourth Circuit's ruling, Manning released the following statement: "While disappointing, we can still raise issues as the government continues to abuse the grand jury process. I don't have anything to contribute to this, or any other grand jury. While I miss home, they can continue to hold me in jail, with all the harmful consequences that brings. I will not give up" (Manning 2019).

On May 9, 2019, Manning was released from custody after the term of the grand jury for which she was subpoenaed expired (Cameron 2019). However, the United States quickly subpoenaed her for a successor grand jury.

On May 16, 2019, after she repeated her refusal to testify, U.S. district judge Anthony Trenga returned her to custody on contempt charges and fined her $500 for every day she was in custody up to 30 days—and $1,000 a day for every day she spent in custody defying the order to testify after that. As of November 2019, she remained in custody based on her refusal to testify.

Juan E. Méndez

Born on December 11, 1944, in Lomas de Zamora, Argentina, Méndez became a lawyer specialized in the defense of political prisoners during the dictatorship of Juan and then Isabel Peron. In August 1975, he changed places with his clients when he was arrested by the police in Buenos Aires.

> On a dark winter night I was detained when I walked into a stakeout in a distant western suburb of Buenos Aires. My captors handed me over to an elite interrogation unit known as SIPBA (Intelligence Service of the Police of the Province of Buenos Aires). By then, I had been handcuffed and blindfolded, and over the next two days I was transported by car to several different places in the suburbs, where I was interrogated by under beatings and application of the electric prod (*picana*). I received five sessions of the electric prod in the course of what I judged to be about twenty-four hours, always by the same torturers and interrogators. (Méndez 2005, 57)

Three decades later, Méndez (2005, 58) remembered the experience as if it were yesterday:

> The *picana* was originally created to be a cattle prod, and when it is used on cattle, is powered by batteries. However, the prod used by police in interrogation is smaller and more flexible. The machine makes a whizzing sound before it is applied, and the operator seems to be able to regulate the intensity or voltage of the discharge. The pain I suffered with each discharge was so intense that my whole body tensed up, many muscles ached for several days after my treatment. When applied in the mouth, face or head, the shock creates the sensation of a blackout.

While the government criminally charged Méndez with theft and weapons offenses, the case was quickly terminated.

"The federal judge who interrupted my torture also cleared me of those charges citing lack of evidence: the car owner did not recognize me even in a highly suggestive lineup, and the police reported that the weapons had been destroyed" (Méndez 2005, 59). Regardless, the Peron regime continued to detain him until it was overthrown in March 1976 in a military coup, and it would take another year of pressure from Amnesty International and others to allow Méndez to go into exile in the United States (Méndez 2005, 59).

For the next decade and a half, he worked for Human Rights Watch, a nongovernmental organization and public charity in the United States that advocates for human rights around the world, becoming its general counsel in 1994 (United Nations 2004). He went on to serve as the executive director of the Inter-American Institute of Human Rights in Costa Rica and as a law professor at Notre Dame University before U.N. secretary general Kofi Annan appointed him as his special advisor on the prevention of genocide in July 2004 (United Nations 2004). In that role, Méndez was the secretary general's point person during U.N. efforts to end the genocide in Darfur, Sudan, despite the efforts of the then U.S. ambassador to the United Nations John Bolton, who refused to let Méndez address the Security Council on the issue (Spiegel Online 2005).

In 2010, Méndez was named the Special Rapporteur on Torture and Other Cruel, Inhuman or Degrading Treatment or Punishment by the Office of the High Commissioner for Human Rights at the United Nations. In that capacity, Méndez attempted to visit Chelsea Manning to follow up on reports that she was being tortured, only to have the United States refuse to let him do so unless accompanied by a guard, who would report whatever Manning said for possible use at her later court martial, which Méndez condemned as a violation of his mandate (MacAskill 2011).

In December 2011, Méndez submitted an *amicus curiae*, or friend-of-the-court, brief at the U.S. Supreme Court in support of the petitioners in *Mohammad v. Palestinian Authority* and their position that the Torture Victim Protection Act, 28 U.S.C 1350, allowed survivors of torture and their families to hold organizations in addition to individuals liable. Unfortunately, in a unanimous decision by Associate Justice Sonia Sotomayor issued on April 18, 2012, the Supreme Court decided to read the statute literally and refuse to allow a lawsuit against an organization like the Palestinian Authority under the Act.

A year later, Méndez publicly advised the United States—and the rest of the world—that holding Manning in solitary confinement for eleven months "can amount to a breach of Article 7 of the International Covenant on Civil and Political Rights, and to an act defined in article 1 or article 16 of the Convention against Torture" (Méndez 2012, 74). He also castigated the United States for continuing to refuse to allow him to meet with Manning in private (Méndez 2012, 75).

Méndez also reminded the United States that it had failed to respond to his requests for information regarding "16 gay and transgender individuals [who] have allegedly been subjected to solitary confinement, torture and ill-treatment while in detention in U.S. immigration facilities . . . Given the lack of any evidences to the contrary, the Special rapporteur believes that the fact reveal that there have been various violations of the provisions under the Convention against Torture, in particular breach of articles 7 and 12. The Special Rapporteur calls on the Government to undertake a prompt and impartial investigation on the conditions of detention, solitary confinement and ill-treatment of the immigrants, prosecute and punish those responsible, and ensure that the victims obtain redress, including fair and adequate compensation, and as full rehabilitation as possible" (Méndez 2012, 75).

On March 11, 2013, Méndez filed an *amicus curiae* in support of two former U.S. military contractors who had allegedly been tortured in Iraq by the United States and who sought U.S. Supreme Court review after the Seventh Circuit Court of Appeals dismissed their lawsuit against the former secretary of defense Donald Rumsfeld. On June 10, 2013, the United States Supreme Court, with Associate Justice Elana Kagan recusing herself, declined to hear the case.

After his term as Special Rapporteur ended in 2016, Méndez continued to serve a variety of international organizations, from the International Commission of Jurists to the entities set up under the accords that ended Colombia's civil war. He is currently a professor of human rights law in residence at American University.

Alberto J. Mora

While Alberto J. Mora may not have succeeded in initially stopping the Bush administration's torture program, he is one of the few lawyers in government service during that period who will likely be vindicated by history for doing his best to do so.

Born in 1952 to Cuban and Hungarian parents (Mora 2008, 121–122), Mora and his family fled Cuba after Fidel Castro and his 26th of July Movement overthrew the dictatorship of Fulgencio Batista in 1959. The Moras moved to Jackson, Mississippi, where Alberto entered high school in 1966 (Mora 2008, 121). He earned a bachelor's in English literature with honors at Swarthmore College in 1974 (Bloom 2008) before joining the U.S. State Department, where he was posted to Lisbon, Portugal, from 1975 through 1978 (Bloom 2008).

After leaving the State Department to attend law school, Mora earned his juris doctorate from the University of Miami in 1981 (Bloom 2008). After several years in private practice focusing on international dispute resolution, Mora became the general counsel of the United States Information Agency from 1989 through 1993 during President George H.W. Bush's administration (Bloom 2008). He later served in the Republican seat on the Broadcasting Board of Governors, now known as the U.S. Agency for Global Media (which supervises the Voice of America, Radio Free Europe, and other propaganda operations directed by the U.S. government), during the administration of President Bill Clinton, as well as serving as "an advocate for Radio Martí, the American news operation aimed at Cuba" (Mayer 2006).

After President George W. Bush took office in 2001, Mora became general counsel of the U.S. Navy, where he "expected to spend most of his time . . . streamlining the budget" (Mayer 2006). However, for Mora, as for many other officials in the administration of Bush the Younger, the 9/11 attacks by al-Qaeda on the Twin Towers, the Pentagon, and Pennsylvania changed everything.

In Mora's case, he became one of the unlikely point men in a battle against the use of torture by the United States against captured al-Qaeda and Taliban fighters and other detainees. How he got there reads more like a television script than history, but that was sadly consistent with that time in America.

According to Mora (2007),

Dave Brant—who reported to me in the Navy because I was what's called the Reporting Senior for NCIS [Naval Criminal Investigation Service]—late on the afternoon of the 17th of December [2002], Dave came to me and without prior warning or announcement said that his people down in Guantanamo, NCIS agents attached to the base and to interrogation activities down there, had reported to him that detainees were being abused. And he felt that the abuse was serious, that it most probably violated American law and certainly violated American values, that his men were upset at being associated with this, and did I want to know more. And I responded to him that I felt I had to know more.

At the time, "I thought, first of all, the abuse of anybody in captivity, certainly within military ranks, or elsewhere, is presumptively illegal. When I heard this, my first thought was that these were rogue elements, that this essentially is activity of undisciplined, unsupervised individuals who almost certainly had escaped some sort of discipline. I thought it was surely a mistake, that it had its origins in discipline, rather than a conscious, deliberate effort" (Mora 2007).

Two days later, Mora learned that Secretary of Defense Donald Rumsfeld had approved the torture methods that NCIS agents considered to be illegal.

"I was horrified. I was dumbfounded. I was concerned. I was stupefied. I was astonished that this could have taken place, that Secretary Rumsfeld himself would have been asked, much less gotten involved in these kinds of matters," Mora (2007) said. Furthermore,

> as I reviewed the documents back in my office after first receiving them, and I looked through them, I saw that the legal memorandum that originated in Guantanamo was wholly inadequate and, as I felt instantaneously, an incompetent piece of legal work to justify that kind of conclusion. And I felt that all of it was some horrific mistake, meaning that—and I felt this for a number of weeks—that clearly both the DOD General Counsel and the Secretary of Defense had made a mistake. They did not understand the legalities of these kinds of actions, they had not thought through the legal issue sufficiently, had not thought through the political issues sufficiently, had not thought through the ethical issues sufficiently, and they just missed it. (Mora 2007)

The seasoned bureaucrat and lawyer that he was, Mora (2007) initially tried to stop the torture at Guantanamo by working through his own chain of command:

> I asked to see Jim Haynes, DOD General Counsel, and I spoke to him about this matter. We had a conversation. I did most of the talking for about an hour. I pointed out to him that a variety of things, but that this was

unlawful behavior, that if you looked at the documents, the documents were completely unbounded. Nowhere in the documents was there any limitation such that interrogation techniques could be applied, but only until the point where they reach the level of cruel, inhuman, and degrading treatment, much less torture, and that the fact that there was no such limitation in the memos could lead to the application, not only of cruelty, but of torture, either through the application of the individual interrogation techniques or in combination, surely. And after the meeting, I was convinced that before the door had swung closed behind me that Jim would be on the phone to the Secretary asking for the rescission of those techniques.

Instead, Mora saw the handwritten notation from Rumsfeld on the torture memo asking why detainees were limited to being put in stress positions for four hours a day when Rumsfeld stood at his desk from eight to ten hours a day (Mora 2007).

"I thought it was attempted to be as a joke. But it would not be interpreted as that by anybody who's going to be looking at this package. It would be seen, possibly, as a wink and a nod to interrogators to blow by these mild restraints and to apply more coercion to the detainees. In implication, the Secretary of Defense found these restraints to be too limiting, that in fact that one could have gone further in the application of coercive techniques to these detainees" (Mora 2007).

Still, Mora pressed on. "Mora said that he did not fear reprisal for stating his opposition to the Administration's emerging policy. 'It never crossed my mind,' he said. 'Besides, my mother would have killed me if I hadn't spoken up. No Hungarian after Communism, or Cuban after Castro, is not aware that human rights are incompatible with cruelty.' He added, 'The debate here isn't only how to protect the country. It's how to protect our values'" (Mayer 2006).

Ultimately, Rumsfeld rescinded the guidelines but turned the matter to a "working group" in which Office of Legal

Counsel John Yoo, who supported the use of torture, was dealt in and Mora was dealt out.

"John Yoo is a very charming, deeply learned individual," Mora (2007) said. After Yoo delivered his conclusions, Mora (2007) challenged him:

> And as he was talking I was becoming more concerned and more alarmed and ultimately I asked him the question, "Well John, does this mean that the President has the authority to order torture?" And he said, "Yes." And I said, "I don't think so." And I was starting to then develop that thought and he holds up his hand and he says, "Wait a second. I've just told you what the law is. Now what you're speaking about now is a matter of legal policy. Now it might be that it's the better legal policy not to permit this, but as a matter of law the President has authority to order this." And I looked at John and I asked him, "Well, John, where does one have this policy discussion?" And he kind of shrugged, looked around and he says, "I don't know. Here in the Pentagon? You guys are the experts on military law." And that was fundamentally the end of our conversation.

Mora thought he had managed to persuade Haynes to bury Yoo's recommendations, but the exact opposite had occurred, with Rumsfeld ultimately choosing to follow Yoo's advice rather than Mora's. He learned the truth in April 2004 when the Abu Ghraib scandal broke. "He [Mora] was further taken aback when he learned, while watching Senate hearings on Abu Ghraib on C-span, that Rumsfeld had signed the working-group report—the draft based on Yoo's opinion—a year earlier, without the knowledge of Mora or any other internal legal critics" (Mayer 2006).

In addition to opposing the use of torture by U.S. military personnel, Mora "vigorously challenged the suspension of habeas corpus for the Guantanamo prisoners and, at the same time, sought to refute the legal framework, constructed to justify widespread wiretapping" (Bloom 2008).

Since leaving government service in 2006, Mora has received a Profile in Courage Award from the John F. Kennedy Foundation and an honorary juris doctorate from Swarthmore.

David A. Passaro

Born in 1966 or 1967, David A. Passaro would eventually achieve the dubious distinction of being the only person who was ever to have successfully criminally prosecuted for his involvement in the CIA's torture program in Afghanistan.

After high school, Passaro entered the Hartford Police Academy in 1990. "He used to chew glass, literally," said Sergeant David Kardys of the Hartford Police Department, who attended the academy with Mr. Passaro. "He was a tough kid" (Dao 2004). Unfortunately for Passaro, "Just months after graduating from the academy, [he] was arrested on felony assault charges following a fight in a parking lot. Though accounts of who started the fight differ, it seems clear that Mr. Passaro badly pummeled another man and the department fired him. Several months later, he pleaded guilty to a misdemeanor charge of breach of peace" (Dao 2004).

Despite pleading guilty to a lesser charge, the misdemeanor conviction was enough for the Harford Police to cut ties with him, so Passaro joined the U.S. Army, eventually becoming a U.S. Army Ranger (Dao 2004).

After the collapse of his first marriage and his departure from the military, the CIA hired Passaro to work as a paramilitary contractor for the Agency in Afghanistan in December 2002 (Dao 2004). On June 18 and 19, 2003, he began to interrogate Abdul Wali, whom Passaro suspected had information about recent attacks on a base run both by American troops and by Afghan soldiers.

According to Hyder Akbar, an Afghan-American who convinced Wali to talk to the Americans, "This was a man who had turned himself in voluntarily. It wasn't the traditional way that people kind of justify torture, the ticking time bomb situation. This was not a situation like that" (PBS 2015). None of that mattered to Passaro, who said more than a decade after the event "Man, I wasn't hired to be nice to these terrorists. I was there to get a job done. I was there to elicit the truth and keep moving" (PBS 2015).

Accordingly, Passaro said,

[I] didn't want [Wali] sleeping any more than two to three hours a night. One of the stress positions was something called the air chair. And that's just hold his arms out until he decided he would change his demeanor. Every time he would sit there, he would do this, and he would drop his arms to his elbows. Well, that's not the air chair. And then I would tap his arms to tell him to get his arms back up underneath. At one point, he lurched out after me, and I slapped him. It was just a quick response. My hands were right here, and it was just to get him off of me. Is that assault? It could be construed as assault, but in the war on terror, and in Afghanistan, in Asadabad, that's not assault. (PBS 2015)

However, other observers, including soldiers from the Eighty-Second Airborne Division, said Passaro reportedly beat Wali "with his hands and feet and a large flashlight" (Dao 2004) over a two-day period until Wali collapsed and died (PBS 2015).

While Passaro would later claim that "anything that I did to Abdul Wali, none of that constitutes torture. In hindsight, I wouldn't have done anything different" (PBS 2015), the U.S. Department of Justice thought otherwise. In 2005, the federal government charged Passaro with two counts of assault with a dangerous weapon and two counts of assault resulting in serious injury—charges that could have resulted in Passaro serving 40 years in prison if convicted (Thompson 2006).

During opening statements, "Assistant U.S. Attorney Pat Sullivan said Passaro told the soldiers they couldn't touch Wali, but that he could, 'because I have special rules'" (Thompson 2006). However, "'David Passaro had no special rules,' Sullivan said. 'He made them up'" (Thompson 2006).

Almost a decade later, Passaro didn't mince words as to what he thought about that argument. "After 9/11, President Bush got on national television, and said, not only are we going to go after the terrorists, but we're going to go after those that harbor the terrorists, and we will do so under any or with any means necessary. *In other words, all the rules and regulations no longer applied*" (PBS 2015; emphasis added).

The jury in Passaro's case felt differently, finding him guilty of one count of felony assault that resulted in serious bodily injury, along with three counts of lesser-included misdemeanor assault charges. The Fourth Circuit Court of Appeals upheld Passaro's conviction in 2009, though it did agree that the district judge had inappropriately enhanced his sentence to more than eight years (AFP 2009).

Passaro was ultimately released after serving six years in prison. Ironically, while his attempt to claim he was only following orders worked about as well for him as it did for the Nazi defendants at Nuremberg (which is to say, not at all), it was the justification used by the Obama administration for not charging other CIA interrogators and for dropping "at least two other" cases of detainees who died at the hands of the Agency, as "the White House has promised not to prosecute anyone for interrogations conducted the Bush years if they adhered to the existing guidelines" (PBS 2015).

Donald H. Rumsfeld

Born on July 9, 1932, in Chicago (Rumsfeld 1945, 1), Rumsfeld grew up in Evanston, Illinois, just outside the city, where he ended up in the newspaper at the age of five after he and his sister nearly drowned (Rumsfeld 1945, 1–2). It was the start of what would be a long career in the public eye—and an especially ironic foreshadowing for a man who would go on to defend the use of waterboarding on prisoners long after he left office (Braw 2011).

After earning a bachelor's degree in political science from Princeton University in 1954, Rumsfeld spent three years as an active duty pilot for the U.S. Navy before becoming a congressional staffer (Lindenauer 2000). Rumsfeld served four terms in the House of Representatives until he resigned in 1969 to join the Nixon administration as the director of the Office of Economic Opportunity (Lindenauer 2000). Surviving the post-Watergate purge of some former Nixon loyalists, Rumsfeld served as President Gerald Ford's chief of staff (in which position he recruited a young Dick Cheney to serve as his deputy; Mann 2006) and as secretary of defense from November 1975 until President Jimmy Carter took office in January 1977.

Rumsfeld abandoned politics for business—at least on the surface—for the next two-and-a-half decades, serving as chief executive officer of G.D Searle & Company and General Instrument Corporation and as chairman of the board of Gilead Sciences, among others (Lindenauer 2000).

In January 2001, Rumsfeld returned to his previous role as secretary of defense—this time under President George W. Bush. Eight months later, American Airlines Flight 77, which had been commandeered by members of al-Qaeda, slammed into the Pentagon just as Rumsfeld was being briefed there about the attacks on the World Trade Center in New York (Harnden 2011). As Rumsfeld recalled a decade later, "I went down the hall until the smoke was so bad that I had to go outside," he said. "I went down, down the hall and then downstairs when the smoke got bad and people said you just can't go any farther. I went outside and there were little pieces of metal spread all over the grass, and the smoke was billowing up, and the flame was very visible and leaping out of the building. There were not a lot of people out there, at that moment, yet" (Harnden 2011).

Rumsfeld did two things after that that no secretary of defense had ever done before him. First, he volunteered himself as a stretcher-bearer to help clear the wounded from the impact area, and second, he refused to be evacuated from the Pentagon as he was supposed to, preferring to make his stand there as long as possible (Harnden 2011).

Then and later, Rumsfeld reportedly preferred pragmatism—to almost an ends-justify-the-means-level—over policy and procedure. A month later, media reports claimed that Rumsfeld was "kicking a lot of glass and breaking doors," after a Predator attack on Mullah Omar, then the leader of the Taliban, reportedly didn't succeed because of legal objections from military lawyers (Hersh 2001), an allegation Rumsfeld denied (Novak 2001).

After the loss of al-Qaeda's formal safe haven in Afghanistan with the fall of the Taliban regime, on January 24, 2002, Rumsfeld wrote a memo on how al-Qaeda prisoners should be treated in American custody.

Noting that, "in war, soldiers get captured [and] in the Geneva Convention, the U.S. and other countries decided it is desirable to recognize that individuals who are legitimately representing their country in uniform and fighting for their country should be treated as 'lawful combatants', and that it benefits all civilized countries to have their soldiers when captured be treated in a humane manner" (Rumsfeld 2002, 1), Rumsfeld went on to declare that "the old models don't fit this new [terrorist] threat" and that "in the case of terrorists, given the reach of terrorist networks and the possible access to weapons of mass destruction, we have no choice but to give priority to speed" (Rumsfeld 2002, 1–2).

Once again, as on the date al-Qaeda targeted his office building, Rumsfeld was willing to sacrifice the rules in pursuit of what he saw as a higher objective. The key difference was that by refusing to leave the Pentagon on 9/11, he put himself at risk—while his attacks on the military's previous policies and procedures with regard to interrogation put hundreds, if not thousands, of people in danger.

Worse was to come a few months later.

"Only a few pieces of paper can change the course of history. On Tuesday, December 2, 2002, Donald Rumsfeld signed one that did" (Sands 2008, 2). That day, Rumsfeld approved a memo from William J. Haynes II, general counsel to the Department of Defense, which called for the approval of a series of new techniques to be used by the military to interrogate Taliban and al-Qaeda prisoners at the U.S. prison at Guantanamo Bay. These included "twelve techniques, aiming at humiliation and sensory deprivation. Stress positions, like standing, for a maximum of four hours. Falsified documents. Isolation for up to thirty days. Interrogation outside the standard interrogation booth. Deprivation of light and auditory stimuli. Hooding during transportation and questioning. Twenty-four hour interrogations. Removal of religious and all other comfort items. Switching away from hot rations to "meals, ready to eat" (MREs). Removal of clothing. Forced grooming, such as shaving of facial hair. And the use of individual phobias, like fear of dogs, to induce stress" (Sands 2008, 4).

While devout Muslim men are not required to grow beards by the tenets of their religion, it is considered to be strongly recommended that they do so, especially by ultra-conservative religious scholars such as those followed by members of the Taliban and al-Qaeda (British Broadcasting Corporation 2010). Thus, forcibly shaving a male prisoner was another way for the military to humiliate them in the hope of breaking their resistance to interrogation.

If those interned at Guantanamo Bay had been classified as prisoners of war, none of this would have been remotely permissible, and Rumsfeld—who both served in the military and had previously been secretary of defense—presumably knew this. As the International Committee of the Red Cross points out, pursuant to the third Geneva Convention, "POWs cannot be prosecuted for taking a direct part in hostilities. Their detention is not a form of punishment, but only aims to prevent further participation in the conflict. They must be released and repatriated without delay after the end of hostilities. The detaining power may prosecute them for possible war crimes, but not for acts of violence that are lawful. . . . POWs must be treated humanely in all circumstances. They are protected against any act of violence, as well as against intimidation, insults, and public curiosity" (International Committee of the Red Cross 2010).

However, thanks to the decision by President George W. Bush, aided and abetted by lawyers like John Yoo and Jay Bybee, that the Taliban and al-Qaeda prisoners *weren't* prisoners of war for purposes of the Geneva Convention, Rumsfeld could not only approve what Haynes asked for but add a flip written comment at the end of the memo by his signature. "I stand for 8–10 hours a day. Why is standing limited to 4 hours?" (Sands 2008, 5).

In accordance with what has historically happened whenever torture is officially tolerated or condoned, these new rougher tactics not just stayed in Guantanamo Bay but affected how prisoners were treated at Abu Ghraib as well by soldiers like Lynndie England and her comrades.

Ironically, it wasn't the eventual leak of the torture memos or the Abu Ghraib scandal that ended Rumsfeld's tenure, but the 2006 midterm elections where the Republican party lost control of the House and the Senate (NBC 2006). Two years later, a report from members of the Senate Armed Services Committee declared that Rumsfeld bore ultimate responsibility for the abuses at Abu Ghraib, a conclusion he rejected (Scott and Mazzetti 2008, A14).

Like most of those who were involved in the approval of torture at the upper levels of the Bush administration, Rumsfeld remains unapologetic about the decisions he made. In a 2011 interview, he quipped that waterboarding was "not as bad as a drone killing you. But waterboarding sells newspapers" (Braw 2011).

Alfredo "Scap" Scappaticci

Born sometime in 1944 in Belfast, Northern Ireland (Teague 2006), Alfredo "Scap" Scappaticci achieved the dubious distinction of being condemned on one side for his activities as the alleged head of the Irish Republican Army's Internal Security Unit, "referred to fearfully as 'the Nutting Squad'—during the 1980s" (Ware 2017), and on the other for his purported work as a double agent for the British, something that he has denied since the allegations first came to light in 2003 (Wallace 2003). In this context, the term "nutting" is Belfast slang for shooting someone in the back of the head.

To some, Scappaticci's transformation from the child of immigrant parents to the purported judge, jury, and sometimes executioner of those who informed on the IRA to the British to an alleged British double agent is a microcosm for what the conflict between the British and Nationalist Irish forces in Northern Ireland have done to the people of Ulster.

"As a boy, Freddie Scappaticci ducked and scuffled on the streets of Belfast, fighting Protestants to fit in with his Catholic friends. His parents had immigrated to Northern Ireland in the 1920s with a wave of other Italian families and settled in the Markets area of south Belfast, where Freddie was born in 1944. The old neighborhood hummed; under historic Georgian terraces, families bustled from churches to butcher shops to apple stalls. The Scappaticcis sold ice cream and earned a reputation as 'terrible nice people'" (Teague 2006). However, the troubles began in earnest in the 1960s, and "before long Scappaticci—who had started to go by the less-Italian name Scap—took to throwing bricks at British squads. 'Freddie was full Belfast,' his childhood acquaintance Victor Notarantonio remembers" (Teague 2006).

Like his onetime friend Gerry Adams, Scappaticci was interned by the British without trial (Teague 2006). "When Scappaticci was released, three years later, he had become a hard-shelled IRA man. He switched from bricks to bullets. His colleagues marveled at his marksmanship, and rumor has it that he killed several soldiers" (Teague 2006).

According to some observers, "It was [Gerry] Adams who reportedly set up the IRA's Internal Security Unit, known colloquially as 'the nutting squad,' in the late 1970s. The group is suspected of having tortured and killed IRA volunteers believed to have collaborated with the British, and Scappaticci, according to reports, became one of its leaders" (Wallace 2003).

The ISU—or the "nutting squad," if one prefers—was tasked with evaluating the political reliability of potential recruits to the Provisional IRA, debriefing IRA members who had been interned or captured after their release to determine if they had given up useful information to the British and interrogating suspected informers (Collins 1997, 217–218, 233–234, 238). According to former ISU member Eamon Collins, who broke with the IRA and wrote a memoir about his experiences, the ISU maintained facilities "set aside for interrogation and torture" (Collins 1997, 350).

According to former Bedfordshire police chief constable Jon Boutcher, who heads up Operation Kenova, which investigates Scappaticci and the ISU's activities, with regard to the nutting squad's actions, "There was no intention to get the truth, these people were brutalised in ways that I in my 35 years as a detective have never seen that level of unwarranted violence. There is nothing noble or justified or right in what happened. Nothing can in any way justify what these people did and it is time that those families were given the truth and Kenova (the police investigation) is a chance to do that" (McHugh 2018).

Meanwhile, sometime in the late 1970s, Scappaticci reportedly was recruited by the British to serve as a double agent after he argued with the IRA's leadership. "Scappaticci, the British intelligence services quickly recognized, had the makings of the perfect agent. A local man, born in Belfast. A credible IRA member. A disillusioned foot soldier. Beaten down. Ready" (Teague 2006). To this day, Scappaticci, denies having been a member of the IRA, but that is contradicted by Collins and others.

Reportedly joining the ISU in 1980 (Teague 2006), Scappaticci—according to Collins—joked about the murders he and his comrades committed as part of their jobs.

> One time I sat in a house with them to await the arrival of some men who had just been released from police custody. The woman of the house had made us tea. John Joe and Scap started reminiscing about past experiences. I asked them whether I would be personally expected to shoot informers. Scap, his mouth full, said that when the time arrived I would have to do it. I asked whether they always told people that they were going to be shot. Scap said it depended on the circumstances. He turned to John Joe and started joking about one informer who had confessed after being offered an amnesty. Scap told the man that he would take him home, reassuring him that he had nothing to worry about. Scap told him to keep the blindfold on for security reasons as they walked away from the car. "It was funny," he said, watching the bastard stumbling and falling, asking me as he felt his way through railings and walls "Is this my house now?" and I'd say "No, not yet, walk on some more . . . and then you shot the fucker in the back of the head," said John Joe, and both of them burst out laughing. (Collins 1997, 297)

Collins was arrested in 1985 and broke under British interrogation, giving up critical details about his work for the IRA from 1978 through the date of his capture ("Murphy 'Most Senior Provo I Met'" 1998). A British court ultimately threw out his confession as obtained "under duress," but upon his release, the IRA subjected him to the same treatment he had handed out to others, interrogating him for several weeks ("Murphy 'Most Senior Provo I Met'" 1998). On January 27, 1999, Collins was beaten and stabbed to death near his home in Newry, Northern Ireland. While his murder remains unsolved as of this writing, police in Northern Ireland believe advances in DNA technology may change that soon (British Broadcasting Corporation 2019).

To the British, until he was unmasked, Scappaticci was a critical intelligence asset who "is said to have passed on the details, which led to the SAS ambush in Gibraltar in which three IRA volunteers, Mairead Farrell, Sean Savage and Danny McCann, were killed in 1988, and to have given vital information about IRA targeting of British military installations in Germany" (Cowan 2003). Furthermore, "in 1990, he is alleged to have set up the arrest of the former Sinn Fein publicity director, Danny Morrison, by leading police to a west Belfast house where Scappaticci was interrogating an IRA informer" (Cowan 2003). However, Scappaticci was said to be linked to the murders of as many as forty people, some of whom were fellow British agents (Cowan 2003).

On December 5, 2018, Scappaticci was charged with possession of "extreme pornographic images" from October 2015 through January 2018 (Operation Kenova 2018). He pled guilty that same day and was sentenced to three months in jail, which was suspended for a year (Operation Kenova 2018).

On April 8, 2019, Boutcher announced he was standing down as chief constable of Bedfordshire in July 2019 in order to focus on Operation Kenova, which he said was "moving into a really important phase" (Operation Kenova 2019). As of this writing, Scappaticci remains free.

George Wickersham

Born on September 19, 1858, Wickersham served as the forty-seventh attorney general of the United States under President

William Howard Taft. After Theodore Roosevelt's third-party candidacy split the Republican vote and denied Taft a second term, Wickersham became the president of the Association of the Bar of the City of New York in 1914 (which is now known as the New York City Bar), a position he held until 1916 (New York City Bar 2018). Following the United States' declaration of war on Germany on April 2, 1917, Wickersham served on the War Trade Board in Cuba, which issued licenses for trade between Cuba and the United States during the duration of the conflict (Department of Justice 2017).

However, his most famous appointment came in 1929, when President Herbert Hoover picked him to chair the National Commission on Law Observance and Enforcement, which quickly became better known as the Wickersham Commission (Department of Justice 2017).

Two years later when the Commission finished its work, it had issued fourteen reports covering "Prohibition; Enforcement of the Prohibition Laws of the United States; Criminal Statistics; Prosecution; Enforcement of the Deportation Laws of the United States; the Child Offender in the Federal System of Justice and the Federal Courts; Criminal Procedure; Penal Institutions, Probation, and Parole; Crime and the Foreign Born; the Cost of Crime; the Causes of Crime (two volumes); and the Police. A fourteenth report, on the controversial Mooney-Billings case, was submitted to the commission but not officially published" (Walker et al. 1997).

Given Wickersham's privileged background and his pedigree as the country's former top law-enforcement official, one might have expected him to soft-pedal the commission's findings on police misconduct or suppress them entirely. Instead, as is clear from that report's first paragraphs, Wickersham did the exact opposite. "The widest inquiry into the shortcomings of the administration of justice, which the President enjoined upon this commission, necessarily involves the duty of investigating the justice of complaints, often made, that in their zeal to accomplish results Government officials themselves frequently lose sight of the fact that they are servants of the law, subject to its mandates and particularly charged with the duty to observe its spirit and its letter" (National Commission on Law Observance and Enforcement 1931, 1). Or, stripped of prolixity and with a dash of Wickersham's sarcasm added, "It is a fundamental principle of our law, constantly reaffirmed by courts and almost as constantly disregarded by many law-enforcement officers, that everyone is presumed to be innocent of crime until convicted" (National Commission on Law Observance and Enforcement 1931, 2).

The Commission found "the third degree—that is the use of physical brutality, or other forms of cruelty, to obtain involuntary confessions or admissions is widespread. . . . Physical brutality, illegal detention, and refusal to allow access of counsel to the prisoner· is common" (National Commission on Law Observance and Enforcement 1931, 4).

Wickersham and his colleagues documented multiple incidents of police torture through the third degree from the West Coast, "Physical brutality, including the third degree, is not much applied in outstanding cases of newspaper prominence. It is said also that persons who retain lawyers with influence may be exempt from third degree. With these and perhaps other minor exceptions third-degree brutality is common in San Francisco" (National Commission on Law Observance and Enforcement 1931, 148), to the Midwest, "The methods described as in use in Chicago include the application of rubber hose to the back or the pit of the stomach, kicks in the shins, beating the shins with a club, blows struck with a telephone book on the side of the victim's head" (National Commission on Law Observance and Enforcement 1931, 126), to the East Coast, "The third degree is widely and brutally employed in New York City. Former prosecuting attorneys have declared this in print and in conversations with the investigators" (National Commission on Law Observance and Enforcement 1931, 90).

The report also provided the first—albeit preliminary—research on the demographics of who tended to be subjected to the third degree. According to Wickersham's investigators, most victims were male, under twenty-five, a person of color and who were (especially in the era before *Gideon v. Wainright*, when an indigent defendant's right to court-appointed counsel hadn't been established) not represented by an attorney (National Commission on Law Observance and Enforcement 1931, 156–160). Furthermore, police were most likely to use the third degree on defendants suspected of committing murder or a robbery (National Commission on Law Observance and Enforcement 1931, 160).

After the report's release, "Federal Bureau of Investigation Chief J. Edgar Hoover immediately launched both internal and external attacks on third-degree practices" (Leo 2008, 71). Thanks to pressure from Hoover and others who had read Wickersham's work, "The use of coercive methods began to decline in the 1930s and 1940s. The decline was uneven—third-degree methods persisted in some places longer than others—but by the mid 1960s custodial police questioning had become psychological in nature. In less than two generations of American policing, the third-degree had virtually disappeared" (Leo 2008, 71).

Besides the commission, Wickersham is known for helping to found the Friends of the Law Library of Congress in 1932 "as a way to help build a great national law library" (Law Library of Congress 2008) and served as president of the Council on Foreign Relations from 1933 until 1936 (Council on Foreign Relations 2018).

Others associated with the commission went on equally significant, if more dramatic, ends. Priscilla Harriet Fansler, who served as the commission's assistant librarian, married Alger Hiss, who would be accused of spying for the Soviet Union during the McCarthy era and ultimately convicted of perjury (Shelton 2012 34).

Wickersham died on January 25, 1936.

John Yoo

Born in Seoul, South Korea, on July 10, 1967, Yoo grew up in the United States with his family, earning an undergraduate degree in history, *summa cum laude*, from Harvard University in 1989, and his juris doctorate from Yale Law School in 1992 (Yoo 2017). After completing a clerkship at the U.S. Court of Appeals for the District of Columbia and for Associate U.S. Supreme Court Justice Clarence Thomas, Yoo served as general counsel for the U.S. Senate Judiciary Committee, before taking the job for which he'd become most famous—or infamous, depending on your point of view—for.

In 2001, Yoo joined the Office of Legal Counsel, which is the arm of the U.S. Department of Justice that provides legal advice to the president and other key policymakers. Just a few weeks after al-Qaeda's successful attack on the Twin Towers and the Pentagon, Yoo argued that Congress could not "place any limits on the president's determinations as to any terrorist threat, the amount of military force to be used in response, or the method, timing and nature of the response" (Golden 2005).

The following January, Yoo argued that the provisions of the Geneva Conventions governing the treatment of prisoners of war didn't apply to either al-Qaeda (because they were a "violent political or organization and not a nation state" [Yoo 2002, 1]) or the Taliban (because "Afghanistan was not—even prior to the beginning of the present conflict—a functioning State" [Yoo 2002, 2]).

That memo "touched off a long, hard-fought battle within the administration, in which lawyers for the State Department and the military services strongly disputed [Yoo's] views" (Golden 2005). Given that the dissenters included the then secretary of state Colin Powell and William Howard Taft IV, the legal adviser to the Department of State (Isikoff 2004), two men with more years of collective experience in government than Yoo had on the planet, one might have expected his conclusions to have been reexamined. Instead, "thereafter, several senior officials said, those lawyers were sometimes excluded from the drafting of more delicate opinions" (Golden 2005).

It likely did Yoo's career no harm that David S. Addington, counsel to Vice President Dick Cheney, was close to him ideologically (Golden 2005) and that Yoo was essentially providing a legal justification for where the George W. Bush administration emotionally wanted to go anyway with regard to evading its obligations under the Convention against Torture and other agreements.

Yoo went on to assist Jay S. Bybee with the creation of the infamous "torture memo" in 2002 (Golden 2005) and to provide the legal justification for the warrantless wiretapping of Americans by the National Security Agency, even though doing so violated federal law, as Yoo admitted (Savage et al. 2016).

Following Yoo's departure from government service, in 2008 the Chief Disciplinary Counsel of the Disciplinary Board of the Supreme Court of Pennsylvania (where Yoo is licensed to practice law) dismissed an ethics complaint brought against him because of his work on the torture memos, finding "many of the witnesses and documents relevant to an investigation into [Yoo's] conduct are beyond the subpoena power of this office" (Clark 2009, 4).

After the inauguration of President Barack Obama, the Office of Professional Responsibility at the U.S. Department of Justice issued a several-hundred-page report accusing Yoo and other OLC attorneys of violating their professional obligations in crafting the memos in 2009. However, Associate Deputy Attorney General David Margolis ultimately declined to refer Yoo's case to the Disciplinary Board of the Supreme Court of Pennsylvania (since Yoo is licensed to practice law there), though he did agree that Yoo showed "poor judgment" (Grindler 2010).

Notwithstanding this decision by the Department of Justice, there were several attempts to hold Yoo and other Bush administration officials legally accountable for the advice they gave policymakers. On November 14, 2006, the Center for Constitutional Rights and Wolfgang Kaleck, a German civil rights attorney, filed a complaint with the federal prosecutor of Germany to investigate and charge Yoo and several other officials. The plaintiffs appealed the decision of the prosecutor not to do so about a year later and on April 21, 2009, the Stuttgart Regional Appeals Court denied the appeal (Center for Constitutional Rights 2009), although the CCR filed a new case in Germany in 2014 that did not involve Yoo.

In 2008, José Padilla, who had been convicted of providing material support to terrorists, sued Yoo for damages Padilla suffered while he was tortured in U.S. military custody. While the U.S. District Court for the Northern District of California initially denied Yoo's claim of immunity, the Ninth Circuit Court of Appeals, relying on an earlier decision by the U.S. Supreme Court, threw Padilla's case out in 2012, "because, prior to a 2004 U.S. Supreme Court decision, the rights of enemy combatants were not 'clearly established', during the 2001 to 2003 time period when Yoo was writing his memos for the DOJ, and because it likewise wasn't clear at the time that 'the specific interrogation techniques allegedly employed against Padilla, however appalling, necessarily amounted to torture'" (Neil 2012).

On the other hand, in May 2012, the Kuala Lumpur War Crimes Tribunal convicted Yoo, along with George W. Bush, Bybee and Addington, and several other former officials, *in absentia* of war crimes (Ridley 2012). It's doubtful that Yoo lost any sleep over this development, as the Tribunal—a project of then former and now current Malaysian prime minister Mahathir Mohamad—had no power to issue arrest warrants or custodial sentences, but simply to "name-and-shame" (Kuppusamy 2007).

As of this writing, Yoo continues to teach at the Boalt Hall School of Law at the University of California Berkeley. He is the author of nine books and a plethora of law journal articles, most focusing in the area of presidential powers and national security.

Yoo came back into the public spotlight in the fall of 2018 during and after the nomination of Bret Kavanaugh to succeed Associate Justice Anthony Kennedy on the U.S. Supreme Court. From 2001 through 2003, Kavanaugh and Yoo were members of a monthly supper group of attorneys connected with the Federalist Society (Kirchgaessner 2018). Evidently, Kavanaugh thought highly of him, as he lobbied the Bush administration to nominate Yoo for a seat on the Ninth Circuit Court of Appeals (Sacks 2018). For reasons that remain unexplained, Kavanaugh referred to Yoo as his "magic bullet" (Sacks 2018) even after Yoo declined interest in the post.

References

AFP. "Court Upholds CIA contractor's Detainee Abuse Conviction," August 11, 2009, https://web.archive.org/web/20120130071733/http://www.google.com/hosted news/afp/article/ALeqM5gSo6iRtgbNNlDhDyO_VcZEm T45MQ (accessed May 19, 2019).

Agee, Philip. *Inside the Company: CIA Diary* (London: Penguin Books, 1975).

Amnesty International. "Nelson Mandela and Amnesty International," July 18, 2014, https://www.amnesty.org.uk/nelson-mandela-and-amnesty-international (accessed April 8, 2014).

Amnesty International. "History: More than 55 Years Protecting Human Rights," 2017, https://www.amnestyusa .org/about-us/history/ (accessed March 31, 2019).

Amnesty International. "Guantánamo Bay: 14 Years of Injustice," January 12, 2018a, https://www.amnesty.org.uk/guantanamo-bay-human-rights (accessed April 1, 2019).

Amnesty International. "USA 'You Don't Have Any Rights Here,'" October 2018b, https://www.amnesty.org/en/latest/research/2018/10/usa-treatment-of-asylum-seekers-southern-border/ (accessed April 8, 2019).

Aptekar, Pavel. "How the Cheka Turned into the FSB," *Vedomosti*, December 20, 2017, https://www.vedomosti .ru/opinion/articles/2017/12/20/745861-vchk-fsb (original in Russian) (accessed May 5, 2019).

Archdiocese of Baltimore. "The Inquisition and Index: Vatican Records Shed Light on Dark Legend," January 19, 2012, https://www.archbalt.org/the-inquisition-and-index-vatican-records-shed-light-on-dark-legend/ (accessed April 10, 2019).

"The Bail Conditions Omar Khadr Must Now Live by," *The Star*, May 7, 2015, https://web.archive.org/web/2017100 7115813/https://www.thestar.com/news/canada/2015/ 05/07/the-rules-khadr-must-live-by-if-he-gets-bail-today .html (accessed May 18, 2019).

Baldauf, Scott. "Firefight Shows Strong Al Qaeda Persistence," *The Christian Science Monitor*, July 29, 2002, https://www .csmonitor.com/2002/0729/p01s01-wosc.html (accessed May 9, 2019).

Barakat, Matthew. "Appeals Court Rejects Chelsea Manning's Effort to Leave Jail," *Miami Herald*, April 22, 2019, https:// www.miamiherald.com/news/nation-world/article22953 6849.html (accessed April 24, 2019).

Beavers, Olivia. "Haspel: I Will Not Bring Back CIA's Interrogation Program," *The Hill*, May 9, 2018, https:// thehill.com/policy/national-security/386887-haspel-i-will-not-bring-back-cias-interrogation-program-under-my (accessed May 19, 2019).

Beccaria, Cesare, and Edward D. Ingraham, trans. *An Essay on Crimes and Punishments* (Philadelphia, PA: Philip H. Nicklin, 1819).

Berenson, Peter. "The Forgotten Prisoners," *The Observer*, May 28, 1961, https://www.theguardian.com/uk/1961/may/ 28/fromthearchive.theguardian (accessed March 31, 2019).

Bessler, John D. "Private: The Birth of American Law: An Italian Philosopher and the American Revolution," *American Constitutional Society*, September 16, 2014, https://www.acslaw.org/acsblog/the-birth-of-american-law-an-italian-philosopher-and-the-american-revolution/ (accessed April 9, 2019).

Bessler, John D. "The Italian Enlightenment and the American Revolution: Cesare Beccaria's Forgotten Influence on American Law." *Mitchell Hamline Law Journal of Public Policy Practice* 37 (1): 1–184 (2017). https://scholarworks .law.ubalt.edu/all_fac/972/ (accessed November 10, 2019).

Bloom, Alfred H. "President Bloom's Charge to Alberto Mora '74," Swarthmore College Commencement, 2008, https:// www.swarthmore.edu/past-commencements/president-blooms-charge-to-alberto-mora-74 (accessed May 22, 2019).

Braw, Elisabeth. "Donald Rumsfeld: Being Waterboarded Is Better Than Being Killed by a Drone," *Huffington Post*, August 1, 2011, https://www.huffpost.com/entry/donald-rumsfeld_b_869534 (accessed May 2, 2019).

British Broadcasting Corporation. "Adams Wants 1984 Shooting Probe," December 14, 2006, http://news.bbc.co .uk/2/hi/uk_news/northern_ireland/6179789.stm (accessed April 28, 2019).

British Broadcasting Corporation. "Are Beards Obligatory for Devout Muslim Men?" June 27, 2010, https://www.bbc .com/news/10369726 (accessed May 5, 2019).

British Broadcasting Corporation. "Chelsea Manning: Wikileaks Source Jailed for Refusing to Testify," March 8, 2019, https://www.bbc.com/news/world-us-canada-4750 1763 (accessed March 10, 2019).

British Broadcasting Corporation. "Eamon Collins: PSNI 'Close to Identifying' IRA Man's Killer," January 27, 2019, https://www.bbc.com/news/uk-northern-ireland-47019728 (accessed May 8, 2019).

British Broadcasting Corporation. "Iraq Closes Abu Ghraib Prison over Security Concerns," April 15, 2014, https:// www.bbc.com/news/world-middle-east-27037455 (accessed April 28, 2019).

Brockes, Emma. "What Happens in War Happens," *The Guardian*, January 2, 2009, https://www.theguardian.com/world/2009/jan/03/abu-ghraib-lynndie-england-interview (accessed April 28, 2019).

Brown, Richard E. "The Life and Work of Donald Olding Hebb: Canada's Greatest Psychologist." 44 *PROC. N.S. INST. SCIpt 1* 44 (Pt 1): 1–25 (2007).

Brown, Richard E. "The Life and Work of Donald Olding Hebb." *Acta Neurologica Taiwanica* 15 (2): 127–142 (June 2006).

Bybee, Jay. "Memorandum for Alberto R. Gonzalez, Counsel to the President," United States Department of Justice, Office of Legal Counsel, August 1, 2002. pp. 1–50 (copy in author's possession).

Cable News Network. "Youngest Guantanamo Detainee Pleads Guilty," October 25, 2010, https://web.archive.org/web/20101026132342/http://www.cnn.com/2010/US/10/25/khadr.plea/ (accessed May 18, 2019).

Cameron, Dell. "Chelsea Manning Has Been Released From Jail," *Gizmodo*, May 9, 2019, https://gizmodo.com/chelsea-manning-has-been-released-from-jail-1834656732 (accessed May 9, 2019).

Carvin, Stephanie. "Yes, Sleep Deprivation Is Torture," *Maclean's*, July 14, 2017, https://www.macleans.ca/opinion/yes-sleep-deprivation-is-torture/ (accessed May 18, 2019).

Center for Constitutional Rights. "Accountability for U.S. Torture: Germany," https://ccrjustice.org/home/what-we-do/our-cases/accountability-us-torture-germany (accessed April 20, 2019).

Central Intelligence Agency. "Book Review-Inside the Company-CIA Diary." *Studies in Intelligence* 19 (2): 35–38 (Summer 1975), https://www.cia.gov/library/center-for-the-study-of-intelligence/kent-csi/vol19no2/pdf/v19i2a06p.pdf (accessed May 23, 2019).

Clark, Kathleen. "Written Testimony of Kathleen Clark: Senate Judiciary Committee Subcommittee on Administrative Oversight and the Courts Hearing on 'What Went Wrong: Torture and the Office of Legal Counsel in the Bush Administration,'" Hearing Date: May 13, 2009, Submitted: May 20, 2009, https://web.archive.org/web/20100612102537/https://law.wustl.edu/news/documents/WrittenTestKathClark.pdf (accessed April 20, 2019).

Collins, Eamon, and Mick McGovern. *Killing Rage* (London: Granta Books, 1997).

Coogan, Tim Pat. *The IRA* (New York: Palgrave, 2002).

Council on Foreign Relations. "Historical Roster of Directors and Officers," 2018, https://www.cfr.org/historical-roster-directors-and-officers (accessed April 26, 2019).

Cowan, Rosie. "He Did the IRA's Dirty Work for 25 Years—and Was Paid £80,000 a Year by the Government," May 11, 2003, *The Guardian*, https://www.theguardian.com/uk/2003/may/12/northernireland.northernireland1 (accessed May 8, 2019).

Dao, James. "The Reach of War: An Accused; A Man of Violence, or Just '110 Percent' Gung-Ho?" *The New York Times*, June 19, 2004, https://www.nytimes.com/2004/06/19/world/the-reach-of-war-an-accused-a-man-of-violence-or-just-110-percent-gung-ho.html (accessed May 19, 2019).

Department of Justice. "Attorney General George Woodward Wickersham," July 5, 2017, https://www.justice.gov/ag/bio/wickersham-george-woodward (accessed April 26, 2019).

Department of Justice. "Office of Legal Counsel: About the Office," https://www.justice.gov/olc (accessed April 30, 2019).

Desmond, Joan Frawley. "U.S. Bishops Back Release of Senate Torture Report," *National Catholic Register*, December 11,

2014, http://www.ncregister.com/daily-news/u.s.-bishops-back-release-of-senate-torture-report (accessed April 10, 2019).

Dewey, John. "The Historic Background of Corporate Legal Personality." *The Yale Law Journal* 35 (6): 655–673 (1926).

DiEdoardo, Christina A. "Resist: 'We Got This,'" *Bay Area Reporter*, November 16, 2017, pp. 9–10.

Encyclopedia Britannica. "Feliks Edmundovich Dzerzhinsky," July 20, 1998, https://www.britannica.com/biography/Feliks-Edmundovich-Dzerzhinsky (accessed May 5, 2019).

Engelberg, Stephen. "Correction: Trump's Pick to Head CIA Did Not Oversee Waterboarding of Abu Zubaydah," *ProPublica*, March 15, 2018, https://www.propublica.org/article/cia-cables-detail-its-new-deputy-directors-role-in-torture (accessed May 19, 2019).

Freedom from Torture. "History," 2017a, https://www.freedomfromtorture.org/about_us/history (accessed April 1, 2019).

Freedom from Torture. "Trustee's Annual Report and Financial Statements for the Year Ended 31 December 2017," 2017b, https://www.freedomfromtorture.org/sites/default/files/documents/trustees_annual_report_and_financial_statements_2017.pdf (accessed April 1, 2019).

Freeman, Alan, and Jeff Sallot. "U.S. Won't Seek Execution of Khadr," *The Globe and Mail*, November 9, 2005, https://web.archive.org/web/20181221183222/https://beta.theglobeandmail.com/news/world/us-wont-seek-execution-of-khadr/article20429907/ (accessed May 18, 2019).

Gazis, Olivia. "CIA Director Nominee Gina Haspel: CIA Releases Timeline of Her Clandestine Career," CBS News, May 1, 2018, https://www.cbsnews.com/news/cia-director-nominee-gina-haspel-cia-releases-timeline-of-her-clandestine-career/ (accessed May 19, 2019).

Golden, Tim. "A Junior Aide Had a Big Role in Terror Policy," *The New York Times*, December 23, 2005, https://www.nytimes.com/2005/12/23/politics/a-junior-aide-had-a-big-rolein-terror-policy.html (accessed April 20, 2019).

Greenhouse, Linda. "Ex CIA Agent Loses Appeal On Passport," *The New York Times*, June 30, 1981, https://www.nytimes.com/1981/06/30/us/ex-cia-agent-loses-appeal-on-passport.html (accessed May 23, 2019).

Grindler, Gary G. "Acting Deputy Attorney General Gary G. Grindler on the OPR Investigation into OLC Memoranda," U.S. Department of Justice, February 26, 2010, https://www.justice.gov/opa/speech/acting-deputy-attorney-general-gary-g-grindler-opr-investigation-olc-memoranda (accessed April 20, 2019).

Groenewegen, Peter. *Eighteenth Century Economics* (London: Routledge, 2002).

Gstalter, Morgan. "Cheney Calls for US to Restart Interrogation Programs," *The Hill*, May 10, 2018, https://thehill.com/homenews/news/387109-cheney-calls-for-the-us-to-restart-enhanced-interrogation-programs (accessed May 19, 2019).

Hamilton, Keegan. "This Is How Trump's Pick for CIA Director Used to Torture Black Site Detainees," *VICE News*, March 13, 2018, https://news.vice.com/en_us/article/vbp98d/this-is-how-trumps-pick-for-cia-director-used-to-torture-black-site-detainees (accessed May 19, 2019).

Hansen, Evan. "Manning-Lamo Chat Logs Revealed," *Wired*, July 13, 2011, https://www.wired.com/2011/07/manning-lamo-logs/ (accessed April 23, 2019).

Harnden, Toby. "9/11 Anniversary: Donald Rumsfeld on How He Survived the September 11 Pentagon Attack," *The*

Telegraph, September 9, 2011, https://www.telegraph.co
.uk/news/worldnews/september-11-attacks/8753250/911-
anniversary-Donald-Rumsfeld-on-how-he-survived-the-
September-11-Pentagon-attack.html (accessed May 2,
2019).

Haspel, Gina. Responses to "Questionnaire for Completion
By Presidential Nominees," Select Committee on
Intelligence, United States Senate, April 28, 2018, https://
www.intelligence.senate.gov/sites/default/files/documents/q-
ghaspel-050918.pdf (accessed May 19, 2019).

Hebb, Donald O. *The Organization of Behavior: A
Neuropsychological Theory* (New York: John Wiley & Sons, 1949).

Hersh, Seymour M. "King's Ransom: How Vulnerable Are the
Saudi Royals?" *The New Yorker*, October 14, 2001, https://
www.newyorker.com/magazine/2001/10/22/kings-ransom
(accessed May 2, 2019).

Hersh, Seymour. "Torture at Abu Ghraib: American Soldiers
Brutalized Iraqis. How Far Up Does the Responsibility
Go?" *The New Yorker*, April 30, 2004, https://www.new
yorker.com/magazine/2004/05/10/torture-at-abu-ghraib
(accessed April 28, 2019).

Hersh, Seymour. "The General's Report: How Antonio
Taguba, Who Investigated the Abu Ghraib Scandal, Became
One of Its Casualties," *The New Yorker*, June 18, 2007,
https://www.newyorker.com/magazine/2007/06/25/the-
generals-report (accessed April 28, 2019).

Hostettler, John. *Cesare Beccaria: The Genius of "On Crimes
and Punishments"* (Dunedin, FL: Waterford Press, 2011).

Human Rights Watch. "United States of America:
Compliance with the Optional Protocol on Convention
on the Rights of the Child on the Involvement of Children
in Armed Conflict: Additional Information for the
Committee on the Rights of the Child," April 15, 2008,

https://www.hrw.org/legacy/pub/2008/children/FLW_
CRC2.pdf (accessed May 18, 2019).

International Committee of the Red Cross. "Prisoners of War
and Detainees Protected under International Humanitarian
Law," October 29, 2010, https://www.icrc.org/en/doc/
war-and-law/protected-persons/prisoners-war/overview-
detainees-protected-persons.htm (accessed May 5, 2019).

Irvine, David R. "LDS Lawyers, Psychologists Had a Hand
in Torture Policies," *The Salt Lake Tribune*, April 29, 2009,
https://web.archive.org/web/20120301090557/http://www
.sltrib.com/opinion/ci_12256286 (accessed April 30, 2019).

Isikoff, Michael. "Memos Reveal War Crimes Warnings,"
Newsweek, May 16, 2004, https://www.newsweek.com/
memos-reveal-war-crimes-warnings-128415 (accessed
April 20, 2019).

Johnson, Eric. "Abu Ghraib Abuse Ringleader Graner
Released from Prison," *Reuters*, August 6, 2011, https://
www.reuters.com/article/us-prisoner-abughraib/abu-
ghraib-abuse-ringleader-graner-released-from-prison-
idUSTRE7752GS20110806 (accessed April 28, 2019).

Kirchgaessner, Stephanie. "Dining Club Emails Reveal
Kavanaugh's Close Ties to Trump's Solicitor General," *The
Guardian*, October 25, 2018, https://www.theguardian
.com/us-news/2018/oct/25/brett-kavanaugh-eureka-club-
noel-francisco-emails (accessed April 20, 2019).

Kiriakou, John. "I Went to Prison for Disclosing the CIA's
Torture. Gina Haspel Helped Cover It Up," *The Washington
Post*, March 16, 2018, https://www.washingtonpost.com/
outlook/i-went-to-prison-for-disclosing-the-cias-torture-
gina-haspel-helped-cover-it-up/2018/03/15/9507884e-
27f8-11e8-874b-d517e912f125_story.html (accessed
May 19, 2019).

Krauss, Clifford. "Threats and Responses: Detainee; Canadian
Teenager Held by U.S. in Afghanistan in Killing of

American Medic," *The New York Times*, September 14, 2002, https://www.nytimes.com/2002/09/14/world/threats-responses-detainee-canadian-teenager-held-us-afghanistan-killing.html (accessed May 9, 2019).

Kuppusamy, Baradan. "Malaysia: Mahathir's War Crimes Court to Name and Shame," *Interpress Service News Agency*, February 15, 2007, http://www.ipsnews.net/2007/02/malaysia-mahathirs-war-crimes-court-to-name-and-shame/ (accessed April 20, 2019).

Laing, Aislinn. "Nelson Mandela's Spear of the Nation: The ANC's Armed Resistance," *The Telegraph*, February 5, 2011, https://www.telegraph.co.uk/news/worldnews/africaand indianocean/southafrica/8304153/Nelson-Mandelas-Spear-of-the-Nation-the-ANCs-armed-resistance.html (accessed April 8, 2019).

Lauchlan, Iain. "Young Felix Dzerzhinsky and the Origins of Stalinism," in Markku Kangaspuro and Vesa Oittinen (eds.), *Essays on Stalinism* (Helsinki: Kikimora Press, 2013), https://www.ed.ac.uk/files/imports/fileManager/wp-iain-lauchlan-YoungFelix.pdf (accessed May 5, 2019).

Law Library of Congress. "The Wickersham Award," 2008, https://www.loc.gov/law/news/articles/2008_wickersham.php (accessed April 26, 2019).

Léglu, Catherine, Rebecca Rist, and Claire Taylor. *The Cathars and the Albigensian Crusade: A Sourcebook* (New York: Routledge, 2014).

Leo, Richard A. *Police Interrogation and American Justice* (Cambridge, MA: Harvard University Press, 2008).

Lewis, Paul. "Bradley Manning Trial Revealed a Lonely Soldier with a Troubled Past," *The Guardian*, August 21, 2013, https://www.theguardian.com/world/2013/aug/21/bradley-manning-lonely-soldier-childhood (accessed April 21, 2019).

Lewis, Paul. "Charles M. Lichenstein, 75, American Envoy at the U.N.," *The New York Times*, August 31, 2002, https://www.nytimes.com/2002/08/31/world/charles-m-lichenstein-75-american-envoy-at-the-un.html (accessed April 29, 2019).

Lindenauer, Andrew. "The Rumsfeld Resume," CBS News, December 28, 2000, https://www.cbsnews.com/news/the-rumsfeld-resume/ (accessed May 2, 2019).

Lionaes, Aase. "Award Ceremony Speech," The Nobel Prize, December 10, 1977, https://www.nobelprize.org/prizes/peace/1977/ceremony-speech/ (accessed March 31, 2019).

Luhn, Alec. "Putin Salutes Russia's Intelligence Agencies on National 'Spies' Day,'" *The Guardian*, December 20, 2015, https://www.theguardian.com/world/2015/dec/20/putin-salutes-russias-intelligence-agencies-on-national-spies-day (accessed May 5, 2019).

MacAskill, Ewen. "Bradley Manning Case Sparks UN Criticism of US Government," *The Guardian*, April 11, 2011, https://www.theguardian.com/world/2011/apr/11/bradley-manning-juan-mendez-torture (accessed April 27, 2019).

Maestro, Marcello. "A Pioneer for the Abolition of Capital Punishment: Cesare Beccaria." *Journal of the History of Ideas* 34 (3): 463–468 (1973).

Mandela, Nelson. *Long Walk to Freedom* (Boston, MA: Back Bay Books, 1995).

Mann, James. "Rumsfeld versus Rumsfeld," *Los Angeles Times*, May 3, 2006, https://www.latimes.com/archives/la-xpm-2006-may-03-oe-mann3-story.html (accessed May 2, 2019).

Manning, Chelsea. Twitter Post, 10:58 A.M., March 8, 2019, https://twitter.com/xychelsea/status/1104094170950578177.

Manning, Chelsea. Twitter Post, 1:19 P.M., April 22, 2019, https://twitter.com/xychelsea/status/1120421891381112840.

Manning, Chelsea. Twitter post, 3:57 P.M., May 16, 2019, https://twitter.com/xychelsea/status/112915892049960 5504.

Mayer, Jane. "The Memo: How an Internal Effort to Ban the Abuse and Torture of Detainees Was Thwarted." *The New Yorker*, February 19, 2006, https://www.newyorker.com/ magazine/2006/02/27/the-memo (accessed May 22, 2019).

McCoy, Alfred W. *Torture and Impunity: The U.S. Doctrine of Coercive Interrogation* (Madison, WI: University of Wisconsin Press, 2012).

McDonald, Henry. "Gerry Adams Appeals 1975 Convictions for Maze Escape Attempts," *The Guardian*, January 16, 2018, https://www.theguardian.com/politics/2018/jan/16/ gerry-adams-appeals-1975-convictions-for-escape-from-maze-prison (accessed April 28, 2019).

McHugh, Michael. "IRA Members 'Told Police They Were Present during Torture Sessions' Says Stakeknife Detective," *The Irish Times*, December 18, 2018, https://www.irish news.com/news/northernirelandnews/2018/12/18/news/ ira-members-told-police-they-were-present-during-torture-sessions-says-stakeknife-detective-1511510/ (accessed May 8, 2019).

Méndez, Juan E. "Torture in Latin America," in Kenneth Roth and Minky Worden (eds.), *Torture: Does It Make Us Safer? Is It Ever OK?* (New York: The New Press, 2005, pp. 57–59).

Méndez, Juan E. "Report of the Special Rapporteur on Torture and Other Cruel, Inhuman or Degrading Treatment or Punishment, Addendum Observations on Communications Transmitted to Governments and Replies Received." A/HRC/19/61/Add.4, February 29, 2012.

Monachesi, Elio. "Pioneers in Criminology. IX. Cesare Beccaria (1738–1794)." *The Journal of Criminal Law, Criminology, and Police Science* 46(4): 439–449 (1955).

Mora, Alberto J. "Torturing Democracy" [Interview], September 17, 2007, https://nsarchive2.gwu.edu/torturing democracy/interviews/alberto_mora.html#initialreports (accessed May 22, 2019).

Mora, Alberto J. *Growing Up in Mississippi*, Judy Tucker and Richard Ford, eds. (University Press of Mississippi, 2008).

Morris, Allison. "'Fringe' Vigilante Dissidents 'behind Attacks' on Gerry Adams' and Bobby Storey's Homes." *The Irish News*, July 19, 2018, https://www.irishnews.com/news/2018/07/19/news/attack-on-gerry-adams-home-the-work-of-fringe-vigilante-dissidents-1385843/ (accessed April 28, 2019).

Muldoon, James, *Popes, Lawyers and Infidels* (Philadelphia, PA: University of Pennsylvania Press, 1979).

"Murphy 'Most Senior Provo I Met,'" *The Independent*, May 9, 1998, https://www.independent.ie/irish-news/murphy-most-senior-provo-i-met-26186332.html (accessed May 8, 2019).

National Commission on Law Observance and Enforcement. "Report on Lawlessness in Law Enforcement" (Washington, D.C.: Government Printing Office, 1931).

NBC News. "Al-Qaida: Dead or Captured," June 22, 2005, http://www.nbcnews.com/id/4686228/ns/world_news-hunt_for_al_qaida/t/al-qaida-dead-or-captured/#.XNUHLY 5KjIU (accessed May 9, 2019).

NBC News. "Rumsfeld Stepping Down," November 8, 2006, http://www.nbcnews.com/id/15622266/ns/politics/t/rumsfeld-stepping-down/#.XM9XJY5KjIU (accessed May 5, 2019).

NBC News. "Ex-CIA Agent Pleads Guilty to Leaking Identity of Covert Operative," October 22, 2012, http://investigations.nbcnews.com/_news/2012/10/22/14626249-ex-cia-agent-pleads-guilty-to-leaking-identity-of-covert-operative?lite&ocid=msnhp (accessed May 19, 2019).

Neil, Martha. "9th Circuit Nixes Padilla Suit against Lawyer John Yoo, Author of So-Called DOJ Torture Memos," *ABA Journal*, May 2, 2012, http://www.abajournal.com/news/article/9th_circuit_nixes_padilla_suit_against_attorney_john_yoo_author_of_so-calle/ (accessed April 20, 2019).

New York City Bar. "Presidents and Officers: Former Association Officers," 2018, https://www.nycbar.org/about/governance/presidents-and-officers (accessed April 26, 2019).

Novak, Robert D. "Targeting the Mullah," *The Washington Post*, October 18, 2001, https://www.washingtonpost.com/archive/opinions/2001/10/18/targeting-the-mullah/63423ec0-bbb9-44a6-a184-ebf9d90e8ef3/?noredirect=on&utm_term=.6389a4eaefba (accessed May 2, 2019).

Operation Kenova. "Man Sentenced for Possession of Extreme Pornographic Images," December 5, 2018, https://www.opkenova.co.uk/man-sentenced-for-possession-of-extreme-pornographic-images (accessed May 8, 2019).

Operation Kenova. "Jon Boutcher to Stand Down as Bedfordshire Chief Constable," April 8, 2019, https://www.opkenova.co.uk/jon-boutcher-to-stand-down-as-bedfordshire-chief-constable (accessed May 8, 2019).

Operation Kenova. "Man Charged with Possession of Extreme Pornographic Images," December 5, 2019, https://www.opkenova.co.uk/man-charged-with-possession-of-extreme-pornographic-images (accessed May 8, 2019).

PBS Newshour. "Convicted Former CIA Contractor Speaks Out about Prisoner Interrogation," April 20, 2015, https://www.pbs.org/newshour/show/convicted-former-cia-contractor-speaks-prisoner-interrogation (accessed May 19, 2019).

PDC. "Dr. PH (Peter) Kooijmans," 2013, https://www.parlement.com/id/vg09llg6f7zn/p_h_peter_kooijmans (accessed April 29, 2019) (original in Dutch).

PDC. "Minister of State and Former Minister of Foreign Affairs Kooijmans Passed Away," February 13, 2013, https://www.parlement.com/id/vj74l7xt8ghm/nieuws/minister_van_staat_en_oud_minister_van (accessed April 29, 2019) (in Dutch).

Peters, Edward. *Torture* (Philadelphia, PA: University of Pennsylvania Press, 1985, 1999).

"Philip Agee: Former CIA Agent Who Accused His Government of 'State Terrorism,'" *The Independent*, January 11, 2008, https://www.independent.co.uk/news/obituaries/philip-agee-former-cia-agent-who-accused-his-government-of-state-terrorism-769468.html (accessed May 22, 2019).

Pilkington, Ed. "Bradley Manning's Treatment Was Cruel and Inhuman, UN Torture Chief Rules," *The Guardian*, March 12, 2012, https://www.theguardian.com/world/2012/mar/12/bradley-manning-cruel-inhuman-treatment-un (accessed May 28, 2018).

Pilkington, Ed. "Bradley Manning Verdict: Cleared of 'Aiding the Enemy' But Guilty of Other Charges," *The Guardian*, July 31, 2013, https://www.theguardian.com/world/2013/jul/30/bradley-manning-wikileaks-judge-verdict (accessed May 28, 2018).

Pilkington, Ed, David Smith, and Lauren Gambino. "Chelsea Manning's Prison Sentence Commuted by Barack Obama," *The Guardian*, January 18, 2017, https://www.theguardian.com/us-news/2017/jan/17/chelsea-manning-sentence-commuted-barack-obama (accessed May 28, 2018).

Ralph, Talia. "Lynndie England, Abu Ghraib Soldier, Still Not Sorry," *Global Post/PRI*, March 19, 2012, https://www.pri.org/stories/2012-03-19/lynndie-england-abu-ghraib-soldier-still-not-sorry (accessed April 28, 2019).

Raz, Mical. "Alone Again: John Zubek and the Troubled History of Sensory Deprivation Research," *Journal of the*

History of the Behavioral Sciences, 49 (4): 379–395 (Fall 2013).

Reis, Mary Robert. "Pope Innocent IV and Church-State Relations, 1243–1254," Loyola University Chicago, Dissertations, Paper 1224, 1972, http://ecommons.luc .edu/luc_diss/1224 (accessed April 9, 2019).

"Report by the Special Rapporteur, Mr. P Kooijmans, Appointed Pursuant to Commission on Human Rights Resolution," 1985/33, UN Doc. E/CN.4/1986/15 (1986).

"Report of the Special Rapporteur, Mr. P. Kooijmans, Pursuant to Commission on Human Rights Resolution," 1992/32, UN Doc. E/CN.4/1993/26 (1992).

Ridley, Yvonne. "Bush Convicted of War Crimes in Absentia," *Foreign Policy Journal*, May 12, 2012, https://www.foreign policyjournal.com/2012/05/12/bush-convicted-of-war-crimes-in-absentia/ (accessed April 20, 2019).

Rumsfeld, Don. "My Autobiography," January 11, 1945, http://library.rumsfeld.com/doclib/sp/83/1946-01-11%20 Autobiography%20%28II-304%29.pdf (accessed May 2, 2019).

Rumsfeld, Donald. "Handling of Al Qaeda Detainees," January 24, 2002, http://library.rumsfeld.com/doclib/ sp/3156/2002-01-23%20Re%20Handling%20of%20 Al%20Qaeda%20Detainees.pdf (accessed May 5, 2019).

Sacks, Mike. Twitter Post, 1:39 p.m., September 6, 2018, https://twitter.com/MikeSacksEsq/status/1037802556 465008640/photo/1 (accessed April 30, 2019).

Sacks, Mike. Twitter Post, 3:12 p.m., September 6, 2018, https://twitter.com/MikeSacksEsq/status/1037825853357 543424 (accessed April 20, 2019).

Sands, Philippe. *Torture Team: Rumsfeld's Memo and the Betrayal of American Values* (New York: Palgrave Macmillan, 2008).

Savage, Charlie, Adam Goldman, and Eileen Sullivan. "Julian Assange Arrested in London as U.S. Unseals Hacking Conspiracy Indictment," *The New York Times*, April 11, 2019, https://www.nytimes.com/2019/04/11/world/europe/julian-assange-wikileaks-ecuador-embassy.html (accessed April 24, 2019).

Savage, Charlie, and Eric Lichtblau. "Classified 2002 Letter on N.S.A. Eavesdropping Is Made Public," *The New York Times*, February 29, 2016, https://www.nytimes.com/2016/03/01/us/politics/classified-2002-letter-on-nsa-eavesdropping-is-made-public.html (accessed April 20, 2019).

Scott, Shane, and Mark Mazzetti. "Senate Panel Report Links Top Bush Administration Officials to Abuse of Detainees," *The New York Times*, December 12, 2008.

Selective Mutism Association. "What Is Selective Mutism?" 2019, https://www.selectivemutism.org/learn/what-is-selective-mutism/ (accessed April 28, 2019).

Shane, Scott. "Philip Agee, 72, Is Dead; Exposed Other C.I.A. Officers," *The New York Times*, January 10, 2008, https://www.nytimes.com/2008/01/10/obituaries/10agee.html (accessed May 23, 2019).

Shelton, Christina. *Alger Hiss: Why He Chose Treason* (New York: Simon & Schuster, 2012).

Shephard, Michelle. "Omar Khadr Repatriated to Canada," *The Star*, September 29, 2012, https://www.thestar.com/news/2012/09/29/omar_khadr_repatriated_to_canada.html (accessed November 10, 2019).

Shephard, Michelle. "Omar Khadr: No Memory of Firefight in Afghanistan," December 13, 2013, *The Star*, https://web.archive.org/web/20170820173141/https://www.thestar.com/news/canada/2013/12/13/omar_khadr_no_memory_of_firefight_in_afghanistan.html (accessed May 18, 2019).

Shephard, Michelle. *Guantanamo's Child: The Untold Story of Omar Khadr* (Mississauga, ON: John Wiley & Sons Canada Ltd., 2008).

Simpkin, John. "Felix Dzerzhinsky," September 1997, https://spartacus-educational.com/RUSDzerzhinsky.htm (accessed May 5, 2019).

Singh, Bilveer. *The Talibanization of Southeast Asia: Losing the War On Terror To Islamist Extremists* (Westport, CT: Praeger Security International, 2007).

Spiegel Online. "SPIEGEL's Daily Take John Bolton Doesn't Want to Hear about Darfur," October 18, 2005, https://www.spiegel.de/international/spiegel-s-daily-take-john-bolton-doesn-t-want-to-hear-about-darfur-a-380360.html (accessed April 27, 2019).

Stanley, Alexandra. "Vatican Is Investigating the Inquisition, in Secret," *The New York Times*, October 31, 1998, https://www.nytimes.com/1998/10/31/world/vatican-is-investigating-the-inquisition-in-secret.html (accessed April 10, 2019).

Stelter, Brian. "How '07 ABC Interview Tilted a Torture Debate," *The New York Times*, April 27, 2009, https://www.nytimes.com/2009/04/28/business/media/28abc.html (accessed May 19, 2019).

Taddonio, Patrice. "CIA Director Nominee Supported Destruction of Torture Tapes," *PBS Frontline*, May 9, 2018, https://www.pbs.org/wgbh/frontline/article/cia-director-nominee-supported-destruction-of-torture-tapes/ (accessed May 19, 2019).

Taguba, Antonio M. "AR 15–6: Investigation of the 800th Military Police Brigade," Department of the Army, Coalition Forces Land Component Command, United States Army Forces Central Command, March 14, 2004. https://nsarchive2.gwu.edu/NSAEBB/NSAEBB140/TR3.pdf (accessed November 10, 2019).

Tasker, John Paul, "Liberal Government Formally Apologizes to Omar Khadr," CBC News, https://web.archive.org/web/20170707164953/http://www.cbc.ca/news/politics/cabinet-explain-omar-khadr-settlement-1.4194467 (accessed May 18, 2019).

Tate, Julie. "Bradley Manning Sentenced to 35 Years in WikiLeaks Case," *The Washington Post*, August 21, 2013, https://www.washingtonpost.com/world/national-security/judge-to-sentence-bradley-manning-today/2013/08/20/85bee184-09d0-11e3-b87c-476db8ac34cd_story.html (accessed May 28, 2018).

Tate, Julie, and Ellen Nakashima. "Judge Refuses to Dismiss Charges against WikiLeaks Suspect Bradley Manning," *The Washington Post*, January 8, 2013, https://www.washingtonpost.com/world/national-security/judge-refuses-to-dismiss-charges-against-wikileaks-suspect-bradley-manning/2013/01/08/2eab1f62-59cb-11e2-beee-6e38f5215402_story.html (accessed May 28, 2018).

Teague, Matthew. "Double Blind: The Untold Story of How British Intelligence Infiltrated and Undermined the IRA," *The Atlantic*, April 2006, https://www.theatlantic.com/magazine/archive/2006/04/double-blind/304710/ (accessed May 7, 2019).

Teotonio, Isabel. "'Canadians Called Me a Liar': Khadr," *The Star*, March 19, 2008, https://www.thestar.com/news/canada/2008/03/19/canadians_called_me_a_liar_khadr.html (accessed May 18, 2019).

Thompson, Estes. "Ex-CIA Contractor on Trial in Beating," *The Washington Post*, August 7, 2006, https://web.archive.org/web/20181003100216/http://www.washingtonpost.com/wp-dyn/content/article/2006/08/07/AR2006080700877.html (accessed May 19, 2019).

Toosi, Nahal. "Trump Taps Former 'Black Site' Prison Operator for CIA Deputy," *Politico*, February 2, 2017, https://www.politico.com/story/2017/02/trump-cia-black-sites-gina-haspel-234565 (accessed May 19, 2019).

Townsend, Mark. "Gita Sahgal's Dispute with Amnesty International Puts Human Rights Group in the Dock." *The Observer*, April 24, 2010, https://www.theguardian.com/world/2010/apr/25/gita-sahgal-amnesty-international (accessed March 31, 2019).

Tusa, Sir John. "Mid-life Crisis for Amnesty?" British Broadcasting Corporation Radio 4, December 28, 2010, https://www.bbc.com/news/world-12022303 (accessed March 31, 2019).

United Nations. *United Nations Yearbook 1984*, https://www.unmultimedia.org/searchers/yearbook/page.jsp?volume=1984&bookpage=1330 (accessed April 29, 2019).

United Nations. *United Nations Yearbook 1984,* https://www.unmultimedia.org/searchers/yearbook/page.jsp?volume=1984&bookpage=813 (accessed April 29, 2019).

United Nations General Assembly. "Optional Protocol to the Convention on the Rights of the Child on the Involvement of Children in Armed Conflict," A/RES/54/263, May 25, 2000, https://www.ohchr.org/Documents/ProfessionalInterest/crc-conflict.pdf (accessed May 18, 2019).

United Nations Secretary-General. "Juan E. Méndez Appointed Special Adviser on Prevention of Genocide" [Appointment], July 14, 2004, https://www.un.org/press/en/2004/sga880.doc.htm (accessed April 27, 2019).

"US Army Rejects Court Martial of Abu Ghraib Commander," *The Guardian*, January 11, 2008, https://www.theguardian.com/world/2008/jan/11/iraq.usa (accessed April 28, 2019).

Van Leeuwen, Marco. "CDA Wassenaar: In Memoriam, Dr. PH (Peter) Kooijmans," February 15, 2013, https://www.wassenaarders.nl/201302151534/politiek/cda-wassenaar-in-memoriam-dr-p-h-peter-kooijmans (accessed April 29, 2019).

Vatican. "Catechism of the Catholic Church," Part III, Sec. 2, Ch.2, Art. 5, II. 2298, http://www.vatican.va/archive/ENG0015/_P80.HTM (accessed April 10, 2019).

Walker, Samuel, and Randolph Boehm. "Records of the Wickersham Commission on Law Observance and Enforcement: Part 1: Records of the Committee on Official Lawlessness," University Publications of America, 1997, http://www.lexisnexis.com/documents/academic/upa_cis/1965_WickershamCommPt1.pdf (accessed April 27, 2019).

Wallace, William. "Trail for Truth on Alleged Spy in IRA Proves Tricky," *Los Angeles Times*, May 19, 2003, https://www.latimes.com/archives/la-xpm-2003-may-19-fg-stakeknife19-story.html (accessed May 7, 2019).

Ware, John. "How, and Why, Did Scappaticci Survive the IRA's Wrath?" *The Irish Times*, April 15, 2017, https://www.irishtimes.com/news/ireland/irish-news/how-and-why-did-scappaticci-survive-the-ira-s-wrath-1.3049139 (accessed May 7, 2019).

Watts, Joe. "Derry Riots: Gerry Adams Demands 'Rationale' for House Bomb Amid Violence Blamed on Dissident Republicans," *The Independent*, July 14, 2018, https://www.independent.co.uk/news/uk/politics/gerry-adams-derry-riots-sinn-fein-explosive-device-northern-ireland-a8447151.html (accessed April 28, 2019).

Weber, Bob. "Alberta Judge Rules Omar Khadr's Sentence Has Ended," *The Globe and Mail*, March 25, 2019, https://www.theglobeandmail.com/canada/article-alberta-judge-rules-omar-khadrs-sentence-has-expired/ (accessed May 18, 2019).

Welch, Francis. "The 'Broadcast Ban' on Sinn Fein," British Broadcasting Corporation, April 5, 2005, http://news.bbc .co.uk/2/hi/uk_news/politics/4409447.stm (accessed April 28, 2019).

"Who Runs Gov: Jay S. Bybee," *The Washington Post*, 2010, https://www.washingtonpost.com/politics/jay-s-bybee/ gIQAAsECAP_print.html?noredirect=on (accessed April 30, 2019).

Yoo, John Choon. "Application of Treaties and Laws to al Qaeda and Taliban Detainees," U.S. Department of Justice, Office of Legal Counsel, January 9, 2002.

Yoo, John Choon. [Curriculum Vitae], 2017, https://works .bepress.com/johnyoo/cv/download/ (accessed April 17, 2019).

Youssef, Nancy. "CIA Fills in Some Blanks on Gina Haspel's Secret Life," *The Wall Street Journal*, March 22, 2018, https://archive.fo/20180322191408/https://www.wsj.com/ articles/cia-fills-in-some-blanks-on-gina-haspels-secret-life-1521745324#selection-2083.0-2083.53 (accessed May 19, 2019).

I am BOU MEN
Former Victim at S
(Toul Sleng Priso
BOU MENG's Docu
Book is 10$ per 1

BOU MENG
SURVIVOR FROM KHMER ROUGE PRISON S-21
USTICE FOR THE FUTURE

BY HUY VANNAK
MYDANS

5 Data and Documents

While the use of torture has plagued humanity from the jurists of Ancient Greece to the CIA interrogators at Guantanamo Bay and at black sites around the world, documenting its use can be far more difficult. While most governments use—or have used—torture against their own citizens or others at some point in their existence, few officials (with the notable exception of Felix Dzerzhinsky during the early days of the Communist regime in the Soviet Union) are willing to publicly speak about it, much less release detailed information on its use.

For this reason, it is often easier to track what governments *say* they are doing to ban torture, such as treaties they have signed against its use, and what the views of their citizens are according to polls, as that information is already public.

To provide as comprehensive a picture as possible, excerpts of several relevant government documents are included in this chapter, including parts of the CIA's KUBARK interrogation manual, which the Agency never intended to become public.

Data

Table 5.1 lists the international conventions and treaties that deal with torture.

During the 1970s, Buo Meng was tortured by the Khmer Rouge regime at the notorious Tuol Sleng prison in Cambodia. He is only one of seven people known to have survived the facility and wrote a book about his experiences there. The prison is now a museum. (Danielal/Dreamstime.com)

Table 5.1   Treaties against Torture

Treaty	Date Entered into Force	Number of Signatories
Geneva Convention	June 19, 1931	53 ratified, 9 state signatories
European Convention on Human Rights (Article 3)	September 3, 1953	47
Inter-American Convention to Prevent and Punish Torture	February 28, 1987	20
Convention against Torture	June 26, 1987	83
Optional Protocol to the Convention against Torture	June 22, 2006	75

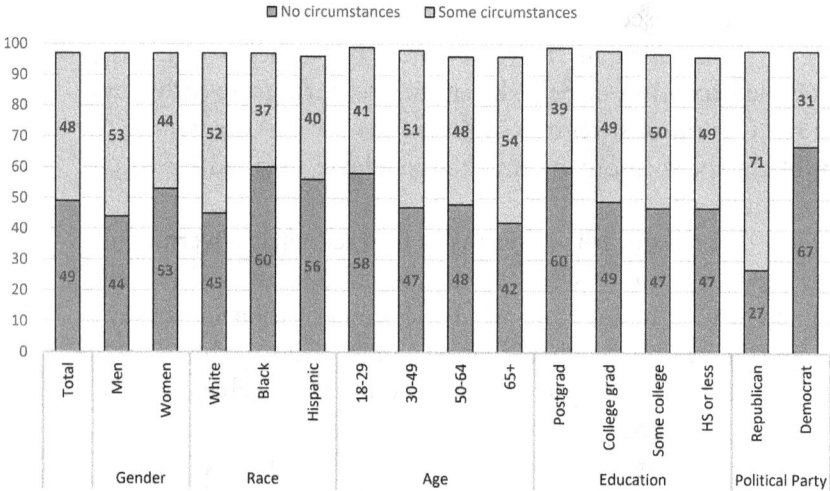

Figure 5.1   U.S. Attitudes toward Torture (2017)

Source: Pew Research Center. "Americans Divided in Views of Use of Torture in U.S. Anti-Terror Efforts." January 26, 2017. Available at https://www.pewresearch.org/fact-tank/2017/01/26/americans-divided-in-views-of-use-of-torture-in-u-s-anti-terror-efforts/.

Figure 5.1, with data from the Pew Research Center, reviews the attitudes toward torture of various demographics within the United States. The poll asked if in support of U.S. anti-terrorism efforts there were "no circumstances" or "some circumstances" in which torture is acceptable.

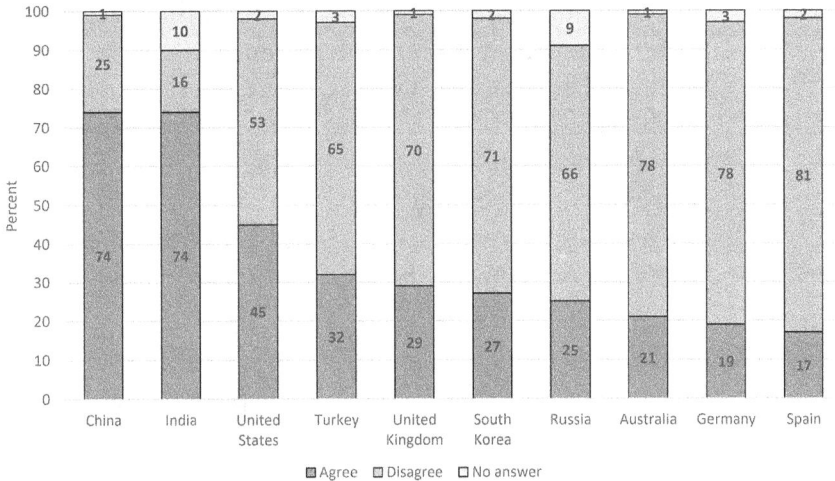

Figure 5.2   World Attitudes toward Torture (2014)

Source: McCarthy, Niall. "The World is Divided on the Use of Torture." *Forbes*, January 26, 2017. Available at https://www.forbes.com/sites/niallmccarthy/2017/01/26/the-world-is-divided-on-the-use-of-torture-infographic/#236379625ac6.

In 2014, Amnesty International conducted a poll to determine worldwide attitudes toward torture. The poll asked if respondents from various countries "Strongly or Somewhat" agreed or disagreed that "torture is justified in some cases to protect the public." See Figure 5.2.

Documents

Assize of Clarendon (1156)

The Assize of Clarendon was promulgated by Henry II of England. It not only created the grand jury system, but helped to spare England of experiencing the worst parts of the resurgence of torture then playing out on the Continent.

1. In the first place the aforesaid king Henry, by thee counsel of all his barons, for the preservation of peace and the observing of justice, has decreed that an inquest shall be made throughout the separate counties, and throughout

the separate hundreds, through twelve of the more lawful men of the hundred, and through four of the more lawful men of each township, upon oath that they will speak the truth: whether in their hundred or in their township there be any man who, since the lord king has been king, has been charged or published as being a robber or murderer or thief; or any one who is a harbourer of robbers or murderers or thieves. And the Justices shall make this inquest by themselves, and the sheriffs by themselves.

2. And he who shall be found through the oath of the aforesaid persons to have been charged or published as being a robber, or murderer, or thief, or a receiver of them, since the lord king has been king, shall be taken and shall go to the ordeal of water, and shall swear that he was not a robber or murderer or thief or receiver of them since the lord king has been king, to the extent of five shillings as far as he knows.

3. And if the lord of him who has been taken, or his steward or his vassals, shall, as his sureties, demand him back within three days after he has been taken, he himself, and his chattels, shall be remanded under surety until he shall have done his law.

4. And when a robber or murderer or thief, or harbourers of them, shall be taken on the aforesaid oath, if the Justices shall not be about to come quickly enough into that county where they have been taken, the sheriffs shall send word to the nearest Justice through some intelligent man, that they have taken such men; and the Justices shall send back word to the sheriffs where they wish those men to be brought before them: and the sheriffs shall bring them before the Justices. And with them they shall bring, from the hundred or township where they were taken, two lawful men to bear record on the part of the county and hundred as to why they were taken; and there, before the Justice, they shall do their law.

5. And in the case of those who shall be taken on the aforesaid oath of this Assize, no one shall have court or justice or chattels save the king himself in his own court, before his own Justices; and the lord king shall have all their chattels. But in the case of those who shall be taken otherwise than through this oath, it shall be as it ordinarily is and ought to be.

6. And the sheriffs who take them shall lead them before the Justice without other summons than they have from him. And when the robbers or murderers or thieves, or receivers of them, who shall be taken through the oath or otherwise, are given over to the sheriffs, they also shall receive them straightway without delay.

7. And, in the different counties where there are no jails, such shall be made in the burgh or in some castle of the king from the money of the king and from his woods if they be near, or from some other neighbouring woods, by view of the servants of the king; to this end, that the sheriffs may keep in them those who shall be taken by the servitors who are accustomed to do this, and through their servants.

8. The lord king wills also that all shall come to the county courts to take this oath; so that no one shall rem main away, on account of any privilege that he has, or of a court or soc that he may have, from coming to take this oath

9. And let there be no one, within his castle or without his castle, nor even in the honour of Wallingford, who shall forbid the sheriffs to enter into his court or his land to take the view of frankpledge; and let all be under pledges: and let them be sent before the sheriffs under free pledge.

10. And, in the cities or Burroughs, let no one have men or receive them in his home or his land or his soc whom he will not take in hand to present before the Justice if they be required; or let them be in frankpledge.

11. And let there be none within a city or Burroughs or castle, or without it, nor also in the honour of Wallingford, who

shall forbid the sheriffs to enter into their land or soc to take those who shall have been charged or published as being robbers or murderers or thieves, or harbourers of the same, or outlawed or accused with regard to the forest, but he (the king) commands that they shall aid them (the sheriffs) to take them (the robbers, etc.).

12. And if any one shall be taken who shall be possessed of robbed or stolen goods, if he be notorious and have evil testimony from the public, and have no warrant, he shall not have law. And if he be not notorious, on account of the goods in his possession, he shall go to the water.

13. And if any one shall confess before lawful men, or in the hundred court, concerning robbery, murder, or theft, or the harbouring of those committing them, and afterwards wish to deny it, he shall not have law.

14. The lord king wishes also that those who shall be tried and shall be absolved by the law, if they be of very bad testimony and are publicly and disgracefully defamed by the testimony of many and public men, shall forswear the lands of the king, so that within eight days they shall cross the sea unless the wind detains them; and, with the first wind which they shall have afterwards, they shall cross the sea; and they shall not return any more to England unless by the mercy of the lord king: and there, and if they return, they shall be outlawed; and if they return they shall be taken as outlaws.

15. And the lord king forbids that any waif, that is vagabond or unknown person, shall be entertained any where except in the burgh, and there he shall not be entertained more than a night, unless he become ill there, or his horse, so that he can show an evident essoin.

16. And if he shall have been there more than one night, he shall be taken and held until his lord shall come to pledge him, or until he himself shall procure safe pledges; and he likewise shall be taken who shall have entertained him.

17. And if any sheriff shall send word to another sheriff that men have fled from his county into another county on account of robbery or murder or theft, or the harbouring of them, or for outlawry, or for a charge with regard to the forest of the king, he (the sheriff who is informed) shall capture them: and even if he learn it of himself or through others that such men have fled into his county, he shall take them and keep them in custody until he have safe pledges from them.

18. And all sheriffs shall cause a register to be kept of all fugitives who shall flee from their counties; and this they shalt do before the county assemblies; and they shall write down and carry their names to the Justices when first they shall come to them, so that they may be sought for throughout all England, and their chattels may be taken for the service of the king.

19. And the lord king wills that, from the time when the sheriffs shall receive the summonses of the itinerant Justices to appear before them with their counties, they shall assemble their counties and shall seek out all who have come anew into their counties since this assize; and they shall send them away under pledge that they will come before the Justices, or they shall keep them in custody until the Justices come to them, and then they shall bring them before the Justices.

20. The lord king forbids, moreover, that monks or canons or any religious house, receive any one of the petty people as monk or canon or brother, until they know of what testimony he is, unless he shall be sick unto death.

21. The lord lying forbids, moreover, that any one in all England receive in his land or his soc or the home under him any one of that sect of renegades who were excommunicated and branded at Oxford. And if any one receive them, he himself shall be at the mercy of the lord king; and the house in which they have been shall be carried without the

town and burned. And each sheriff shall swear that he will observe this, and shall cause all his servitors to swear this, and the stewards of the barons, and all the knights and free tenants of the counties.

22. And the lord king wills that this assize shall be kept in his kingdom as long as it shall please him.

Source: Henderson, Ernest F. *Select Historical Documents of the Middle Ages* (London: George Bell and Sons, 1896).

Heinrich Himmler's Memo on the Third Degree (June 12, 1942)

This English translation of an order by Henrich Himmler, then acting head of the Nazi SD, through Heinrich Müller, head of the Gestapo, calls for the use of the "third degree" on certain prisoners.

Subject: Third degree

In order to simplify things the Decree of the Chief of the Security police and the SD of 1.7.37 Bk. No. 28 (II) 301/37 Secret (to be destroyed according to sealed orders) will be superseded by the following new ruling, with immediate effect:

1. Third degree may only be applied if it is clear from preliminary investigation that the prisoner can give information on important facts, as social or subversive to the State and to the Reich, but will not disclose what he knows, and the information cannot be obtained by investigation.

2. Third degree may, under this supposition, only be employed against Communists, Marxists, Jehovah's Witnesses, saboteurs, terrorists, members of resistance movements, parachute agents, anti-social elements, Polish or Soviet-Russian loafers or tramps. In all other cases, my permission must first be obtained.

3. Third degree may not be used to extort confessions of a prisoner's own crimes. Also this method may not be employed

against persons who are temporarily detained by law for further investigations.

My previous permission is also necessary in exceptional cases.

4. Third degree can, according to the circumstances, consist, among other methods, of very simple diet (water and bread), hard bunk, dark cell, deprivation of sleep, exhaustion drill, but also in the administration of flogging (for more than 20 strokes a doctor must be consulted).

Source: Document No. 1531-PS. *Nazi Conspiracy and Aggression*, Volume 4. Office of the United States Chief Counsel for Prosecution of Axis Criminality. Washington, D.C.: Government Printing Office, 1976.

Convention for the Protection of Human Rights and Fundamental Freedoms (November 4, 1950)

This convention, unlike the UN Declaration of Human Rights, was enforceable. It was signed on November 4, 1950, but did not go into effect until September 3, 1953. Drafted by the Council of Europe, it currently has been signed by forty-seven member states. This excerpt from the introduction and Section 1 of the Convention outlines some of the rights and freedoms assured to all.

The governments signatory hereto, being members of the Council of Europe,

> Considering the Universal Declaration of Human Rights proclaimed by the General Assembly of the United Nations on 10th December 1948;
>
> Considering that this Declaration aims at securing the universal and effective recognition and observance of the Rights therein declared;
>
> Considering that the aim of the Council of Europe is the achievement of greater unity between its members and

that one of the methods by which that aim is to be pursued is the maintenance and further realisation of human rights and fundamental freedoms;

Reaffirming their profound belief in those fundamental freedoms which are the foundation of justice and peace in the world and are best maintained on the one hand by an effective political democracy and on the other by a common understanding and observance of the human rights upon which they depend;

Being resolved, as the governments of European countries which are like-minded and have a common heritage of political traditions, ideals, freedom and the rule of law, to take the first steps for the collective enforcement of certain of the rights stated in the Universal Declaration,

Have agreed as follows:

Article 1—Obligation to respect human rights

The High Contracting Parties shall secure to everyone within their jurisdiction the rights and freedoms defined in Section I of this Convention.

Section I—Rights and freedoms
Article 2—Right to life

1. Everyone's right to life shall be protected by law. No one shall be deprived of his life intentionally save in the execution of a sentence of a court following his conviction of a crime for which this penalty is provided by law.

2. Deprivation of life shall not be regarded as inflicted in contravention of this article when it results from the use of force which is no more than absolutely necessary:

   a) in defence of any person from unlawful violence;

b) in order to effect a lawful arrest or to prevent the escape of a person lawfully detained;

c) in action lawfully taken for the purpose of quelling a riot or insurrection.

Article 3—Prohibition of torture

No one shall be subjected to torture or to inhuman or degrading treatment or punishment.

Article 4—Prohibition of slavery and forced labour

1. No one shall be held in slavery or servitude.

2. No one shall be required to perform forced or compulsory labour.

3. For the purpose of this article the term "forced or compulsory labour" shall not include:

   a. any work required to be done in the ordinary course of detention imposed according to the provisions of Article 5 of this Convention or during conditional release from such detention;

   b. any service of a military character or, in case of conscientious objectors in countries where they are recognised, service exacted instead of compulsory military service;

   c. any service exacted in case of an emergency or calamity threatening the life or well-being of the community;

   d. any work or service which forms part of normal civic obligations.

. . .

Source: Council of Europe. Treaty No. 005. Available at https://www.coe.int/en/web/conventions/full-list/-/conventions/treaty/005.

CIA Report on Using Torture to Induce Assassination (January 22, 1954)

This report from the first deployment of the CIA's ARTICHOKE team evaluated if it could induce a foreign official to commit an assassination via the use of drugs or other torture methods. The goal of Project ARTICHOKE was to study interrogation methods, including mind control using hypnosis, chemicals, and other experiments.

1. The ARTICHOKE Team visited [redacted] during period 8 January to 15 January 1954. The purpose of the visit was to give an evaluation of a hypothetical problem, namely: Can an individual of ****** descent be made to perform an act of attempted assassination involuntarily under the influence of ARTICHOKE?

2. PROBLEM:

    a. The essential elements of the problem are as follows:

        i. As a "trigger mechanism" for a bigger project, it was proposed that an individual of ****** descent, approximately 35 years old, well educated, proficient in English and well established socially and politically in the ****** Government be induced under ARTICHOKE to perform an act, involuntarily, of attempted assassination against a prominent ****** politician or if necessary, against an American official. The SUBJECT was formerly in [redacted] employ but has since terminated and is now employed with the ****** Government. According to all available information, the SUBJECT would offer no further cooperation with [redacted]. Access to the SUBJECT would be extremely limited, probably limited to a single social meeting. Because the SUBJECT is a heavy drinker, it was proposed that the individual could be surreptitiously drugged through the medium of an alcoholic cocktail at a social party, ARTICHOKE applied and the SUBJECT induced to perform the act of attempted assassination at some later date. All of the above was to be accomplished at one involuntary uncontrolled social meeting. After the act of attempted assassination was performed, it was assumed that the SUBJECT would be taken into custody by the ****** Government and thereby "disposed of." Other than the personal reassurances by [redacted] means of security involving the project, techniques, personnel, and disposal of the SUBJECT were no indicated. Whether the proposed act of attempted assassination was carried out or not by the SUBJECT was of no great significance in relation to the overall project.

3. CONCLUSIONS:

   a. In answer to the hypothetical question, can an individual of ****** descent be made to perform an act of attempted assassination, involuntarily, under ARTICHOKE, according to the above conditions, the answer in this case was probably "No" because of the limitations imposed operationally as follows:

      i. The SUBJECT would be an involuntary and unwitting SUBJECT.

      ii. We would have none, or at most, very limited physical control and custody of the SUBJECT.

      iii. Access to the SUBJECT is strictly limited to a social engagement among a mixed group of both cleared and uncleared personnel.

4. The final answer was that in view of the fact that successful completion of this proposed act of attempted assassination was insignificant to the overall project; to wit, whether it

was even carried out or not, that under "crash conditions" and appropriate authority from Headquarters, the ARTI-CHOKE Team *would* undertake the problem in spite of the operational limitations.

Source: Central Intelligence Agency, "ARTICHOKE Report," January 22, 1954, Copy H B-113, Available at https://www .cia.gov/library/readingroom/docs/DOC_0000140399.pdf.

CIA Counterintelligence Manual (1963)

This manual, known as KUBARK, describes the techniques to be used in torturing detainees during interrogation. This excerpt reviews techniques meant to coerce information out of a detainee.

The following are the principal coercive techniques of interrogation: arrest, detention, deprivation of sensory stimuli through solitary confinement or similar methods, threats and fear, debility, pain, heightened suggestibility and hypnosis, narcosis, and induced regression. This section also discusses the detection of malingering by interrogatees and the provision of appropriate rationalizations for capitulating and cooperating.

C. Arrest

The manner and timing of arrest can contribute substantially to the interrogator's purposes. What we aim to do is to ensure that the manner of arrest achieves, if possible, surprise, and the maximum amount of mental discomfort in order to catch the suspect off balance and to deprive him of the initiative. One should therefore arrest him at a moment when he least expects it and when his mental and physical resistance is at its lowest. The ideal time at which to arrest a person is in the early hours of the morning because surprise is achieved then, and because a person's resistance physiologically as well as psychologically is at its lowest If a person cannot be arrested in the early hours . . ., then the next best time is in the evening. . . .

D. Detention

If, through the cooperation of a liaison service or by unilateral means, arrangements have been made for the confinement of a resistant source, the circumstances of detention are arranged to enhance within the subject his feelings of being cut off from the known and the reassuring, and of being plunged into the strange. Usually his own clothes are immediately taken away, because familiar clothing reinforces identity and thus the capacity for resistance. (Prisons give close hair cuts and issue prison garb for the same reason.) If the interrogate© is especially proud or neat, it may be useful to give him an outfit that is one or two sizes too large and to fail to provide a belt, so that he must hold his pants up. . . .

E. Deprivation of Sensory Stimuli

The chief effect of arrest and detention, and particularly of solitary confinement, is to deprive the subject of many or most of the sights, sounds, tastes, he has grown accustomed . . . The apparent reason for these effects is that a person cut off from external stimuli turns his awareness inward, upon himself, and then projects the contents of his own unconscious outwards, so that he endows his faceless environment with his own attributes, fears, and forgotten memories. . . .

F. Threats and Fear

The threat of coercion usually weakens or destroys resistance more effectively than coercion itself. The threat to inflict pain, for example, can trigger fears more damaging than the immediate sensation of pain. In fact, most people underestimate their capacity to withstand pain. The same principle holds for other fears: sustained long enough, a strong fear of anything vague or unknown induces regression, whereas the materialization of the fear, the infliction of some form of punishment, is likely to come as a relief. The subject finds that he can hold out, and his resistances are strengthened. . . . The effectiveness of a threat depends not only on what sort of person the interrogatee is and whether he believes that his questioner can and will carry the threat out but also on the interrogator's reasons for threatening. If the interrogator threatens because he is angry, the subject frequently senses the fear of failure underlying the anger and is strengthened in his own resolve to resist. Threats delivered coldly are more effective than those shouted in rage. It is especially important that a threat not be uttered in response to the interrogatee's own expressions of hostility. These, if ignored, can induce feelings of guilt, whereas retorts in kind relieve the subject's feelings. . . .

G. Debility

No report of scientific investigation of the effect of debility upon the interrogatee's powers of resistance has been discovered. For centuries interrogators have employed various methods of inducing physical weakness: prolonged constraint; prolonged exertion; extremes of heat, cold, or moisture; and deprivation or drastic reduction of food or sleep. Apparently the assumption is that lowering the source's physiological resistance will lower his psychological capacity for opposition. If this notion were valid, however, it might reasonably be expected that those subjects who are physically weakest at the beginning of an interrogation would be the quickest to capitulate, a concept not supported by experience. The available evidence suggests that resistance is sapped principally by psychological rather than physical pressures. The threat of debility—for example, a brief deprivation of food—may induce much more anxiety than prolonged hunger, which will result after a while in apathy and, perhaps, eventual delusions or hallucinations. In brief, it appears probable that the techniques of inducing debility become counter-productive at an early stage. . . .

H. Pain

Everyone is aware that people react very differently to pain. . . . The wide range of individual reactions to pain may be partially explicable in terms of early conditioning. The person whose first encounters with pain were frightening and intense may be more violently affected by its later infliction than one whose original experiences were mild. Or the reverse may be true, and the man whose childhood familiarized him with pain may dread it less, and react less, than one whose distress is heightened by fear of the unknown. The individual remains the determinant.

It has been plausibly suggested that, whereas pain inflicted on a person from outside himself may actually focus or intensify his will to resist, his resistance is likelier to be sapped by pain which he seems to inflict upon himself. . . .

Interrogatees who are withholding but who feel qualms of guilt and a secret desire to yield are likely to become intractable if made to endure pain. The reason is that they can then interpret the pain as punishment and hence as expiation. There are also persons who enjoy pain and its anticipation and who will keep back information that they might otherwise divulge if they are given reason to expect that withholding will result in the punishment that they want. Persons of considerable moral or intellectual stature often find in pain inflicted by others a confirmation of the belief that they are in the hands of inferiors, and their resolve not to submit is strengthened.

Intense pain is quite likely to produce false confessions, concocted as a means of escaping from distress. A time-consuming delay results, while investigation is conducted and the admissions are proven untrue. During this respite the interrogate can pull himself together. He may even use the time to think up new, more complex "admissions" that take still longer to disprove. KUBARK is especially vulnerable to such tactics because the interrogation is conducted for the sake of information and not for police purposes.

If an interrogatee is caused to suffer pain rather late in the interrogation process and after other tactics have failed, he is almost certain to conclude that the interrogator is becoming desperate. He may then decide that if he can just hold out against this final assault, he will win the struggle and his freedom. And he is likely to be right. Interrogatees who have withstood pain are more difficult to handle by other methods. The effect has been not to repress the subject but to restore his confidence and maturity.

I. Heightened Suggestibility and Hypnosis

Hypnosis offers one advantage not inherent in other interrogation techniques or aids: the post-hypnotic suggestion. Under favorable circumstances it should be possible to administer a silent drug to a resistant source, persuade him as the drug takes effect that he is slipping into a hypnotic trance, place him under actual hypnosis as consciousness is returning, shift his frame of reference so that his reasons for resistance become reasons for cooperating, interrogate him, and conclude the session by implanting the suggestion that when he emerges from trance he will not remember anything about what has happened. . . .

J. Narcosis

Just as the threat of pain may more effectively induce compliance than its infliction, so an interrogatee's mistaken belief that he has been drugged may make him a more useful interrogation subject than he would be under narcosis. . . . In the interrogation situation, moreover, the effectiveness of a placebo may be enhanced because of its ability to placate the conscience. The subject's primary source of resistance to confession or divulgence may be pride, patriotism, personal loyalty to superiors, or fear of retribution if he is returned to their hands. Under such circumstances his natural desire to escape from stress by complying with the interrogator's wishes may become decisive if he is provided an acceptable rationalization for compliance. "I was drugged" is one of the best excuses. . . .

K. The Detection of Malingering

The detection of malingering is obviously not an interrogation technique, coercive or otherwise. But the history of interrogation is studded with the stories of persons who have attempted, often successfully, to evade the mounting pressures of interrogation by feigning physical or mental illness. KUBARK interrogators may encounter seemingly sick or irrational interrogatees at times and places which make it difficult or next-to-impossible to summon medical or other professional assistance. . . . Most persons who feign a mental or physical illness do not know enough about it to deceive the well- informed. . . .

Source: CIA, *KUBARK Counterintelligence Interrogation*, July 1963 (released January 1997), pp. 85–102. Available through the National Security Archive, https://nsarchive2.gwu.edu/ NSAEBB/NSAEBB122/, document 1b.

Convention against Torture (December 10, 1984)

This United Nations treaty, adopted in 1984, came into force on June 26, 1987. The Convention defines torture, requires signatories to prevent torture in their jurisdictions, and creates a Committee against Torture to monitory implementation and address concerns.

The States Parties to this Convention,

Considering that, in accordance with the principles proclaimed in the Charter of the United Nations, recognition of the equal and inalienable rights of all members of the human family is the foundation of freedom, justice and peace in the world,

Recognizing that those rights derive from the inherent dignity of the human person,

Considering the obligation of States under the Charter, in particular Article 55, to promote universal respect for, and observance of, human rights and fundamental freedoms,

Having regard to article 5 of the Universal Declaration of Human Rights and article 7 of the International Covenant on Civil and Political Rights, both of which provide that no one shall be subjected to torture or to cruel, inhuman or degrading treatment or punishment,

Having regard also to the Declaration on the Protection of All Persons from Being Subjected to Torture and Other Cruel, Inhuman or Degrading Treatment or Punishment, adopted by the General Assembly on 9 December 1975,

Desiring to make more effective the struggle against torture and other cruel, inhuman or degrading treatment or punishment throughout the world,

Have agreed as follows:

Part I

Article 1

1. For the purposes of this Convention, the term "torture" means any act by which severe pain or suffering, whether physical or mental, is intentionally inflicted on a person for such purposes as obtaining from him or a third person information or a confession, punishing him for an act he or a third person has committed or is suspected of having committed, or intimidating or coercing him or a third person, or for any reason based on discrimination of any kind, when such pain or suffering is inflicted by or at the instigation of or with the consent or acquiescence of a public official or other person acting in an official capacity. It does not include pain or suffering arising only from, inherent in or incidental to lawful sanctions.

2. This article is without prejudice to any international instrument or national legislation which does or may contain provisions of wider application.

Article 2

1. Each State Party shall take effective legislative, administrative, judicial or other measures to prevent acts of torture in any territory under its jurisdiction.

2. No exceptional circumstances whatsoever, whether a state of war or a threat of war, internal political instability or any other public emergency, may be invoked as a justification of torture.

3. An order from a superior officer or a public authority may not be invoked as a justification of torture.

Article 3

1. No State Party shall expel, return ("refouler") or extradite a person to another State where there are substantial grounds for believing that he would be in danger of being subjected to torture.

2. For the purpose of determining whether there are such grounds, the competent authorities shall take into account all relevant considerations including, where applicable, the existence in the State concerned of a consistent pattern of gross, flagrant or mass violations of human rights.

Article 4

1. Each State Party shall ensure that all acts of torture are offences under its criminal law. The same shall apply to an attempt to commit torture and to an act by any person which constitutes complicity or participation in torture.

2. Each State Party shall make these offences punishable by appropriate penalties which take into account their grave nature.

. . .

Article 9

1. States Parties shall afford one another the greatest measure of assistance in connection with criminal proceedings brought in respect of any of the offences referred to

in article 4, including the supply of all evidence at their disposal necessary for the proceedings.

2. States Parties shall carry out their obligations under paragraph I of this article in conformity with any treaties on mutual judicial assistance that may exist between them.

Article 10

1. Each State Party shall ensure that education and information regarding the prohibition against torture are fully included in the training of law enforcement personnel, civil or military, medical personnel, public officials and other persons who may be involved in the custody, interrogation or treatment of any individual subjected to any form of arrest, detention or imprisonment.

2. Each State Party shall include this prohibition in the rules or instructions issued in regard to the duties and functions of any such person.

Article 11

Each State Party shall keep under systematic review interrogation rules, instructions, methods and practices as well as arrangements for the custody and treatment of persons subjected to any form of arrest, detention or imprisonment in any territory under its jurisdiction, with a view to preventing any cases of torture.

. . .

Part II

Article 17

1. There shall be established a Committee against Torture (hereinafter referred to as the Committee) which shall carry out the functions hereinafter provided. The Committee shall consist of ten experts of high moral standing and recognized competence in the field of human rights, who

shall serve in their personal capacity. The experts shall be elected by the States Parties, consideration being given to equitable geographical distribution and to the usefulness of the participation of some persons having legal experience.

. . .

Article 20

1. If the Committee receives reliable information which appears to it to contain well-founded indications that torture is being systematically practised in the territory of a State Party, the Committee shall invite that State Party to co-operate in the examination of the information and to this end to submit observations with regard to the information concerned.

2. Taking into account any observations which may have been submitted by the State Party concerned, as well as any other relevant information available to it, the Committee may, if it decides that this is warranted, designate one or more of its members to make a confidential inquiry and to report to the Committee urgently.

3. If an inquiry is made in accordance with paragraph 2 of this article, the Committee shall seek the co-operation of the State Party concerned. In agreement with that State Party, such an inquiry may include a visit to its territory.

4. After examining the findings of its member or members submitted in accordance with paragraph 2 of this article, the Commission shall transmit these findings to the State Party concerned together with any comments or suggestions which seem appropriate in view of the situation.

. . .

Source: United Nations Office of the High Commissioner for Human Rights. Available at https://www.ohchr.org/en/profes sionalinterest/pages/cat.aspx.

U.S. Senate Ratification of the Convention against Torture (October 27, 1990)

While the U.S. Senate did consent to ratify the Convention against Torture, they did so with the reservations outlined in the following text. Some concluded that these reservations stripped the Convention of most of its force.

Resolved, (two-thirds of the Senators present concurring therein),

That the Senate advise and consent to the ratification of The Convention Against Torture and Other Cruel, Inhuman or Degrading Treatment or Punishment, adopted by unanimous agreement of the United Nations General Assembly on December 10, 1984, and signed by the United States on April 18, 1988,

Provided that:

I. The Senate's advice and consent is subject to the following reservations:

1. That the United States shall implement the Convention to the extent that the Federal Government exercises legislative and judicial jurisdiction over the matters covered therein; to the extent that constituent units exercise jurisdiction over such matters, the Federal Government shall take appropriate measures, to the end that the competent authorities of the constituent units may take appropriate measures for the fulfillment of this Convention.

    That the United States considers itself bound by the obligation under Article 16 to prevent "cruel, inhuman or degrading treatment or punishment," only insofar as the term "cruel, inhuman or degrading treatment or punishment" means the cruel, unusual and inhumane treatment or punishment prohibited by the Fifth, Eighth, and/or Fourteenth Amendments to the Constitution of the United States.

2. That pursuant to Article 30(2) the United States declares that it does not consider itself bound by Article 30(1), but reserves the right specifically to agree to follow this or any other procedure for arbitration in a particular case.

II. The Senate's advice and consent is subject to the following understandings, which shall apply to the obligations of the United States under this Convention:

1. (a) That with reference to Article 1, the United States understands that, in order to constitute torture, an act must be specifically intended to inflict severe physical or mental pain or suffering and that mental pain or suffering refers to prolonged mental harm caused by or resulting from: (1) the intentional infliction or threatened infliction of severe physical pain or suffering; (2) the administration or application, or threatened administration or application, of mind altering substances or other procedures calculated to disrupt profoundly the senses or the personality; (3) the threat of imminent death; or (4) the threat that another person will imminently be subjected to death, severe physical pain or suffering, or the administration or application of mind altering substances or other procedures calculated to disrupt profoundly the senses or personality.

(b) That the United States understands that the definition of torture in Article 1 is intended to apply only to acts directed against persons in the offender's custody or physical control.

(c) That with reference to Article 1 of the Convention, the United States understands that "sanctions" includes judically-imposed sanctions and other enforcement actions authorized by United States law or by judicial interpretation of such law provided that such sanctions or actions are not clearly prohibited under international law.

(d) That with reference to Article 1 of the Convention, the United States understands that the term "acquiescence" requires that the public official, prior to the activity constituting torture, have awareness of such activity and thereafter breach his legal responsibility to intervene to prevent such activity.

(e) That with reference to Article 1 of the Convention, the United States understands that noncompliance with applicable legal procedural standards does no per se constitute torture.

2. That the United States understands the phrase, "where there are substantial grounds for believing that he would be in danger of being subjected to torture," as used in Article 3 of the Convention, to mean "if it is more likely than not that he would be tortured."

3. That it is the understanding of the United States that Article 14 requires a State Party to provide a private right of action for damages only for acts of torture committed in territory under the jurisdiction of that State Party.

4. That the United States understands that international law does not prohibit the death penalty, and does not consider this Convention to restrict or prohibit the United States from applying the death penalty consistent with the Fifth, Eighth and/or Fourteenth Amendments to the Constitution of the United States, including any constitutional period of confinement prior to the imposition of the death penalty.

III. The Senate's advice and consent is subject to the following declarations:

1. That the United States declares that the provisions of Articles 1 through 16 of the Convention are not self-executing.

2. That the United States declares, pursuant to Article 21, paragraph 1, of the Convention, that it recognizes the competence of the Committee against Torture to receive and consider communications to the effect that a State Party claims that another State Party is not fulfilling its obligations under the Convention. It is the understanding of the United States that, pursuant to the above mentioned article, such communications shall be accepted and processed only if they come from a State Party which has made a similar declaration.

Source: *Congressional Record*, October 27, 1990. Washington, D.C.: Government Printing Office, 1990, S36198–S36199.

Memo from John Yoo to William Haynes (January 9, 2002)

This memo, from Deputy Assistant Attorney General John Yoo to William Haynes, general counsel of the Department of Defense, concludes the War Crimes Act of 1996 did not apply to American operations in Afghanistan against the Taliban and Al Qaeda, except for the Act's bar on torture.

RE: Application of Treaties and Laws to al Qaeda and Taliban Detainees

You have asked for our Office's views concerning the effect of international treaties and federal laws on the treatment of individuals detained by the U.S. Armed Forces during the conflict in Afghanistan. In particular, you have asked whether certain treaties forming part of the laws of armed conflict apply to the conditions of detention and the procedures for trial of members of al Qaeda and the Taliban militia. We conclude that these treaties do not protect members of the al Qaeda organization, which as a non-State actor cannot be a party to the international agreements governing war. We further conclude that that President has sufficient grounds to find that these treaties do not protect members of the Taliban militia.

This memorandum expresses no view as to whether the President should decide, as a matter of policy, that the U.S. Armed Forces should adhere to the standards of conduct in those treaties with respect to the treatment of prisoners.

We believe it most useful to structure the analysis of these questions by focusing on the War Crimes Act, 18 U.S.C. § 2441 (Supp. III 1997) ("WCA"). The WCA directly incorporates several provisions of international treaties governing the laws of war into the federal criminal code. Part I of this memorandum describes the WCA and the most relevant treaties that it incorporates: the four 1949 Geneva Convention, which generally regulate the treatment of non-combatants, such as prisoners of war ("POWs"), the injured and sick, and civilians.

Part II examines whether al Qaeda detainees can claim the protections of these agreements. Al Qaeda is merely a violent political movement or organization and not a nation-state. As a result, it is ineligible to be a signatory to any treaty. Because of the novel nature of this conflict, moreover, we do not believe that al Qaeda would be included in non-international forms of armed conflict to which some provisions of the Geneva Conventions might apply. Therefore, neither the Geneva Conventions nor the WCA regulate the detention of al Qaeda prisoners captured during the Afghanistan conflict.

Part III discuses whether the same treaty provisions, as incorporated through the WCA apply to the treatment of captured members of the Taliban militia. We believe that the Geneva Conventions do not apply for several reasons. First, the Taliban was not a government and Afghanistan was not—even prior to the beginning of the present conflict—a functioning State during the period in which they engaged in hostilities against the United States and its allies. Afghanistan's status as a failed state is ground alone to find that members of the Taliban militia are not entitled to enemy POW status under the Geneva Conventions. Further, it is clear that the President has the constitutional authority to suspend our treaties with Afghanistan pending the restoration of a legitimate government capable of performing Afghanistan's treaty obligations. Second, it appears from the public evidence that the Taliban militia may have been so intertwined with al Qaeda as to be functionally indistinguishable from it. To the extent that the Taliban militia was more akin to a non-governmental organization that used military force to pursue its religious and political ideology than a functioning government, its members would be on the same legal footing as al Qaeda.

In part IV, we address the question whether any customary international law of armed conflict may apply to the al Qaeda or Taliban militia members detained during the course of the Afghanistan Conflict. We conclude that customary international law, whatever its source and content, does not bind the President or restrict the actions of the United States military, because it does not constitute federal law recognized under the Supremacy Clause of the Constitution. The President, however, has the constitutional authority as Commander in Chief to interpret and apply the customary or common laws of war in such a way that they would extend to the conduct of members of both al Qaeda and the Taliban, and also to the conduct of the U.S. Armed Forces towards members of those groups taken as prisoners in Afghanistan.

. . .

Conclusion

For the foregoing reasons, we conclude that neither the federal War Crimes Act nor the Geneva Conventions would apply to the detention condition in Guantanamo Bay, Cuba, or to trial by military commission of al Qaeda or Taliban Prisoners. We also conclude that customary international law has no binding legal effect on either the President or the military because it is not federal law, as recognized by the Constitution. Nonetheless, we also believe that the President, as Commander in Chief, has the constitutional authority to impose the customary laws of war on both the al Qaeda and Taliban groups and the U.S. Armed Forces.

Source: "Application of Treaties and Laws to Al Qaeda and Taliban Detainees." January 2, 2002. Available at the National Security Archive, https://nsarchive2.gwu.edu/torturingdemocracy/documents/, document 9.

Memo from Jay Bybee to Alberto Gonzales (August 1, 2002)

This memo, from Assistant Attorney General Jay Bybee to Alberto Gonzales, counsel to the president, asserts that the Convention against Torture only barred "extreme" breaches of its terms and suggested possible defenses for the United States to assert if was accused of engaging in torture.

You have asked for our Office's views regarding the standards of conduct under the Convention Against Torture and Other Cruel, Inhuman and Degrading Treatment or Punishment as implemented by Sections 2340–2340A of title 18 of the United States Code. As we understand it, this question has arisen in the context of the conduct of interrogations outside of the United States. We conclude below that Section 2340A proscribes acts inflicting, and that are specifically intended to inflict, severe pain or suffering, whether mental or physical. Those acts must be of an extreme nature to rise to the level of torture within the meaning of Section 2340A and the Convention. We further conclude that certain acts may be cruel, inhuman, or degrading, but still not produce pain and suffering of the requisite intensity to fall within Section 2340A's proscription against torture. We conclude by examining possible defenses that would negate any claim that certain interrogation methods violate the statute.

In Part I, we examine the criminal statue's text and history. We conclude that for an act to constitute torture as defined in

Section 2340, it must inflict pain that is difficult to endure. Physical pain amounting to torture must be equivalent to intensity to the pain accompanying serious physical injury, such as organ failure, impairment of bodily function, or even death. For purely mental pain or suffering to amount to torture under Section 2340, it must result in significant psychological harm of significant duration, e.g., lasting for months or even years. We conclude that the mental harm also must result from one of the predicate acts listed in the statute, namely: threats of imminent death; threats of infliction of the kind of pain that would amount to physical torture; infliction of such physical pain as a means of psychological torture; use of drugs or other procedures designed to deeply disrupt the senses, or fundamentally alter an individual's personality; or threatening to do any of these things to a third party. The legislative history simply reveals that Congress intended for the statute's definition to track the Convention's definition of torture and the reservations, understandings, and declarations that the United States submitted with its ratification. We conclude that the statute, taken as a whole, makes plain that it prohibits only extreme acts.

In Part II, we examine the text, ratification history, and negotiating history of the Torture Convention. We conclude that the treaty's text prohibits only the most extreme [Page 2] acts by reserving criminal penalties solely for torture and declining to require such penalties for "cruel, inhuman, or degrading treatment or punishment." This confirms our view that the criminal statute penalizes only the most egregious conduct. Executive branch interpretations and representations to the Senate at the time of ratification further confirm that the treaty was intended to reach only the most extreme conduct.

In Part III, we analyze the jurisprudence of the Torture Victims Protection Act, 28 U.S.C. §§ 1350 note (2000), which provides civil remedies for torture victims, to predict the standards that courts might follow in determining what actions reach the threshold of torture in the criminal context. We conclude from these cases that courts are likely to take at totality-of-the-circumstances approach, and will look to an entire course of conduct, to determine whether certain acts will violate Section 2340A. Moreover, these cases demonstrate that most often torture involves cruel and extreme physical pain. In Part IV, we examine international decisions regarding the use of sensory deprivation techniques. These cases make clear that while many of these techniques may amount to cruel, inhuman and degrading treatment, they do not produce pain or suffering of the necessary intensity to meet the definition of torture. From these decisions, we conclude that there is a wide range of such techniques that will not rise to the level of torture.

In Part V, we discuss whether Section 2340A may be unconstitutional if applied to interrogations undertaken of enemy combatants pursuant to the President's Commander-in-Chief powers. We find that in the circumstances of the current war against al Qaeda and its allies, prosecution under Section 2340A may be barred because enforcement of the statute would represent an unconstitutional infringement of the President's authority to conduct war. In Part VI, we discuss defenses to an allegation that an interrogation method might violate the statute. We conclude that, under the current circumstances, necessity or self-defense may justify interrogation methods that might violate Section 2340A.

. . .

Conclusion

For the foregoing reasons, we conclude that torture as defined in and proscribed by Sections 2340–2340A, covers only extreme acts. Severe pain is generally of the kind difficult for the victim to endure. Where the pain is physical, it must be of an intensity akin to that which accompanies serious physical injury such as death or organ failure. Severe mental pain requires suffering not just at the moment of infliction but it also requires lasting psychological harm, such as seen in mental disorders like posttraumatic stress disorder. Additionally, such severe mental pain can arise only from the predicate acts listed in Section 2340. Because the acts inflicting torture are extreme, there is significant range of acts that though they might constitute cruel, inhuman, or degrading treatment or punishment fail to rise to the level of torture.

Further, we conclude that under the circumstances of the current war against al Qaeda and its allies, application, of Section 2340A to interrogations undertaken pursuant to the President's Commander-in-Chief powers may be unconstitutional. Finally, even if an interrogation method might violate Section 2340A, necessity or self-defense could provide justifications that would eliminate any criminal liability.

Source: "Standards for Conduct for Interrogation under 18 U.S.C. 2340–2340A." August 1, 2002. Available at the National Security Archive, https://nsarchive2.gwu.edu/torturing democracy/documents/, document 22.

Executive Order 13491: Ensuring Lawful Interrogations (January 22, 2009)

With this executive order, President Barack Obama prohibited the use of torture by U.S. personnel and directed the closure of CIA detention facilities.

By the authority vested in me by the Constitution and the laws of the United States of America, in order to improve the effectiveness of human intelligence-gathering, to promote the safe, lawful, and humane treatment of individuals in United States custody and of United States personnel who are detained in armed conflicts, to ensure compliance with the treaty obligations of the United States, including the Geneva Conventions, and to take care that the laws of the United States are faithfully executed, I hereby order as follows:

Section 1. Revocation. Executive Order 13440 of July 20, 2007, is revoked. All executive directives, orders, and regulations inconsistent with this order, including but not limited to those issued to or by the Central Intelligence Agency

(CIA) from September 11, 2001, to January 20, 2009, concerning detention or the interrogation of detained individuals, are revoked to the extent of their inconsistency with this order. Heads of departments and agencies shall take all necessary steps to ensure that all directives, orders, and regulations of their respective departments or agencies are consistent with this order. Upon request, the Attorney General shall provide guidance about which directives, orders, and regulations are inconsistent with this order.

. . .

Sec. 3. Standards and Practices for Interrogation of Individuals in the Custody or Control of the United States in Armed Conflicts.

(a) Common Article 3 Standards as a Minimum Baseline. Consistent with the requirements of the Federal torture statute, 18 U.S.C. 2340–2340A, section 1003 of the Detainee Treatment Act of 2005, 42 U.S.C. 2000dd, the Convention Against Torture, Common Article 3, and other laws regulating the treatment and interrogation of individuals detained in any armed conflict, such persons shall in all circumstances be treated humanely and shall not be subjected to violence to life and person (including murder of all kinds, mutilation, cruel treatment, and torture), nor to outrages upon personal dignity (including humiliating and degrading treatment), whenever such individuals are in the custody or under the effective control of an officer, employee, or other agent of the United States Government or detained within a facility owned, operated, or controlled by a department or agency of the United States.

(b) Interrogation Techniques and Interrogation-Related Treatment. Effective immediately, an individual in the custody or under the effective control of an officer, employee, or other agent of the United States Government, or detained within a facility owned, operated, or controlled by a department or agency of the United States, in any armed conflict, shall not be subjected to any interrogation technique or approach, or any treatment related to interrogation, that is not authorized by and listed in Army Field Manual 2–22.3 (Manual). Interrogation techniques, approaches, and treatments described in the Manual shall be implemented strictly in accord with the principles, processes, conditions, and limitations the Manual prescribes. Where processes required by the Manual, such as a requirement of approval by specified Department of Defense officials, are inapposite to a department or an agency other than the Department of Defense, such a department or agency shall use processes that are substantially equivalent to the processes the Manual prescribes for the Department of Defense. Nothing in this section shall preclude the Federal Bureau of Investigation, or other Federal law enforcement agencies, from continuing to use authorized, non-coercive techniques of interrogation that are designed to elicit voluntary statements and do not involve the use of force, threats, or promises.

(c) Interpretations of Common Article 3 and the Army Field Manual. From this day forward, unless the Attorney General with appropriate consultation provides further guidance, officers, employees, and other agents of the United States Government may, in conducting interrogations, act in reliance upon Army Field Manual 2–22.3, but may not, in conducting interrogations, rely upon any interpretation of the law governing interrogation—including interpretations of Federal criminal laws, the Convention Against Torture, Common Article 3, Army Field Manual 2–22.3, and its predecessor document, Army Field Manual 34–52 —issued by the Department of Justice between September 11, 2001, and January 20, 2009.

Sec. 4. Prohibition of Certain Detention Facilities, and Red Cross Access to Detained Individuals.

(a) CIA Detention. The CIA shall close as expeditiously as possible any detention facilities that it currently operates and shall not operate any such detention facility in the future.

(b) International Committee of the Red Cross Access to Detained Individuals. All departments and agencies of the Federal Government shall provide the International Committee of the Red Cross with notification of, and timely access to, any individual detained in any armed conflict in the custody or under the effective control of an officer, employee, or other agent of the United States Government or detained within a facility owned, operated, or controlled by a department or agency of the United States Government, consistent with Department of Defense regulations and policies.

. . .

Source: 74 *Federal Register* 4893, January 27, 2009. Available at https://www.govinfo.gov/app/details/DCPD-200900007.

NOT
in Our Name

Dr. Marti...

REEDC

Det...

6 Resources

This first part of the chapter reviews research strategies for obtaining information on torture. The second part provides specific sources and serves two purposes. First, it is a consolidated list of some of those sources cited in other chapters, broken down by subject. Second, it includes some sources which, while not discussed in this text, are valuable for further research and worth including on that basis.

Where appropriate, some works are cited in multiple sections.

Research Strategies

The Freedom of Information Act

While it can be cumbersome and time consuming, in the United States the federal Freedom of Information Act can be a powerful tool in the hands of researchers, especially when time is not of the essence. (Despite the time limits set out in the statute, many federal agencies routinely take far longer to process—let alone substantively respond to—requests than they did a few decades ago.)

The first place to look is the agency's or entity's electronic Freedom of Information Act (FOIA) reading room, which allows for downloads of a selection of documents that the agency has released to earlier requesters in full or in part. While not every released document is in the online reading room, it does serve as a valuable place to start.

At a 2007 Martin Luther King Jr. Day protest, hundreds of activists march through the streets of Detroit condemning torture and demanding the impeachment of then-President George W. Bush for his administration's involvement in torture in Iraq and elsewhere. (Jim West/Alamy)

A careful choice of search terms is important. For example, the CIA is unlikely to characterize the waterboarding of a prisoner as "torture" in a written document, even for internal use, but would probably refer to it instead as "enhanced interrogation" or even as "waterboarding."

Central Intelligence Agency Reading Room

> https://www.cia.gov/library/readingroom/home

Federal Bureau of Investigation Reading Room ("The Vault")

> https://vault.fbi.gov/

Department of Homeland Security Reading Room ("FOIA Library")

> https://www.dhs.gov/foia-library

United States Air Force Reading Room

> https://www.afhra.af.mil/Home/FOIA-Reading-Room/

United States Army Reading Room

> https://www.foia.army.mil/readingroom/

United States Marine Corps Reading Room

> https://www.hqmc.marines.mil/Agencies/USMC-FOIA/
> USMC-FOIA-Reading-Room/

United States Navy Reading Room

> https://www.secnav.navy.mil/foia/readingroom/Site
> Pages/Home.aspx

United States Department of State ("Virtual") Reading Room

> https://foia.state.gov/Search/Search.aspx

Assuming the document you want and which you believe the agency possesses isn't available in the reading room, you'll need to draft a request letter under the Freedom of Information Act to the appropriate office within the agency. The reading room links listed here also have links to the FOIA office within each agency with information on how to submit a request.

There are nonprofit entities like MuckRock that can assist you with this (as of this writing, a $20 fee covers up to four requests submitted through their site) but it's fairly straightforward to draft your own FOIA letter and submit it by U.S. mail or electronic mail (as the agency prefers). The Reporters Committee for Freedom of the Press (RCFP) offers a similar service as MuckRock, but its doesn't appear to have a fee at this time, though registration is required.

MuckRock

https://www.muckrock.com/

Reporter's Committee for Freedom of the Press/iFOIA

https://www.ifoia.org/

MuckRock and RCFP/iFOIA can also be powerful resources when doing research on the possible involvement of state, county, and city governments in torture, for example through the treatment of prisoners by the police or sheriff's department. These requests are governed through state open meeting/public records laws and in some cases, such as in the City and County of San Francisco, local sunshine ordinances.

Congressional and Federal Government Reports

As a significant bill (e.g., the War Crimes Act of 1996) moves through the federal legislative process in the United States, the committee considering it will usually prepare a report on the measure, which can be an invaluable source to determine what the members who backed the bill were thinking at the time they voted on it and what they intended it to do. In addition, Congress produces a plethora of reports each session through its committee hearings, which can also be good sources. Some of these reports remain classified, like the Senate's report on

CIA torture (where only the executive summary has been released in redacted form), but the majority are not.

Beginning with the 104th Congress (1995–1996), these reports are available from https://www.congress.gov at no charge. Reports from previous congresses may be available from the National Archives' site at https://www.archives.gov but, as their holdings are much larger and their search engine is not as robust in my experience, it's best to have at least a partial title or bill number before checking the National Archives.

Another good source is the Government Publishing Office (GPO), which facilitates searches not only of official U.S. government publications but the Congressional Record (the journal of what members say on the House and Senate floor) via https://www.govinfo.gov/. The GPO is continuously expanding their resources by adding new publications and larger date ranges.

Older records that cannot be accessed online are usually available in government depository libraries; a searchable list can be found at https://catalog.gpo.gov/fdlpdir/FDLPdir.jsp.

U.S. National Archives

On the federal level, the National Archives is located in Washington, D.C., with a much larger facility, known as Archives II, in College Park, Maryland. In addition, the National Archives and Records Administration (NARA) (which runs the Archives) has facilities in seventeen states around the country, in addition to the libraries of former presidents (which NARA also runs).

While not all of NARA's records are digitized and their Web interface can be awkward on occasion, dealing directly with NARA staff can be rewarding.

The National Archives has put together a digital overview for how the process works at https://www.archives.gov/research/start.

Access to online research is summarized at https://www.archives.gov/research/start/online-tools.

Searches are free, as is downloading those records that have been digitized. NARA does charge a reproduction fee for those that are not made available in electronic form.

State Government Reports

States vary greatly as to the breadth and depth of the reports their legislative and executive branch agencies produce, as well as what percentage of that work is accessible online (as opposed to visiting the State Library or Archive). They can still be good resources when researching a particular local instance of torture (e.g., abuse of detainees in jails or state prisons if the issue has come to the public's attention).

United Nations Documents

The United Nations has made (and is making) a real effort to make their documents and reports available online, but getting a specific document can still take some work. A good place to start is the U.N.'s Official Document Search System, at https://www.un.org/en/sections/general/documents/index.html.

The ODS search link at https://documents.un.org/prod/ods.nsf/home.xsp allows for both a keyword and full-text search of the documents. For a specific committee report, use the Info Quest search at https://lib-unique.un.org/DPI/DHL/unique.nsf?Open.

Canadian Government Documents

In 1985, the Canadian Parliament passed the Access to Information Act, which—in theory—was supposed to enable researchers and members of the public to access federal government documents. Unfortunately, as with the American Freedom of Information Act, the Canadian Access to Information Act's reality has—in the eyes of many—fallen far short of its promise.

As an initial matter, only those persons who are (a) Canadian citizens (wherever they reside) or (b) lawful permanent residents of Canada may explicitly make requests under the Act, although the current (as of June 2019) government has allowed persons and corporations "present" in Canada (e.g., asylees) to also make requests.

The government encourages the public to submit their requests electronically through a central clearing website at https://atip-aiprp.tbs-sct.gc.ca/en/Home/Welcome.

The service charges $5 per request and requires users to submit proof that they qualify to use the Act along with their request. Under the law, the service is supposed to transfer the request to the relevant government agency or entity, which then has thirty days to respond to the applicant (from the date the agency or entity gets the request from the service) with either the documents or an explanation as to the status of the request.

It's also possible to search the service for *completed* requests by keyword. In June 2019, a search on the "torture" keyword came up with eleven prior requests, some of which appear to have located a sizable number of documents (though, unlike the FOIA electronic reading rooms in the United States, one still has to request an electronic copy of the previously released documents, which the agency must process before they're released, so it's impossible to say how much has been redacted from the index page).

In addition, the Canadian government provides a list of its designated Access to Information and Privacy Coordinators for each agency or entity covered by the Act, so it is possible to submit the request directly to the appropriate entity to expedite matters. A list of access to information and privacy coordinators by institution is at https://www.tbs-sct.gc.ca/ap/atip-aiprp/coord-eng.asp.

The Access to Information Act also differs from its American counterpart in how it handles exemptions to disclosure and in the discretion it gives the head of the particular government body holding the records. For example, "the head of a government institution *shall* refuse to disclose to disclose any record requested under this Act that contains information that was obtained in confidence from (a) the government of a foreign state or an institution thereof; (b) an international organization of states or an institution thereof; (c) the government of a province or an institution thereof; (d) a municipal or regional government established by or pursuant to an Act of the legislature of a province or an institution of such a government; or (e) an aboriginal government" (Access to Information Act, R.S.C., 1985, c. A-1, s13) (emphasis added).

On the other hand, the head of the agency

> *may* refuse to disclose any record requested under this Act that contains information the disclosure of which could reasonably be expected to be injurious to the conduct of international affairs, the defence of Canada or any state allied or associated with Canada or the detection, prevention or suppression of subversive or hostile activities, including, without restricting the generality of the foregoing, any such information (a) relating to military tactics or strategy, or relating to military exercises or operations undertaken in preparation for hostilities or in connection with the detection, prevention or suppression of subversive or hostile activities; (b) relating to the quantity, characteristics, capabilities or deployment of weapons or other defence equipment or of anything being designed, developed, produced or considered for use as weapons or other defence equipment; (c) relating to the characteristics, capabilities, performance, potential, deployment, functions or role of any defence establishment, of any military force, unit or personnel or of any organization or person responsible for the detection, prevention or suppression of subversive or hostile activities; (d) obtained or prepared for the purpose of intelligence relating to (i) the defence of Canada or any state allied or associated with Canada, or (ii) the detection, prevention or suppression of subversive or hostile activities; (e) obtained or prepared for the

purpose of intelligence respecting foreign states, international organizations of states or citizens of foreign states used by the Government of Canada in the process of deliberation and consultation or in the conduct of international affairs; (f) on methods of, and scientific or technical equipment for, collecting, assessing or handling information referred to in paragraph (d) or (e) or on sources of such information; (g) on the positions adopted or to be adopted by the Government of Canada, governments of foreign states or international organizations of states for the purpose of present or future international negotiations; (h) that constitutes diplomatic correspondence exchanged with foreign states or international organizations of states or official correspondence exchanged with Canadian diplomatic missions or consular posts abroad; or (i) relating to the communications or cryptographic systems of Canada or foreign states used (i) for the conduct of international affairs, (ii) for the defence of Canada or any state allied or associated with Canada, or (iii) in relation to the detection, prevention or suppression of subversive or hostile activities. (Access To Information Act, R.S.C., 1985, c. A-1, s15; emphasis added)

The Access to Information Act only applies to federal government records. Each province has its own legislation for access to its documents, but since the main entities in Canada that are likely to interact with torture (e.g., the RCMP and CSIS) are federal, a detailed discussion of provincial open records act laws is beyond the scope of this chapter.

British Government Documents

Thanks to a major overhaul on how the British government handled the declassification and release of public documents in the mid-2000s, the process for accessing such documents is much more straightforward. To request documents that are "closed" and have not been previously released, visit https://www.nationalarchives.gov.uk/contact/contactform.asp, which is administered by the UK's National Archives.

Requests can also be made in writing to Enquiry Service, The National Archives, Kew, Richmond, Surrey TW9 4DU United Kingdom.

In contrast to their Canadian counterparts, the National Archives in the UK does not charge a fee for searching closed records (though it will if you request help to find an already-released document present in its files) and doesn't require requesters to be UK citizens, requesters to be permanent residents, or even that requesters live in the UK.

Of course, like their counterpart statutes in the United States and Canada, the British Freedom of Information Act has exemptions—most notably, any information that was "directly or indirectly supplied" to a public entity by British law enforcement, security, and intelligence services.

The Act applies to England, Wales, and Northern Ireland. Scotland is covered by a separate statute enacted by the Scottish Parliament: the Freedom of Information Act (Scotland) (2002); the Scottish Information Commissioner maintains a useful website at http://www.itspublicknowledge.info/home/ScottishInformationCommissioner.aspx with information on how to make open record requests in Scotland.

The Internet Archive/Wayback Machine

The Internet Archive is probably best known for its Wayback Machine (https://archive.org/web/), which continually crawls the Web taking snapshots of websites that are then stored for posterity, something that can be useful if the site is later changed or deleted altogether. The Wayback Machine has recently added a feature that allows users to not only save the page at will, but to generate a static URL (which points back to their servers) so the page can be preserved for citation purposes.

However, the Wayback Machine is only a small part of what the Internet Archive (https://archive.org/) does. It also archives everything from newscasts to books, as well as documents uploaded by users.

User-submitted documents can be a powerful tool, but documents may have been redacted or otherwise edited, so use caution when evaluating their usefulness.

Specific Sources

Academic Journals

The following articles from academic journals, organized by topic, may often be accessed through public, school, or university libraries. They provide a general overview of torture.

Conrad, Courtenay R., and Ritter Emily Hencken. "Treaties, Tenure, and Torture: The Conflicting Domestic Effects of International Law." *The Journal of Politics* 75 (2): 397 (2013).

Crane, Jonathan K. "Perspectives on Torture: Reports from a Dialogue Including Christian, Judaic, Islamic, and Feminist Viewpoints." *Journal of Religious Ethics* 39 (4): 585–588 (2011).

Hare, Caspar. "Torture—Does Timing Matter?" *Journal of Moral Philosophy* 11 (4): 385–394 (2014).

Kahn, Paul W. "Torture and Democratic Violence." *Ratio Juris* 22 (2): 244–259 (2009).

Kahn, Paul W. "Torture and the Dream of Reason." *Social Research* 78 (3): 747 (2011).

Keller, Linda M. "Is Truth Serum Torture?" *American University International Law Review* 20 (3) (February 2005): 521–612.

Lebowitz, Michael J. "The Value of Claiming Torture: An Analysis of Al-Qaeda's Tactical Lawfare Strategy and Efforts to Fight Back." *Case Western Reserve Journal of International Law* 43 (1/2): 357 (2010).

Lewis, Michael W. "A Dark Descent into Reality: Making the Case for an Objective Definition of Torture." *Washington & Lee Law Review* 67 (1): 77–136 (2010).

Majima, Shunzo. "Just Torture?" *Journal of Military Ethics* 11 (2): 136–148 (2012).

Miles, Steven H. "Accountability for Doctors Who Torture." *The American Journal of Bioethics* 14 (3) (2014).

Platt, Susan Noyes. "Intimate Violence: Artists' Responses to Illegal Detention and Torture." *Brown Journal of World Affairs* 19 (2): 163–183 (2013).

Schiller, Juliet A. "Using Torture against Women." *Peace Review* 26 (3): 388–393 (2014).

Wisnewski, J. Jeremy. *Understanding Torture* (Edinburgh University Press, 2010).

Governmental and United Nations Reports

While public reports on torture prepared by governmental entities, particularly those concerning governments that are accused of engaging in torture, should be read with a skeptical eye, they form an important part of the public body of knowledge on the subject. In many instances, investigators for governmental entities have far greater access to both decision-makers and documents than private historians do, especially for relatively recent events. In contrast, governmental manuals, legal advice memoranda, and internal reports that their authors did not intend to become public can be a treasure trove of the actions by an agency or a decision-maker, as well as their motivations for taking those actions.

Bush, George W. "Inaugural Address." January 20, 2001, https://www.presidency.ucsb.edu/node/211268 (accessed July 11, 2019).

Bush, George W. "Humane Treatment of al Qaeda and Taliban Detainees" (The White House, 2002).

Bush, George W. "Interpretation of the Geneva Conventions Common Article 3 as Applied to a Program of Detention and Interrogation Operated by the Central Intelligence Agency." Executive Order 13440, Sec. 2 (c), July 20, 2007, https://fas.org/irp/offdocs/eo/eo-13440.htm (accessed November 10, 2019).

Bybee, Jay. "Memorandum for Alberto R. Gonzalez, Counsel to the President" (United States Department of Justice, Office of Legal Counsel, August 1, 2002 (copy in author's possession).

Caproni, Valerie. "Custodial Interrogation for Public Safety and Intelligence-Gathering Purposes of Operational Terrorists Arrested Inside the United States" (Federal Bureau of Investigation, October 21, 2010), 333-HQ-Cl595552-OGC. Unclassified.

Central Intelligence Agency. "Kubark Counterintelligence Interrogation." C01297486, July 1963, Secret, Approved for release February 25, 2014. https://www.cia.gov/library/readingroom/home (accessed November 24, 2019)

Central Intelligence Agency. "Psychological Operations in Guerrilla Warfare" [Contra Handbook]. C02194646, Secret, Approved for release November 7, 2017. https://www.cia.gov/library/readingroom/home (accessed November 24, 2019)

Central Intelligence Agency. "Disposition Memorandum: Alleged Use of Unauthorized Interrogation Techniques." December 6, 2006, C05959918, Top Secret, Approved for release June 10, 2016. https://www.cia.gov/library/readingroom/home (accessed November 24, 2019)

Central Intelligence Agency, Office of the Inspector General, "Report of Investigation—The Rendition and Detention of German Citizen Khalid Al-Masri." C06541725, July 16, 2007, Top Secret, Approved for release June 10, 2016.

https://www.cia.gov/library/readingroom/home (accessed November 24, 2019)

Clark, Kathleen. "Written Testimony of Kathleen Clark: Senate Judiciary Committee Subcommittee on Administrative Oversight and the Courts Hearing on 'What Went Wrong: Torture and the Office of Legal Counsel in the Bush Administration.'" Hearing date May 13, 2009, Submitted May 20, 2009, https://web .archive.org/web/20100612102537/https://law.wustl.edu/ news/documents/WrittenTestKathClark.pdf (accessed April 20, 2019).

Committee against Torture, United Nations. "Concluding Observations on the Seventh Periodic Report of Canada." December 21, 2018, CAT/C/CAN/CO/7, https:// tbinternet.ohchr.org/_layouts/15/treatybodyexternal/ Download.aspx?symbolno=CAT%2fC%2fCAN%2fCO% 2f7&Lang=en (accessed June 10, 2019).

Crumpton, Henry. "Operational Review of CIA Detainee Program." C06541530, Central Intelligence Agency, May 12, 2004, Top Secret, Approved for release June 10, 2016.

Dawit Isaak v Republic of Eritrea. Decision of the African Commission on Human and Peoples Rights on the Preliminary Objection, Communication 428/12, April 27, 2018, http://www.achpr.org/files/sessions/19th-eo/comunications/428.12/decision_on_communication_ 428_12_eng.pdf

Federal Bureau of Investigation. *Legal Handbook for Special Agents*, 1987, 2003, https://vault.fbi.gov/Legal%20Handbook %20for%20FBI%20Special%20Agents/Legal%20 Handbook%20for%20FBI%20Special%20Agents%20 Part%201%20of%201/view (accessed January 27, 2019).

Gonzales, Alberto R. "Decision re Application of the Geneva Convention on Prisoners of War to the Conflict with Al Queda and the Taliban" (January 25, 2002).

Government Printing Office. *Public Papers of the Presidents of the United States: George W. Bush*, Book II (September 11, 2001).

Grieve, Dominic. "Detainee Mistreatment and Rendition: 2001–2010," Intelligence and Security Committee of Parliament, June 28, 2018, http://isc.independent.gov.uk/files/20180628_HC1113_Report_Detainee_Mistreatment_and_Rendition_2001_10.pdf (accessed June 10, 2019).

Grieve, Dominic. "Detainee Mistreatment and Rendition: Current Issues," Intelligence and Security Committee of Parliament, June 28, 2018, http://isc.independent.gov.uk/files/20180628_HC1114_Report_Detainee_Mistreatment_and_Rendition-Current_Issues.pdf (accessed June 10, 2019).

Guantanamo Review Task Force. "Final Report." Department of Justice, Department of Defense, Department of State, Department of Homeland Security, Office of the Director of National Intelligence, Joint Chiefs of Staff, January 22, 2010, https://www.justice.gov/sites/default/files/ag/legacy/2010/06/02/guantanamo-review-final-report.pdf (accessed June 8, 2019).

House Judiciary Committee. "War Crimes Act of 1996." Report Number 104–698, 104th Congress 2nd Session.

Jacobsmeyer, Paul J. Letter to Jason Leopold. 13-F-1139, February 12, 2014, https://www.documentcloud.org/documents/1020057-guantanamo-parole-list.html (accessed May 27, 2018).

Kean, Thomas H., and Lee Hamilton. "The 9/11 Commission Report: Final Report of the National Commission on Terrorist Attacks Upon the United States" (National Commission on Terrorist Attacks upon the United States, 2004).

Kuppusamy, Baradan. "Malaysia: Mahathir's War Crimes Court to Name and Shame." *Interpress Service News Agency*, February 15, 2007, http://www.ipsnews.net/2007/02/

malaysia-mahathirs-war-crimes-court-to-name-and-shame/ (accessed April 20, 2019).

Mendez, Juan E. "Report of the Special Rapporteur on Torture and other Cruel, Inhuman or Degrading Treatment or Punishment, Addendum Observations on Communications Transmitted to Governments and Replies Received," A/HRC/19/61/Add.4, February 29, 2012.

Nachmanoff, Arnold. "Brazil—More Torture Reports Could Complicate Medici Visit [to Dr. [Henry] Kissinger]." National Security Council, February 11, 1971, LOC HAK 11-6-24-6, Secret, Declassified in part November 30, 2010.

National Commission on Law Observance and Enforcement. "Report on Lawlessness in Law Enforcement." Government Printing Office, 1931.

Obama, Barack H. "Ensuring Lawful Interrogations." Executive Order 13491, January 22, 2009.

Obama, Barack H. "Review and Disposition of Individuals Detained at the Guantánamo Bay Naval Base and Closure of Detention Facilities." Executive Order 13492, January 22, 2009.

Reidy, Aisling. *The Prohibition of Torture: A Guide to the Implementation of Article 3 of the European Convention on Human Rights* (Strasbourg: Council of Europe, 2003).

Report by the Special Rapporteur, Mr. P. Kooijmans, appointed pursuant to Commission on Human Rights resolution 1985/33, UN Document E/CN.4/1986/15 (1986).

Report of the Special Rapporteur, Mr. P. Kooijmans, pursuant to Commission on Human Rights resolution 1992/32, UN Document E/CN.4/1993/26 (1992).

Ridley, Yvonne. "Bush Convicted of War Crimes in Absentia." *Foreign Policy Journal*, May 12, 2012, https://www .foreignpolicyjournal.com/2012/05/12/bush-convicted-of-war-crimes-in-absentia/ (accessed April 20, 2019).

"Robben Island Guidelines for the Prohibition and Prevention of Torture in Africa." African Commission on Human and Peoples' Rights, Conclusion Date: October 23, 2002, https://apt.ch/en/robben-island-guidelines/ (accessed November 10, 2019).

Taguba, Antonio M. "AR 15–6: Investigation of the 800th Military Police Brigade" (Department of the Army, Coalition Forces Land Component Command, United States Army Forces Central Command, March 14, 2004).

Trump, Donald J. "Protecting America through Lawful Detention of Terrorists." Executive Order 13823 (January 30, 2018).

United Nations. "Report of the Committee against Torture." General Assembly, Seventy-Third Session, Supplement No. 44 A/73/44 (2018).

U.S. Department of Defense. "JTF-GTMO Detainee Assessment." JTF-GTMO-CDR, 20311208 (December 8, 2006).

U.S. Senate Select Committee on Intelligence. "Committee Study of the Central Intelligence Agency's Detention and Interrogation Program." Findings and Conclusions, Executive Summary (2012).

Wainstein, Eleanor S. "The Cross and Laporte Kidnappings, Montreal, October 1970." Rand Corporation Report for Department of State and Defense Advanced Research Projects Agency, R-1986/1-DOS/ARPA (February 1977).

Walker, Samuel, and Randolph Boehm. "Records of the Wickersham Commission on Law Observance and Enforcement: Part 1: Records of the Committee on Official Lawlessness" (University Publications of America, 1997), http://www.lexisnexis.com/documents/academic/upa_cis/1965_WickershamCommPt1.pdf (accessed April 27, 2019).

WikiLeaks. "Iraq War Logs." https://wikileaks.org/irq/ (accessed May 28, 2018).

Yoo, John. "Application of Treaties and Laws to al Qaeda and Taliban Detainees" (U.S. Department of Justice, Office of Legal Counsel, January 9, 2002).

While not a governmental document per se, the following book is an excellent compendium to the torture memos issued under the Bush Administration, together with commentary.

Cole, David. *The Torture Memos* (New York: The New Press, 2009).

Similarly, The New York Times *prepared an excellent concordance to the torture memos, which is useful to researchers (and which hopefully will remain online on their site for the foreseeable future).* Time *magazine has done the same with regard to the interrogation program under the Bush administration.*

Berenson, Tessa. "A Timeline of the Interrogation Program." *Time*, December 9, 2014, http://time.com/3625181/ senate-torture-report-timeline/ (accessed May 28, 2018).

The New York Times. "A Guide to the Memos on Torture." https://archive.nytimes.com/www.nytimes.com/ref/inter national/24MEMO-GUIDE.html (accessed May 26, 2018).

Nongovernmental Organizations

For our purposes, a nongovernmental organization is any organization not directly or indirectly controlled by a nation-state or governmental entity with a voluntary membership that is not engaged in armed struggle. Examples include advocacy groups like Amnesty International and Human Rights Watch.

Amnesty International. "History: More than 55 Years Protecting Human Rights." 2017, https://www.amnestyusa .org/about-us/history/ (accessed March 31, 2019).

Amnesty International. "USA 'You Don't Have Any Rights Here,'" October 2018, https://www.amnesty.org/en/latest/research/2018/10/usa-treatment-of-asylum-seekers-southern-border/ (accessed April 8, 2019)

Amnesty International UK. "Nelson Mandela and Amnesty International," July 18, 2014, https://www.amnesty.org.uk/nelson-mandela-and-amnesty-international (accessed April 8, 2014).

Amnesty International UK. "Guantánamo Bay: 14 years of injustice," January 12, 2018, https://www.amnesty.org.uk/guantanamo-bay-human-rights (accessed April 1, 2019).

Association for the Prevention of Torture, Center for Justice and International Law. "Torture in International Law: A Guide to Jurisprudence," Geneva, APT/CEJIL 2008, https://www.apt.ch/content/files_res/jurisprudenceguide.pdf (accessed October 18, 2018).

Berenson, Peter. "The Forgotten Prisoners," *The Observer*, May 28, 1961, https://www.theguardian.com/uk/1961/may/28/fromthearchive.theguardian (accessed March 31, 2019).

Center for Constitutional Rights. "Accountability for U.S. Torture: Germany," https://ccrjustice.org/home/what-we-do/our-cases/accountability-us-torture-germany (accessed April 20, 2019).

Freedom from Torture. "History," 2017, https://www.freedomfromtorture.org/about_us/history (accessed April 1, 2019).

Freedom from Torture. "Trustee's Annual Report and Financial Statements for the year ended 31 December 2017," https://www.freedomfromtorture.org/sites/default/files/documents/trustees_annual_report_and_financial_statements_2017.pdf (accessed April 1, 2019).

Human Rights Watch. "United States of America: Compliance with the Optional Protocol on Convention on the Rights of the Child on the Involvement of Children in Armed Conflict: Additional information for the

Committee on the Rights of the Child," April 15, 2008, https://www.hrw.org/legacy/pub/2008/children/FLW_CRC2.pdf (accessed May 18, 2019).

International Committee of the Red Cross. "Prisoners of War and Detainees Protected under International Humanitarian Law," October 29, 2010, https://www.icrc.org/en/doc/war-and-law/protected-persons/prisoners-war/overview-detainees-protected-persons.htm (accessed May 5, 2019).

Laing, Aislinn. "Nelson Mandela's Spear of the Nation: the ANC's Armed Resistance," *The Telegraph*, February 5, 2011, https://www.telegraph.co.uk/news/worldnews/africaandindianocean/southafrica/8304153/Nelson-Mandelas-Spear-of-the-Nation-the-ANCs-armed-resistance.html (accessed April 8, 2019).

Lionæs, Aase. "Award Ceremony Speech," *The Nobel Prize*, December 10, 1977, https://www.nobelprize.org/prizes/peace/1977/ceremony-speech/ (accessed March 31, 2019).

The Rendition Project. "Abu Zubaydah," https://www.therenditionproject.org.uk/prisoners/zubaydah.html (accessed May 27, 2018).

Townsend, Mark. "Gita Sahgal's Dispute with Amnesty International Puts Human Rights Group in the Dock." *The Observer*, April 24, 2010, https://www.theguardian.com/world/2010/apr/25/gita-sahgal-amnesty-international (accessed March 31, 2019).

Tusa, Sir John. "Mid-life Crisis for Amnesty?" British Broadcasting Corporation Radio 4, December 28, 2010, https://www.bbc.com/news/world-12022303 (accessed March 31, 2019).

Testimony from Torture Survivors

Testimony and commentary from those who have been tortured and who have lived to tell about it is vital to research in the field. While some of those stories remain inaccessible as of this writing—for example, that of the remaining detainees being held by the United States at Guantanamo Bay—ideally that too will change in the years to come. In non-biographical books where a single person's statements are emphasized, the person whose testimony is given in the citation is shown in parentheses, for example, "(Gerry Adams)."

Collins, Eamon, McGovern, Mick. *Killing Rage* (New York: Granta Books, 1997).

Coogan, Tim Pat. *The IRA* (New York: Palgrave, 2002, pp. 628–629) (Gerry Adams).

Hicks, David. *Guantanamo: My Journey* (New York: Random House, 2012).

Mandela, Nelson. *Long Walk to Freedom* (Boston: Back Bay Books, 1995).

Manning, Chelsea. Twitter post, March 8, 2019, 10:58 A.M. https://twitter.com/xychelsea/status/11040941709505 78177.

Mendez, Juan E. "Torture in Latin America," in Kenneth Roth and Minky Worden (eds.), *Torture: Does It Make Us Safer? Is It Ever OK?* (New York: The New Press, 2005, pp. 57–59) (Juan E. Mendez).

Newton, Huey. *Revolutionary Suicide* (San Diego: Harcourt Brace Jovanovich, 1973; New York: Penguin Books, 2009).

Slahi, Mohamedou Ould. *Guantánamo Diary: Restored Edition* (Boston: Back Bay Books, 2017).

Teotonio, Isabel. "'Canadians Called Me a Liar': Khadr," *The Star*, March 19, 2008, https://www.thestar.com/news/canada/2008/03/19/canadians_called_me_a_liar_khadr .html (accessed May 18, 2019) (Omar Khadr).

You Don't Like the Truth: Four Days Inside Guantanamo [DVD]. Directed by Luc Côté and Patricio Henríquez (Montréal: Films Transit International, 2010).

The Interrogators

For several reasons, there isn't a lot of public scholarship on interrogation—with or without the use of torture—from or about the perspective of interrogators or their helpers, but these do exist.

Chornik, Katia. "Music and Torture in Chilean Detention Centers: Conversations with an Ex-Agent of Pinochet's Secret Police." *The World of Music*, 2 (1): 51–65 (2013). New Series.

Collins, Eamon, and Mick McGovern. *Killing Rage* (New York: Granta Books, 1997).

Granhag, Pär Anders, Steven Kleinman, and Simon Oleszkuewicz. "The Scharff Technique: On How to Effectively Elicit Intelligence from Human Sources." *International Journal of Intelligence and CounterIntelligence* 29 (1): 135 (2016).

Mackey, Chris, and Greg Miller. *The Interrogators: Task Force 500 and America's Secret War against Al Qaeda* (Boston: Back Bay Books, 2005).

PBS Newshour. "Convicted Former CIA Contractor Speaks Out about Prisoner Interrogation," April 20, 2015, https://www.pbs.org/newshour/show/convicted-former-cia-contractor-speaks-prisoner-interrogation (accessed May 19, 2019).

Rieff, David. "The Bureaucrat of Torture." *World Policy Journal* 19 (1): 105 (2002).

Toliver, Raymond F. *The Interrogator: The Story of Hanns Joachim Scharff, Master Interrogator of the Luftwaffe* (Atglen, PA: Schiffer Publishing, 1997).

Wahl, Rachel. "Justice, Context, and Violence: Law Enforcement Officers on Why They Torture." *Law & Society Review* 48 (4): 807 (2014).

Wilber, Del Quintin. "FBI Gets an Unexpected Lesson from a Former Interrogator for The Nazis." *Los Angeles Times*, June 10, 2016, http://www.latimes.com/nation/

la-na-fbi-nazi-interrogator-20160610-snap-story.html
(accessed May 6, 2018).

Winkler, Gary S. *Tortured: Lynndie England, Abu Ghraib and the Photographs that Shocked the World* (Santa Fe, NM: Bad Apple Books, 2009).

Torture in the United States and Canada

This section focuses on the use of torture within the continental United States (including Alaska and Hawaii) and Canada and not on the use of torture by American or Canadian forces or agents on U.S. military bases or black sites abroad.

Baram, Marcus. "WikiLeaks' Iraq War Logs: U.S. Troops Abused Prisoners for Years After Abu Ghraib." *Huffington Post*, October 22, 2010, https://www.huffingtonpost.com/2010/10/22/wikileaks-iraq-war-logs-i_n_772658.html, accessed May 28, 2018.

Becker, Steven W. "When Judges Judge Themselves: The Chicago Police Torture Scandal and the Continuing Quest for Justice in the Case of People V. Keith Walker." *DePaul Journal for Social Justice* 3 (2): 115–137 (2010).

Bélanger, Claude. "Readings in Quebec History: October Crisis," August 23, 2000, http://faculty.marianopolis.edu/c.belanger/quebechistory/readings/october.htm (accessed January 27, 2019).

Bélanger, Claude. "Chronology of the October Crisis, 1970, and Its Aftermath," August 23, 2000, http://faculty.marianopolis.edu/c.belanger/quebechistory/chronos/october.htm (accessed January 27, 2019).

Bloche, M. Gregg. "Toward a Science of Torture?" *Texas Law Review* 95 (6): 1329–1355 (2017).

Boyd, Nan Alamilla. *Wide Open Town: A History of Queer San Francisco to 1965* (University of California Press, 2003).

Browne, Christopher G. "Tortured Prosecuting: Closing the Gap in Virginia's Criminal Code by Adding a Torture Statute." *William and Mary Law Review*, 1: 269 (2014).

Canadian Broadcasting Corporation. "The October Crisis: October 1970: The FLQ, the Kidnappings and the Response," October 4, 2010, https://www.cbc.ca/news/canada/the-october-crisis-1.973762.

Canadian Broadcasting Corporation. "'Just Watch Me,' Pierre Trudeau and the October Crisis," June 21, 2018, https://www.cbc.ca/archives/just-watch-me-pierre-trudeau-and-the-october-crisis-1.4676740 (accessed November 10, 2019).

Canadian Broadcasting Corporation. "The October Crisis," 2001, https://www.cbc.ca/history/episcontentse1ep16 ch1pa4le.html (accessed January 27, 2019).

Davis, Kevin. "Under Questioning: The Chicago Police Legacy of Extracting False Confessions Is Costing the City Millions." *ABA Journal*, July 2018, http://www.abajournal .com/magazine/article/chicago_police_false_confessions (accessed January 20, 2019).

Del Rosso, Jared. "The Toxicity of Torture: The Cultural Structure of US Political Discourse of Waterboarding." *Social Forces* 93 (1): 383.

DiEdoardo, Christina Ann Marie. *Lanza's Mob: The Mafia and San Francisco* (Santa Barbara, CA: ABC-CLIO, 2016).

DiEdoardo, Christina A. "Resist: 'We Got This,'" *Bay Area Reporter*, November 16, 2017, pp. 9–10.

Dubin, Krista, Andrew R. Milewski, Joseph Shin, and Thomas P. Kalman. "Medical Students' Attitudes toward Torture, Revisited." *Health And Human Rights* 19 (2): 265–277 (2017).

Eisenhower, William D. "Torture in the Naked Public Square." *Ethics & Behavior* 27 (5): 423–435 (2017).

Front de libération du Québec. "FLQ Manifesto 1970." Damien Claude Bélanger, ed. http://faculty.marianopolis .edu/c.belanger/quebechistory/docs/october/documents/ FLQManifesto.pdf (accessed January 26, 2019).

Green, Carla. "Transgender Honduran Woman's Death in US 'Ice Box' Detention Prompts Outcry," *The Guardian*,

May 31, 2018, https://www.theguardian.com/us-news/2018/may/31/roxana-hernandez-transgender-honduran-woman-dies-us-ice-box (accessed March 11, 2019).

Ha, Tu Thanh. "Jacques Cinq-Mars Was a Tough, Rule-Bending Montreal Police Captain," *The Globe and Mail*, December 1, 2016, updated April 10, 2017, https://www.theglobeandmail.com/news/national/jacques-cinq-mars-was-a-tough-rule-bending-montreal-police-captain/article33130058/ (accessed January 27, 2019).

Jenkins, David. "Rethinking Suresh: Refoulement to Torture under Canada's Charter of Rights and Freedoms." *Alberta Law Review* 47 (1): 125–160 (2009).

Jowanna, Matthew J. "Torture, American Style: A Recipe for Civil Tort Immunity." *McGeorge Law Review* 42 (2): 243–295.

Kappeler, Victor E. "A Brief History of Slavery and the Origins of American Policing," http://plsonline.eku.edu/insidelook/brief-history-slavery-and-origins-american-policing (accessed May 1, 2018).

Kerness, Bonnie. "Torture in U.S. Prisons." *Peace Review* 23 (3): 364–368 (2011).

Lawler, Orpheli Garcia. "What Happened to Roxana Hernández, the Trans Woman Who Died in ICE Custody?" *New York Magazine: The Cut*, December 5, 2018, https://www.thecut.com/2018/12/roxana-hernndez-a-transgender-woman-died-in-ice-custody.html.

Leo, Richard A. *Police Interrogation and American Justice* (Harvard University Press, 2008).

Lowell, A. Lawrence. "The Judicial Use of Torture." *Harvard Law Review* 11 (4): 220–233 (1897).

Lowth, Mary. "Does Torture Work? Donald Trump and the CIA." *The British Journal of General Practice: The Journal of the Royal College of General Practitioners* 67 (656): 126 (2017).

Moreau, Julie. "LGBTQ Migrants 97 Times More Likely to Be Sexually Assaulted in Detention, Report Says," NBC News, June 6, 2018, https://www.nbcnews.com/feature/nbc-out/lgbtq-migrants-97-times-more-likely-be-sexually-assaulted-detention-n880101 (accessed March 11, 2019).

The New York Times. "To Abolish the Third Degree," July 6, 1902.

The New York Times. "Yes, Declaim against Torture," December 15, 1984.

The New York Times. "A Master Terrorist Is Nabbed," April 6, 2002.

The New York Times. "No Penalty for Torture," September 5, 2012.

Pertiz, Ingrid. "October Crisis Hit Unknowns The Hardest," *The Globe and Mail*, October 16, 2000, updated April 7, 2018, https://www.theglobeandmail.com/news/national/october-crisis-hit-unknowns-the-hardest/article1042856/ (accessed January 26, 2019).

Pilkington, Ed. "Bradley Manning's Treatment Was Cruel and Inhuman, UN Torture Chief Rules," *The Guardian*, March 12, 2012, https://www.theguardian.com/world/2012/mar/12/bradley-manning-cruel-inhuman-treatment-un (accessed May 28, 2018).

Pilkington, Ed. "Bradley Manning Verdict: Cleared of 'Aiding the Enemy' but Guilty of Other Charges," *The Guardian*, July 31, 2013, https://www.theguardian.com/world/2013/jul/30/bradley-manning-wikileaks-judge-verdict (accessed May 28, 2018).

Pilkington, Ed, David Smith, and Lauren Gambino. "Chelsea Manning's Prison Sentence Commuted by Barack Obama," *The Guardian*, January 18, 2017, https://www.theguardian.com/us-news/2017/jan/17/chelsea-manning-sentence-commuted-barack-obama (accessed May 28, 2018).

Raz, Mical. "Alone Again: John Zubek and the Troubled History of Sensory Deprivation Research." *Journal of the History of the Behavioral Sciences*, 49 (4): 379–395 (Autumn, Fall 2013).

Riebman, Elliott. "How and Why a Code of Silence between State's Attorneys and Police Officers Resulted in Unprosecuted Torture." *DePaul Journal for Social Justice* 9 (2): 1–30 (2016).

Seligman, Scott D. *The Third Degree: The Triple Murder That Shook Washington and Changed American Criminal Justice* (University of Nebraska Press, 2018).

Seville, Lisa Riordan, Hannah Rappleye, and Andrew W. Lehren. "22 Immigrants Died in ICE Detention Centers During the Past 2 Years," *NBC News*, January 6, 2019, https://www.nbcnews.com/politics/immigration/22-immigrants-died-ice-detention-centers-during-past-2-years-n954781 (accessed March 11, 2019).

Sobol, Rosemary, Jeremy Gorner, and David Heinzmann. "Disgraced ex-Chicago Police Cmdr. Jon Burge, Accused of Presiding over Decades of Brutality and Torture, Has Died," *Chicago Tribune*, September 19, 2018, https://www.chicagotribune.com/news/local/breaking/ct-met-jon-burge-dead-20180919-story.html (accessed January 20, 2019).

St. Vincent, Sarah H. "Coercion's Common Threads: Addressing Vagueness in the Federal Criminal Prohibitions on Torture by Looking to State Domestic Violence Laws." *Michigan Law Review* 109 (5): 813 (March 2011).

Stuart, Tessa. "Trump's Family Separation Policy Was Exponentially Worse than Previously Known," *Rolling Stone*, January 17, 2019, https://www.rollingstone.com/politics/politics-news/family-separation-thousands-779254/ (accessed March 10, 2019).

Stueck, Adam. "A Place under Heaven: Amerindian Torture and Cultural Violence in Colonial New France, 1609–1729." *Dissertations* (2009–), 2012, Paper 174, http://epublications.marquette.edu/dissertations_mu/174 (accessed June 7, 2019).

Tate, Julie. "Bradley Manning Sentenced to 35 years in WikiLeaks Case," *The Washington Post*, August 21, 2013, https://www.washingtonpost.com/world/national-security/judge-to-sentence-bradley-manning-today/2013/08/20/85bee184-09d0-11e3-b87c-476db8ac34cd_story.html (accessed May 28, 2018).

Tate, Julie, and Ellen Nakashima. "Judge Refuses to Dismiss Charges against WikiLeaks Suspect Bradley Manning," *The Washington Post*, January 8, 2013, https://www.washingtonpost.com/world/national-security/judge-refuses-to-dismiss-charges-against-wikileaks-suspect-bradley-manning/2013/01/08/2eab1f62-59cb-11e2-beee-6e38f5215402_story.html (accessed May 28, 2018).

Voreh, Erika. "The United States' Convention against Torture RUDS: Allowing the Use of Solitary Confinement in Lieu of Mental Health Treatment in U.S. Immigration Detention Centers." *Emory International Law Review* 33 (2): 287–310 (January 2019).

Watkins, John Elfreth. "Charges of the THIRD DEGREE Ordeal," *San Francisco Chronicle*, October 16, 1910.

Wisnewski, J. Jeremy. "Unwarranted Torture Warrants: A Critique of the Dershowitz Proposal." *Journal of Social Philosophy* 39 (2): 308–321 (2008).

Wright, Robert. *Trudeaumania: The Rise to Power of Pierre Elliott Trudeau* (Toronto: HarperCollins, 2016).

Torture by United States and Canadian Personnel Abroad (or with Their Cooperation)

This section focuses on the use of torture by American or Canadian forces or agents on U.S. military bases or black sites abroad.

Alexander, Janet Cooper. "John Yoo's War Powers: The Law Review and the World." *California Law Review* 100 (2): 331–364 (April 2012).

Alkadry, Mohamad G., and Matthew T. Witt. "Abu Ghraib and the Normalization of Torture and Hate." *Public Integrity* 11 (2): 135–53 (2009).

Baksh, Nazim, and Terrence McKenna. "Documents Show CSIS and RCMP's Role in Post-9/11 Torture of 3 Canadians in Syria," *CBC News*, September 19, 2016, https://www.cbc.ca/news/canada/terrorism-torture-syria-canadians-1.3669425 (accessed on June 10, 2019).

Bassiouni, M. Cherif. "The Institutionalization of Torture under the Bush Administration." *Case Western Reserve Journal of International Law* 37 (2/3): 389 (2006).

Berenson, Tessa. "A Timeline of the Interrogation Program," *Time*, December 9, 2014, http://time.com/3625181/senate-torture-report-timeline/ (accessed May 28, 2018).

Black, Crofton, and Sam Raphael. "Revealed: The Boom and Bust of the CIA's Secret Torture Sites," *The Bureau of Investigative Journalism*, October 14, 2015, https://www.thebureauinvestigates.com/stories/2015-10-14/revealed-the-boom-and-bust-of-the-cias-secret-torture-sites (accessed May 27, 2018).

Boehm, Dana Carver. "Waterboarding, Counter-Resistance, and the Law of Torture: Articulating the Legal Underpinnings of U.S. Interrogation Policy." *University of Toledo Law Review* 41 (1): 1–41 (2009).

Braw, Elisabeth. "Donald Rumsfeld: Being Waterboarded Is Better Than Being Killed by a Drone," *Huffington Post*, August 1, 2011, https://www.huffpost.com/entry/donald-rumsfeld_b_869534 (accessed May 2, 2019).

British Broadcasting Corporation. "Bush Admits to CIA Secret Prisons," September 7, 2006, http://news.bbc.co.uk/2/hi/5321606.stm (accessed May 28, 2018).

British Broadcasting Corporation. "Poland 'Helped in CIA Rendition,' European Court Rules," July 24, 2014, http://www.bbc.com/news/world-europe-28460628 (accessed May 27, 2018).

British Broadcasting Corporation. "Lithuania and Romania Complicit in CIA Torture—European Court," May 31, 2018, http://www.bbc.com/news/world-europe-44313905 (accessed May 31, 2018).

British Broadcasting Corporation. "Chelsea Manning: Wikileaks Source Jailed for Refusing to Testify," March 8, 2019, https://www.bbc.com/news/world-us-canada-47501763 (accessed March 10, 2019).

Bruck, Connie. "Why Obama Has Failed to Close Guantánamo," *The New Yorker*, August 1, 2016, https://www.newyorker.com/magazine/2016/08/01/why-obama-has-failed-to-close-guantanamo (accessed May 28, 2018).

Campion-Smith, Bruce. "Canada Will Use Intelligence Gained through Torture if It Will Save Lives," *The Star*, September 25, 2017, https://www.thestar.com/news/canada/2017/09/25/canada-will-use-intelligence-gained-through-torture-if-it-will-save-lives.html (accessed June 10, 2019).

Caplan, Gerald. "How Can Canada Condone Torture?" *The Globe and Mail*, November 24, 2016, https://www.theglobeandmail.com/news/politics/how-can-canada-condone-torture/article33018131/ (accessed June 10, 2019).

Carvin, Stephanie. "Yes, Sleep Deprivation Is Torture," *Maclean's*, July 14, 2017, https://www.macleans.ca/opinion/yes-sleep-deprivation-is-torture/ (accessed May 18, 2019).

Dao, James. "The Reach of War: An Accused; A Man of Violence, or Just '110 Percent' Gung-Ho?" *The New York Times*, June 19, 2004, https://www.nytimes.com/2004/06/19/world/the-reach-of-war-an-accused-a-man-of-violence-or-just-110-percent-gung-ho.html (accessed May 19, 2019).

Davis, Marsha, director. *Doctors of the Dark Side* [film]. (Soundview Media Partners, 2011).

Einolf, Christopher J. "The Fall and Rise of Torture: A Comparative and Historical Analysis." *Sociological Theory* 25 (2): 101–121 (2007).

Engelberg, Stephen. "Correction: Trump's Pick to Head CIA Did Not Oversee Waterboarding of Abu Zubaydah," *ProPublica*, March 15, 2018, https://www.propublica.org/article/cia-cables-detail-its-new-deputy-directors-role-in-torture (accessed May 19, 2019).

Golden, Tim. "A Junior Aide Had a Big Role In Terror Policy," *The New York Times*, December 23, 2005, https://www.nytimes.com/2005/12/23/politics/a-junior-aide-had-a-big-rolein-terror-policy.html (accessed April 20, 2019).

Gordon, Leslie A. "Unknown Knowns: Torture Lawsuits against Rumsfeld May Revive a 40-Year-Old Liability Case." *ABA Journal* 98 (2): 13 (2012).

Grindler, Gary G. "Acting Deputy Attorney General Gary G. Grindler on the OPR Investigation into OLC Memoranda," U.S. Department of Justice, February 26, 2010, https://www.justice.gov/opa/speech/acting-deputy-attorney-general-gary-g-grindler-opr-investigation-olc-memoranda (accessed April 20, 2019).

Hajjar, Lisa. "CIA: Kubark's Very Long Shadow," *Al Jazeera*, August 6, 2012, https://www.aljazeera.com/indepth/opinion/2012/08/201285121033592843.html (accessed May 19, 2018).

Hagan, John, Gabrielle Ferrales, and Guillermina Jasso. "Collaboration and Resistance in the Punishment of Torture in Iraq: A Judicial Sentencing Experiment." *Wisconsin International Law Journal* 28 (1): 1–38 (2010).

Hall, Amy Laura. "Torture and Television in the United States." *Muslim World* 103 (2): 267–286 (April 2013).

Hamilton, Keegan. "This Is How Trump's Pick for CIA Director Used to Torture Black Site Detainees," March 13,

2018, *VICE News*, https://news.vice.com/en_us/article/
vbp98d/this-is-how-trumps-pick-for-cia-director-used-to-
torture-black-site-detainees (accessed May 19, 2019).

Hersh, Seymour. "Torture at Abu Ghraib: American Soldiers
Brutalized Iraqis. How Far Up Does the Responsibility
Go?" *The New Yorker*, April 30, 2004, https://www.new
yorker.com/magazine/2004/05/10/torture-at-abu-ghraib
(accessed April 28, 2019).

Hersh, Seymour. "The General's Report: How Antonio
Taguba, Who Investigated the Abu Ghraib Scandal,
Became One of Its Casualties," *The New Yorker*, June 18,
2007, https://www.newyorker.com/magazine/2007/06/25/
the-generals-report (accessed April 28, 2019).

Hodgson, Godfrey. "The U.S.-European Torture Dispute: An
Autopsy." *World Policy Journal* 22 (4): 7 (2005).

Irvine, David R. "LDS Lawyers, Psychologists Had a Hand in
Torture Policies," *The Salt Lake Tribune*, April 29, 2009,
https://web.archive.org/web/20120301090557/http://www.
sltrib.com/opinion/ci_12256286 (accessed April 30, 2019).

Isikoff, Michael. "Memos Reveal War Crimes Warnings,"
Newsweek, May 16, 2004, https://www.newsweek.com/
memos-reveal-war-crimes-warnings-128415 (accessed
April 20, 2019).

Jindia, Shilpa. "Secret Surveillance and the Legacy of
Torture Have Paralyzed the USS Cole Bombing Trial
at Guantanamo," *The Intercept*, March 5, 2018, https://
theintercept.com/2018/03/05/guantanamo-trials-abd-al-
rahim-al-nashiri/ (accessed May 27, 2018).

Johnson, Eric. "Abu Ghraib Abuse Ringleader Graner
Released from Prison," *Reuters*, August 6, 2011, https://
www.reuters.com/article/us-prisoner-abughraib/abu-
ghraib-abuse-ringleader-graner-released-from-prison-
idUSTRE7752GS20110806 (accessed April 28, 2019).

Kiriakou, John. "I Went to Prison for Disclosing the CIA's
Torture. Gina Haspel Helped Cover It Up," March 16, 2018,

The Washington Post, https://www.washingtonpost.com/ outlook/i-went-to-prison-for-disclosing-the-cias-torture-gina-haspel-helped-cover-it-up/2018/03/15/9507884e-27f8-11e8-874b-d517e912f125_story.html (accessed May 19, 2019).

Kramer, Paul. "The Water Cure: Debating Torture and Counterinsurgency—A Century Ago," *The New Yorker*, February 17, 2008, https://www.newyorker.com/magazine/ 2008/02/25/the-water-cure (accessed June 22, 2019).

Lazreg, Marnia, and Eric Weitz. *Torture and the Twilight of Empire: From Algiers to Baghdad* (Princeton University Press, 2008).

Mayer, Andre. "CIA Torture Report: Why Canada Can't Claim Innocence," December 10, 2014, *CBC News,* https://www .cbc.ca/news/cia-torture-report-why-canada-can-t-claim-innocence-1.2867716 (accessed June 10, 2019).

Mayer, Jane. "The Memo: How an Internal Effort to Ban the Abuse and Torture of Detainees Was Thwarted," *The New Yorker*, February 19, 2006, https://www.newyorker.com/ magazine/2006/02/27/the-memo (accessed May 22, 2019).

McChesney, John. "The Death of an Iraqi Prisoner," *National Public Radio*, October 27, 2005, https://www.npr.org/ templates/story/story.php?storyId=4977986, accessed May 27, 2018.

Mora, Alberto J. "Torturing Democracy" [Interview], September 17, 2007, https://nsarchive2.gwu.edu/torturin gdemocracy/interviews/alberto_mora.html#initialreports (accessed May 22, 2019).

The New York Times. "A Master Terrorist Is Nabbed," April 6, 2002, p. A14.

Owens, Patricia. "Torture, Sex and Military Orientalism." *Third World Quarterly* 31 (7): 1041 (2010).

Peralta, Eyder. "'Torture Report': A Closer Look at When and What President Bush Knew," *National Public Radio*, December 16, 2014, https://www.npr.org/sections/thetwo-way/2014/12/16/369876047/torture-report-a-closer-look-at-when-and-what-president-bush-knew (accessed May 25, 2018).

Phillips, Kristine. "Duterte Keeps Lashing Out at the United States—Over Its Atrocities a Century Ago." *The Washington Post*, July 24, 2017, https://www.washingtonpost.com/news/worldviews/wp/2017/07/24/philippiness-duterte-keeps-lashing-out-at-the-united-states-over-its-atrocities-a-century-ago/ (accessed November 24, 2019)

Pilkington, Ed. "Guantánamo Detainee to Testify on 'Unspeakable Torture' by CIA Agents," *The Guardian*, May 10, 2017, https://www.theguardian.com/us-news/2017/may/10/guantanamo-detainee-abu-zubaydah-cia-torture-hearing (accessed May 27, 2018).

Pitzke, Marc. "Outrage, Applause, Indifference: US Reacts to WikiLeaks Iraq Documents," *Spiegel Online*, October 23, 2010, http://www.spiegel.de/international/world/outrage-applause-indifference-us-reacts-to-wikileaks-iraq-documents-a-724974.html (accessed May 28, 2018).

Priest, Dana. "CIA Holds Terror Suspects in Secret Prisons," *Washington Post*, November 2, 2005, http://www.washingtonpost.com/wp-dyn/content/article/2005/11/01/AR2005110101644.html (accessed May 28, 2018).

Ralph, Talia. "Lynndie England, Abu Ghraib Soldier, Still Not Sorry," *Global Post/PRI*, March 19, 2012, https://www.pri.org/stories/2012-03-19/lynndie-england-abu-ghraib-soldier-still-not-sorry (accessed April 28, 2019).

Scott, Shane, and Mark Mazzetti. "Senate Panel Report Links Top Bush Administration Officials to Abuse of Detainees," *The New York Times*, December 12, 2008.

Shaw, Christopher. "The International Proscription against Torture and the United States' Categorical and Qualified Responses." *Boston College International & Comparative Law Review* 32 (2): 289–303 (2009).

Shephard, Michelle. *Guantanamo's Child: The Untold Story of Omar Khadr* (John Wiley & Sons Canada, 2008).

Shephard, Michelle. "Omar Khadr Repatriated to Canada," *The Star*, September 29, 2012, https://web.archive.org/web/20121001214723/http://www.thestar.com/news/article/1264337--omar-khadr-repatriated-to-canada (accessed May 18, 2019).

Shephard, Michelle. "Omar Khadr: No Memory of Firefight in Afghanistan." *The Star*, December 13, 2013, https://web.archive.org/web/20170820173141/https://www.thestar.com/news/canada/2013/12/13/omar_khadr_no_memory_of_firefight_in_afghanistan.html (accessed May 18, 2019).

Singh, Bilveer. *The Talibanization of Southeast Asia: Losing the War on Terror to Islamist Extremists* (Westport, CT: Praeger Security International, 2007).

Slater, Jerome. "Tragic Choices in the War on Terrorism: Should We Try to Regulate and Control Torture?" *Political Science Quarterly (Academy of Political Science)* 121 (2) (2006).

Smith, D. H. "American Atrocities in the Philippines: Some New Evidence." *Pacific Historical Review* 55 (2): 281–283 (1986).

Soldz, Stephen. "Fighting Torture and Psychologist Complicity." *Peace Review* 23 (1): 12–20 (2011).

The Star. "The Bail Conditions Omar Khadr Must Now Live By," May 7, 2015, https://web.archive.org/web/20171007115813/https://www.thestar.com/news/canada/2015/05/07/the-rules-khadr-must-live-by-if-he-gets-bail-today.html (accessed May 18, 2019).

Taddonio, Patrice. "CIA Director Nominee Supported Destruction of Torture Tapes," *PBS Frontline*, May 9, 2018, https://www.pbs.org/wgbh/frontline/article/cia-director-nominee-supported-destruction-of-torture-tapes/ (accessed May 19, 2019).

Tasker, John Paul. "Liberal Government Formally Apologizes to Omar Khadr," *CBC News*, https://web.archive.org/web/20170707164953/http://www.cbc.ca/news/politics/cabinet-explain-omar-khadr-settlement-1.4194467 (accessed May 18, 2019).

Teotonio, Isabel. "Canadians Called Me a 'Liar': Khadr." *The Star*, March 19, 2008, https://www.thestar.com/news/canada/2008/03/19/canadians_called_me_a_liar_khadr.html (accessed May 18, 2019).

Thompson, Estes. "Ex-CIA Contractor on Trial in Beating," *The Washington Post*, August 7, 2006, https://web.archive.org/web/20181003100216/http://www.washingtonpost.com/wp-dyn/content/article/2006/08/07/AR2006080700877.html (accessed May 19, 2019).

Toosi, Nahal. "Trump Taps former 'Black Site' Prison Operator for CIA Deputy," *Politico*, February 2, 2017, https://www.politico.com/story/2017/02/trump-cia-black-sites-gina-haspel-234565 (accessed May 19, 2019).

Waldron, Jeremy. "Torture and Positive Law: Jurisprudence for the White House." *Columbia Law Review* 105 (6): 1681 (2005).

Webster, Paul. "Canadian Soldiers and Doctors Face Torture Allegations," *The Lancet*, April 28, 2007, https://www.thelancet.com/pdfs/journals/lancet/PIIS0140673607606515.pdf (accessed June 10, 2019).

Welch, Richard. "American Atrocities in the Philippines: The Indictment and the Response." *Pacific Historical Review* 43 (2): 233 (1974). doi:10.2307/3637551.

Wills, Matthew. "The Ugly Origins of America's Involvement in the Philippines," *JSTOR Daily*, May 10, 2017, https://daily.jstor.org/the-ugly-origins-of-americas-involvement-in-the-philippines/ (accessed June 22, 2019).

Youssef, Nancy. "CIA Fills In Some Blanks on Gina Haspel's Secret Life," *The Wall Street Journal*, March 22, 2018, https://archive.fo/20180322191408/https://www.wsj.com/articles/cia-fills-in-some-blanks-on-gina-haspels-secret-life-1521745324#selection-2083.0-2083.53 (accessed May 19, 2019).

Torture in Europe, Africa, and Asia

This section focuses on the use of torture within Europe, Africa, and Asia.

Amnesty International. *Torture in Greece: The First Torturers' Trial 1975* (Amnesty International Publications, 1977).

Ansgar Kelly, Henry. "Judicial Torture in Canon Law and Church Tribunals: From Gratian to Galileo." *Catholic Historical Review* 101 (4): 754 (2015).

Aptekar, Pavel. "How the Cheka Turned into the FSB," *Vedomosti*, December 20, 2017, https://www.vedomosti.ru/opinion/articles/2017/12/20/745861-vchk-fsb (Orig. in Russian) (accessed May 5, 2019).

Archdiocese of Baltimore. "The Inquisition and Index: Vatican Records Shed Light on Dark Legend," January 19, 2012, https://www.archbalt.org/the-inquisition-and-index-vatican-records-shed-light-on-dark-legend/ (accessed April 10, 2019).

Bishop, Jordan. "Aquinas on Torture." *New Blackfriars* 87 (1009): 229–237 (2006).

Cahill, Carmen. *Bad Faith: A Forgotten History of Family, Fatherland and Vichy France* (New York: Alfred A. Knopf, 2006).

Central Intelligence Agency. "Communist Control Techniques: An Analysis of the Methods Used by Communist State Police in the Arrest, Interrogation and Indoctrination of Persons Regarded as 'Enemies of the State,'" 25X1A8a, April 2, 1956, Secret, Approved for release September 26, 2000.

Cobain, Ian, and Ewen MacAskill. "True Scale of UK Role in Torture and Rendition after 9/11 Revealed," *The Guardian*, June 28, 2018, https://www.theguardian.com/uk-news/2018/jun/28/uk-role-torture-kidnap-terror-suspects-after-911-revealed (accessed June 10, 2019).

Collins, Eamon, and Mick McGovern. *Killing Rage* (New York: Granta Books, 1997).

Conant, Lisa. "Who Files Suit? Legal Mobilization and Torture Violations in Europe." *Law & Policy* 38 (4): 280–303 (2016).

Coogan, Tim Pat. *The IRA* (New York: Palgrave, 2002).

Donadio, Rachel. "Italy Convicts 23 Americans for C.I.A. Renditions," *The New York Times*, November 4, 2009, https://www.nytimes.com/2009/11/05/world/europe/05italy.html (accessed October 14, 2018).

Elliott, Mark. "Torture, Deportation and Extra-Judicial Detention: Instruments of the 'War on Terror.'" *Cambridge Law Journal* 68 (2): 245–48 (2009).

"The FLQ Situation," 1970–10–15, RG2, Privy Council Office, Series A-5-a, Volume 6359 Access Code: 90, http://central.bac-lac.gc.ca/.redirect?app=cabcon&id=137&lang=eng (accessed January 26, 2019).

Forje, Gima H. "Combating Torture in Africa: A Cal on Governments and Civil Society." *International Journal on World Peace* 26 (3): 97–101 (2009).

Gagarin, Michael. "The Torture of Slaves in Athenian Law." *Classical Philology* 91 (1): 1–18 (1996).

Gaskarth, Jami. "Entangling Alliances? The UK's Complicity in Torture in the Global War on Terrorism." *International Affairs* 87 (4): 945–964 (2011).

Gasper, Brandie. "Examining the Use of Evidence Obtained under Torture: The Case of the British Detainees May Test the Resolve of the European Convention in the Era of Terrorism." *American University International Law Review* 21 (2): 277–325 (2006).

Ginger, Henry. "Greece, Facing Expulsion, Quits Council of Europe." *The New York Times*, December 13, 1969, p. 1.

Honoré, Tony. *Ulpian: Pioneer of Human Rights*, 2nd ed. (Oxford University Press, 1982, 2002).

Lauchlan, Iain. "Young Felix Dzerzhinsky and the Origins of Stalinism," in Markku Kangaspuro and Vesa Oittinen (eds.), *Essays on Stalinism* (Helsinki: Kikimora Press, 2013), https://www.ed.ac.uk/files/imports/fileManager/wp-iain-lauchlan-YoungFelix.pdf (accessed May 5, 2019).

Lazreg, Marnia, and Eric Weitz. *Torture and the Twilight of Empire: From Algiers to Baghdad* (Princeton University Press, 2008).

Léglu, Catherine, Rebecca Rist, and Claire Taylor. *The Cathars and the Albigensian Crusade: A Sourcebook* (New York: Routledge, 2014).

Luhn, Alec. "Putin Salutes Russia's Intelligence Agencies on National 'Spies' Day,'" *The Guardian*, December 20, 2015, https://www.theguardian.com/world/2015/dec/20/putin-salutes-russias-intelligence-agencies-on-national-spies-day (accessed May 5, 2019).

McAuley, James. "France's Macron Admits to Military's Systematic Use of Torture in Algeria," *The Washington Post*, September 13, 2018, https://www.washingtonpost.com/world/europe/frances-macron-admits-to-militarys-systematic-use-of-torture-in-algeria-war/2018/09/13/6b0e85cc-b729-11e8-94eb-3bd52dfe917b_story.html (accessed October 18, 2018).

McDonald, Henry. "Gerry Adams Appeals 1975 Convictions for Maze Escape Attempts," *The Guardian*, January 16, 2018, https://www.theguardian.com/politics/2018/jan/16/gerry-adams-appeals-1975-convictions-for-escape-from-maze-prison (accessed April 28, 2019).

McQuigg, Ronagh. "How Effective Is the United Nations Committee against Torture?" *European Journal of International Law* 22 (3): 813–828 (2011).

Menéndez, Agustín José. "Torture through Rendition in Europe: A Past That Will Not Pass Away." *European Law Journal* 24 (2/3): 118–123 (2018).

Muldoon, James. *Popes, Lawyers and Infidels* (University of Pennsylvania Press, 1979).

Peters, Edward. *Torture* (University of Pennsylvania Press, 1985, 1999).

Polina, Levina. "Links between Criminal Justice Procedure and Torture: Learning from Russia." *New Criminal Law Review: An International and Interdisciplinary Journal* 16 (1): 104 (2013).

Reis, Mary Robert. "Pope Innocent IV and Church-State Relations, 1243–1254," Dissertations, Paper 1224, Loyola University Chicago (1972), http://ecommons.luc.edu/luc_diss/1224 (accessed April 9, 2019).

Skillbeck, Rupert. "The UK Is 'Getting Worse' on Torture and Ill-Treatment Both at Home and Abroad," OpenDemocracyUK, May 7, 2019, https://www.opendemocracy.net/en/opendemocracyuk/uk-getting-worse-torture-and-ill-treatment-both-home-and-abroad/

Stanley, Alexandra. "Vatican Is Investigating the Inquisition, in Secret," *The New York Times*, October 31, 1998, https://www.nytimes.com/1998/10/31/world/vatican-is-investigating-the-inquisition-in-secret.html (accessed April 10, 2019).

Stevenson, William. *A Man Called Intrepid*, 8th ed. (New York: Ballentine Books, 1978).

Sullivan, Andrew. "Verschärfte Vernehmung," *The Atlantic*, May 29, 2007, https://www.theatlantic.com/daily-dish/archive/2007/05/-versch-auml-rfte-vernehmung/228158/ (accessed May 4, 2018).

Tanner, Murray Scot. "Shackling the Coercive State." *Problems of Post-Communism* 47 (5): 13 (2000).

Tetley, William. "The October Crisis: Appendix D," *Canada's Human Rights History*, https://historyofrights.ca/wp-content/uploads/documents/FLQ_appendixd.pdf (accessed January 27, 2019).

Tetley, William. "The October Crisis: Appendix E," *Canada's Human Rights History*, https://historyofrights.ca/wp-content/uploads/documents/FLQ_appendixe.pdf (accessed January 27, 2019).

U.S. Holocaust Museum. "Forced Sterilization," https://www.ushmm.org/learn/students/learning-materials-and-resources/mentally-and-physically-handicapped-victims-of-the-nazi-era/forced-sterilization (accessed May 4, 2018).

Vargo, Marc E. *Women of the Resistance: Eight Who Defied the Third Reich* (Jefferson, NC: McFarland & Company, 2012).

Studies on Torture

These sources review the research on torture by academics in the field.

Ames, David R., and Alice J. Lee. "Tortured Beliefs: How and When Prior Support for Torture Skews the Perceived Value of Coerced Information." *Journal of Experimental Social Psychology* 60: 86–92 (September 2015).

Beaudoin, Cynthia H. "Torture: Paradigms, Practices, and Policies." *Albany Law Review* 67 (2): 331–334 (2003).

Boulanger, Ghislaine. "The American Psychological Association: From Impunity to Shame." *International*

Journal of Applied Psychoanalytic Studies 14 (2): 108–115 (2017).

Choi, Hyunjung, Hoon-Jin Lee, and Hwa-Young Lee. "The Effects of Torture-Related Stressors on Long-Term Complex Post-Traumatic Symptoms in South Korean Torture Survivors." *International Journal of Psychology* 52: 57–66 (December 2017).

Conrad, Courtenay R. "Divergent Incentives for Dictators: Domestic Institutions and (International Promises Not To) Torture." *The Journal of Conflict Resolution* 58 (1): 34 (2014).

Crosby, Sondra S., and Gilbert Benavidez. "From Nuremberg to Guantanamo Bay: Uses of Physicians in the War on Terror." *American Journal of Public Health* 108 (1): 36–41 (2018).

Davis, Michael. "Torture and the Inhumane." *Criminal Justice Ethics* 26 (2): 29 (2007).

Del Rosso, Jared. "The Toxicity of Torture: The Cultural Structure of US Political Discourse of Waterboarding." *Social Forces* 93 (1): 383 (2014).

Dosi, Giovanni, and Andrea Roventini. "The Irresistible Fetish of Utility Theory: From 'Pleasure and Pain' to Rationalising Torture." *Intereconomics* 51 (5): 286–287 (2016).

Duberstein, John. "Excluding Torture: A Comparison of the British and American Approaches to Evidence Obtained by Third Party Torture." *North Carolina Journal of International Law & Commercial Regulation* 32 (1): 159–193 (2006).

Franklin, James. "Evidence Gained from Torture: Wishful Thinking, Checkability, and Extreme Circumstances." *Cardozo Journal of International & Comparative Law* 17 (2): 281–90 (2009).

Gilinskiy, Yakov. "Torture by the Russian Police: An Empirical Study." *Police Practice & Research* 12 (2): 163–171 (2011).

Green, Debbie, Andrew Rasmussen, and Barry Rosenfeld. "Defining Torture: A Review of 40 Years of Health Science Research." *Journal of Traumatic Stress* 23 (4): 528–531 (2010).

Janzen, D. Bruce, Jr. "First Impressions and Last Resorts: The Plenary Power Doctrine, the Convention against Torture, and Credibility Determinations in Removal Proceedings." *Emory Law Journal* 6: 1235 (2018).

Kelly, Tobias. "The Cause of Human Rights: Doubts about Torture, Law, and Ethics at the United Nations." *The Journal of the Royal Anthropological Institute* 17 (4): 728 (2011).

Koh, Harold Hongju, and Henry Shue. "Why Torture Doesn't Work: The Neuroscience of Interrogation." *Political Psychology* 37 (5): 753–757 (2016).

Ledwidge, Frank. "The Optional Protocol to the Convention against Torture (OPCAT): A Major Step Forward in the Global Prevention of Torture." *Helsinki Monitor* 17 (1): 69–82 (2006).

Levinson, Sanford. "Slavery and the Phenomenology of Torture." *Social Research* 74 (1): 149 (2007).

Matthews, Richard. "An Empirical Critique of 'Interrogational' Torture." *Journal of Social Philosophy* 43 (4): 457–470 (2012).

Mayer, Jeremy D., and Naoru Koizumi. "Is There a Culture or Religion of Torture? International Support for Brutal Treatment of Suspected Terrorists." *Studies in Conflict & Terrorism* 40 (9): 758–771 (2017).

Michels, Moritz, and Martin Wieser. "From Hohenschönhausen to Guantanamo Bay: Psychology's Role in the Secret Services of the GDR and the United States." *Journal of the History of the Behavioral Sciences* 54 (1): 43–61 (2018).

Miles, Steven H. "Military Doctors and Deaths by Torture: When a Witness Becomes an Accessory." *The American Journal of Bioethics* 13 (5): 1–2 (2013).

Mumford, Andrew. "Minimum Force Meets Brutality: Detention, Interrogation and Torture in British Counter-Insurgency Campaigns." *Journal of Military Ethics* 11 (1): 10–25 (2012).

Rakatansky, Herbert. "Doctors and Torture." *Medicine And Health, Rhode Island* 92 (8): 286–287 (2009).

Rejali, Darius. "Modern Torture as a Civic Marker: Solving a Global Anxiety with a New Political Technology." *Journal of Human Rights* 2 (2): 153 (2003).

Reynolds, Vikki. "Doing Justice: A Witnessing Stance in Therapeutic Work alongside Survivors of Torture and Political Violence." *Studies in Meaning* 4: 157–184 (January 2010).

Said, Wadie E. "Political Asylum and Torture: A Comparative Analysis." *Third World Quarterly* 27 (5): 871 (2006).

Schoen, Sarah. "The Culture of Interrogation: Evaluating Detainees at Guantanamo Bay." *International Journal of Applied Psychoanalytic Studies* 14 (2): 133–142 (2017).

Schubert, Carla C., and Raija-Leena Punamäki. "Mental Health among Torture Survivors: Cultural Background, Refugee Status and Gender." *Nordic Journal of Psychiatry* 65 (3): 175–182 (2011).

Sharma, Mandira. "Making Laws Work: Advocacy Forum's Experiences in Prevention of Torture in Nepal." *Sur: International Journal on Human Rights* 11 (20): 200–211 (2014).

Simpson, James. "No Brainer: The Early Modern Tragedy of Torture." *Religion & Literature* 43 (3): 1–23 (2011).

Skoglund, Lena. "Diplomatic Assurances against Torture— An Effective Strategy? A Review of Jurisprudence and Examination of the Arguments." *Nordic Journal of International Law* 77 (4): 319–364 (2008).

Steinhoff, Uwe. "Torture—The Case for Dirty Harry and against Alan Dershowitz." *Journal of Applied Philosophy* 23 (3): 337–353 (2006).

Suedfeld, Peter. "Torture, Interrogation, Security, and Psychology: Absolutistic versus Complex Thinking." *Analyses of Social Issues & Public Policy* 7 (1): 55–63 (December 2007).

Sullivan, Christopher Sullivan. "The (in)Effectiveness of Torture for Combating Insurgency." *Journal of Peace Research* 51 (3): 388 (2014).

Sussman, David. "Defining Torture." *Case Western Reserve Journal of International Law* 37 (2/3): 225 (2006).

Sveaass, Nora, Felice Gaer, and Claudio Grossman. "Rehabilitation in Article 14 of the Convention against Torture and Other Cruel, Inhuman, or Degrading Treatment or Punishment." *International Lawyer* 51 (1): 1–24 (2018).

Tarrant, Mark, Nyla R. Branscombe, Ruth Warner, and Dale Weston. "Social Identity and Perceptions of Torture: It's Moral When We Do It." *Journal of Experimental Social Psychology* 48 (2): 513–518 (March 2012).

Thienel, Tobias. "The Admissibility of Evidence Obtained by Torture under International Law." *European Journal of International Law* 17 (2): 349–367 (2006).

Tindale, Christopher W. "The Logic of Torture: A Critical Examination." *Social Theory & Practice* 22 (3): 349 (1996).

Turner, Ian. "Human Rights and Antiterrorism: A Positive Legal Duty to Infringe Freedom from Torture?" *Studies in Conflict & Terrorism* 35 (11): 760–778 (2012).

Viki, G. Tendayi, Daniel Osgood, and Sabine Phillips. "Dehumanization and Self-Reported Proclivity to Torture Prisoners of War." *Journal of Experimental Social Psychology* 49 (3), 325–328 (May 2013).

Wolfendale, Jessica. "Training Torturers: A Critique of the 'Ticking Bomb' Argument." *Social Theory & Practice* 32 (2): 269 (2006).

Yemini, Moran. "Conflictual Moralities, Ethical Torture: Revisiting the Problem of 'Dirty Hands.'" *Ethical Theory and Moral Practice* 17 (1): 163 (2014).

Treaties and UN Resolutions

While the effect of a treaty is largely dependent on whether or not it has an enforcement mechanism, its language can assist scholars a great deal in determining the status of what the global community believes is or isn't torture.

"ASEAN Human Rights Declaration." Association of Southeast Asian Nations, Conclusion Date: November 18, 2012, https://www.asean.org/storage/images/ASEAN_RTK_2014/6_AHRD_Booklet.pdf (accessed January 4, 2019).

"Convention against Torture." United Nations Human Rights Office of the High Commissioner, Conclusion Date: December 10, 1984, https://www.ohchr.org/en/professional interest/pages/cat.aspx (accessed November 10, 2019).

"Convention for the Protection of Human Rights and Fundamental Freedoms." Council of Europe, https://www.coe.int/en/web/conventions/full-list/-/conventions/treaty/005 (accessed May 26, 2019).

"Treaty of Amity and Cooperation in Southeast Asia." Association of Southeast Asian Nations, Conclusion Date: February 24, 1976, https://asean.org/treaty-amity-cooperation-southeast-asia-indonesia-24-february-1976/ (accessed November 10, 2019).

United Nations. 183rd Plenary Meeting, PV 183, Dec. 10, 1948, 933. http://undocs.org/A/PV.183 (accessed May 6, 2018).

United Nations. "Optional Protocol to the International Covenant on Civil and Political Rights," http://www.ohchr.org/EN/ProfessionalInterest/Pages/OPCCPR1.aspx (accessed May 20, 2018).

United Nations General Assembly. "Optional Protocol to the Convention on the Rights of the Child on the Involvement of Children in Armed Conflict," A/RES/54/ 263, May 25, 2000, https://www.ohchr.org/Documents/ ProfessionalInterest/crc-conflict.pdf (accessed May 18, 2019).

United Nations Human Rights Office of the High Commissioner. "Convention against Torture and Other Cruel, Inhuman or Degrading Treatment or Punishment," General Assembly Resolution 39/46 of 10 December 1984, http://www.ohchr.org/EN/ProfessionalInterest/Pages/CAT .aspx (accessed May 22, 2018).

United Nations Human Rights Office of the High Commissioner. "Status of Ratification International Dashboard," http://indicators.ohchr.org/ (accessed May 20, 2018).

"Universal Declaration of Human Rights." United Nations, http://www.ohchr.org/EN/UDHR/Documents/UDHR_ Translations/eng.pdf (accessed May 6, 2018).

7 Chronology

This chapter sets out the timeline not only for the events discussed in this book, but their wider historical context. Because this book covers almost three thousand years of recorded history regarding the use of torture and enhanced interrogation, from ancient Greece to the United States in the mid-twenty-first century, this chronology should be viewed as a starting point for further research, rather than its end.

8th–5th century B.C.E   Greek city states move away from *argon*, or trial-by-feud, to a rudimentary system of litigation to settle disputes.

4th century BCE   Aristotle writes *Rhetoric*, in which he discusses how to use *basanos*, or evidence procured from slaves under torture, as part of a case.

4th century BCE   Demosthenes declares that evidence obtained through torture is always accurate.

60–27 BCE   As Rome transitions from a republic to the authoritarianism of the First and Second Triumvirates and then to an empire under Augustus, the use of torture becomes more frequent and fewer citizens can claim immunity from its use.

Aerial via of the headquarters of the Central Intelligence Agency in Langley, Virginia. From the late 1950s through the present, the CIA's key role in the development of new torture technology and techniques is rivaled only by the Agency's ability to avoid any real consequences for its involvement in torture. (Library of Congress)

476 CE   With the fall of the last emperor in the West, the Roman Empire collapses, signaling a return to a justice system that relies more on religious oaths and self-help than torture.

600 CE   Torture comes into use in Japan.

1100 CE   Russian officials begin to use torture.

1166 CE   King Henry II of England creates a procedure where grand juries of local citizens would present evidence of crimes to royal judges who rode circuit around the realm, with cases proceeding to trial before a jury of residents. Since the jury can consider circumstantial evidence, there is less of a need for a confession, and thus for torture, by judicial bodies. Torture continues to be used in England for investigative purposes.

1252 CE   Pope Innocent IV approves the use of torture against those the Catholic Church deems to be heretics as part of the Inquisition.

13th century to 19th century CE   Torture becomes widely used both as a tool by investigators and as a method of obtaining a confession before magistrates across medieval Europe. As the years pass, torture before magistrates is normalized by regulation of its intensity and before whom it must take place, with some countries banning its use entirely.

14th century CE   French law distinguishes between judicial torture (to gain a confession) and investigative torture for the first time.

1652 CE   Dutch settlers introduce torture to what would become South Africa. The practice continues until Britain captures the colony in 1795.

1754 CE   Prussia becomes the first European state to ban the use of torture.

1764 CE   Italian criminologist Cesare Beccaria writes *On Crimes and Punishments* and attacks both the utility of torture and the philosophical justifications for its use.

1769 CE   British judge William Blackstone declares torture to be "an engine of the state, not of law" and suggests its use be excluded in criminal cases.

1801 CE   Czar Alexander I bans the use of torture in Russia. Notwithstanding this edict, the use of torture outlives both his regime and that of his royal family.

1870s CE   Alexander "Clubber" Williams, an inspector with the New York City Police Department (NYPD) declares there is "more law at the end of a policeman's night stick than in any ruling of the U.S. Supreme Court." Thanks to Williams and officers like him, use of the "third degree," a euphemism for torturing suspects, becomes endemic in the United States.

1879 CE   Japan bans the use of torture.

1890 CE   The U.S. Supreme Court declines to extend the 8th Amendment's prohibition against cruel and unusual punishment to state police forces in *In re Kemmler.*

1902 CE   *The New York Times* informs its readers that the NYPD maintains a sensory-deprivation cell at the Tombs, the city's jail, where even the toughest prisoners can reportedly be made to crack within hours.

1910 CE   U.S. Senator Frank Brandegee leads a select committee on the use of torture by federal police forces. Because of the Supreme Court's ruling in *Kemmler*, the state and local police, who are the most enthusiastic practitioners of the "third degree," go unexamined.

July 28, 1914 CE   World War I begins. By the time it concludes in November 1918, some European countries are rethinking their prior moves away from the use of torture.

March 1917   Czar Nicholas II is overthrown in Russia. The provisional government that replaces him is itself ousted eight months later by the Bolsheviks.

July 1918   Felix Dzerzhinsky, founder of the Cheka and the OGPU, the first two secret services dedicated to protecting the Bolshevik state, declares, "We stand for organized terror—this should be frankly stated—terror being absolutely indispensable in current revolutionary conditions." Notwithstanding a formal prohibition of its use under Russian and later, Soviet, law, Dzerzhinsky and his successors engage in torture on a mass scale, including mock executions.

October 1922   Benito Mussolini seizes power in Italy after being asked to form a government by King Victor Emmanuel III following the March on Rome by Mussolini's fascist party. Shortly thereafter, his OVRA secret police begins using torture against the regime's enemies, both real and imagined.

1929   The *Encyclopedia Britannica* deems the term "third degree" worthy of inclusion and explanation.

1929   French police begin to imitate their American colleagues' use of torture for investigative purposes.

1931   In the United States, the Wickersham Commission releases its report titled Lawlessness in Law Enforcement, which focuses on the use of the "third degree" by police across the country.

January 30, 1933   President Paul von Hindenburg names Adolf Hitler the chancellor of Germany. Though his Nazi party lacks a majority in the Reichstag, Germany's parliament, with the help of centrist parties, Hitler pushes through an enabling act that permits him to rule by decree. Soon after, Nazi officials begin to use torture on a regular basis.

1934   Nazis begin compulsive sterilization of Germans they consider "unfit" to reproduce as a means of carrying out their racist eugenic policies.

1937   Henrich Himmler's subordinates in the Nazi *Schutzstaffel*, or SS, a paramilitary and security police force set up by the Nazis, coin the term "*Verschärfte Vernehmung*," or "enhanced interrogation," to describe torture that would not leave obvious marks.

September 1, 1939   Nazi Germany invades Poland. Britain and France declare war and World War II begins.

1942   Himmler orders the use of the "third degree" against "[C]ommunists, Marxists, Jehovah's Witnesses, saboteurs, terrorists, members of resistance movements, antisocial elements, refractory elements, or Polish or Soviet vagabonds" both in Germany and occupied Europe.

1943–1944 The Vichy French *Milice*, or militia, begins operations against the French resistance and in support of the Nazi occupation force. Due in part to its use of torture, the *Milice* are quickly compared to the Nazi *Gestapo* because of their viciousness and cruelty.

1943–1945 Hanns Joachim Scharff, an enlisted man in the Luftwaffe, the German air force, eschews the use of both torture and *Verschärfte Vernehmung* in his work interrogating captured Allied pilots. Notwithstanding (or because) of this, he becomes known as the most effective interrogator in Hitler's service, interviewing over 500 air crews and getting information from at least 480 of them. After the war, he trains interrogators with the FBI in his technique and consults with the U.S. Air Force to teach its personnel how to resist it.

November 1945 to October 1946 Following the unconditional surrender of Nazi Germany, the Allied powers place the surviving top members of Hitler's regime on trial for war crimes at Nuremberg. The tribunal is the first international body to successfully try war crimes in the twentieth century and has a major influence in the creation of international law by the nascent United Nations.

September 1947 The Central Intelligence Agency (CIA) is founded in the United States.

1948 The UN General Assembly passes the Universal Declaration of Human Rights. Article 5 of the Declaration specifically bans torture.

1949 The CIA launches Project BLUEBIRD, which is intended to help its agents resist torture and other interrogation techniques used by opposing intelligence services.

November 1950 The Council of Europe approves the European Convention on Human Rights. Unlike the United Nations' declaration, the Convention can be enforced through the European Court of Human Rights.

1951   The CIA initiates Project ARTICHOKE, which was designed to develop "any method by which we can get information from a person against his will and without his knowledge." This includes the creation of black sites for ARTICHOKE interrogators around the world.

1951   In a project funded by the Canadian Research Board following a Montreal meeting between the CIA, British and Canadian intelligence, McGill University professor Donald O. Hebb learns subjecting volunteers to sensory deprivation for twenty-four to forty-eight hours can induce virtual psychosis, confirming what was written about the NYPD's sensory deprivation cell at the Tombs in 1902.

Early 1950s   Cornell University researchers on the CIA payroll discover the most effective KGB torture technique was simply forcing prisoners to stand for long periods. The discovery influences the use of stress positions by American interrogators from then on.

1954   Algerian nationalists rebel against the French government, starting the Algerian War for Independence. The French respond with harsh military measures, including the indiscriminate use of torture, such as waterboarding, against civilians. Foreign correspondent Edward Behr estimates that thousands—if not tens of thousands—of Algerians died at the hands of French torturers.

1956   A CIA report titled "Communist Control Techniques" concludes that "the effects of isolation, anxiety, fatigue, lack of sleep, uncomfortable temperatures, and chronic hunger . . . do, of course, constitute torture and physical coercion. All of them lead to serious disturbances of many bodily processes." By this time, of course, the CIA was using many of the same tactics.

May 1961   California repeals its vagrancy statute, thereby depriving its police of a tool they used to make pretext arrests of members of disfavored groups, many of which were subjected to the "third degree."

June 1961   In *Mapp v. Ohio*, the U.S. Supreme Court requires state courts to exclude illegally obtained evidence from criminal proceedings.

1961   British lawyer Peter Benenson forms Amnesty International (AI) in London. The group soon becomes one of the most effective anti-torture advocates of the 1960s and 1970s.

1963   The CIA issues its *KUBARK Counterintelligence Interrogation Manual*, KUBARK being the Agency's code name for itself. The manual advises that *threats* to inflict physical pain or administer drugs are often more effective than actually doing so when it comes to extracting information. It also candidly states that the main difference between CIA and KGB interrogation techniques is that the KGB usually attempted to "convert" a broken subject to their worldview as the last act, while the Agency historically did not. The authors consider this reticence on the part of the CIA to be an error, because "If the interrogatee remains semi-hostile or remorseful after a successful interrogation has ended, less time may be required to complete his conversion (and conceivably to create an enduring asset) than might be needed to deal with his antagonism if he is merely squeezed and forgotten."

June 1966   In *Miranda v. Arizona*, the U.S. Supreme Court excludes statements made by prisoners to their interrogators unless those prisoners have been informed of their right to counsel. Writing for the Court, Chief Justice Earl Warren declares that the intent of the decision is to end the use of the "third degree" by removing the motivation for its use.

December 1966   The U.N. General Assembly approves the International Covenant on Civil and Political Rights. Among other things, the treaty prohibits torture and medical experimentation on unwilling subjects.

April 1967–July 1974   Following a coup, a military *junta* rules Greece for seven years. Thanks to advocacy work by AI, Greece withdraws from the Council of Europe in 1969 just ahead of its expulsion based on reports of the use of torture by the military. Following the regime's collapse in 1974, some of those responsible are placed on trial in 1975.

1971   The Republic of Ireland accuses the United Kingdom before the European Court of Human Rights of violating the European Convention on Human Rights in its treatment of Irish Republican Army suspects in Northern Ireland.

1972   Amnesty International launches a worldwide campaign to ban torture, which aggravates so many governments that it finds itself banned from using UNESCO facilities in Paris.

1975   The UN General Assembly adopts the Declaration of the Protection of All Persons from being subjected to Torture and other Cruel, Inhuman or Degrading Treatment or Punishment. While high minded, like most UN resolutions, it lacks a means of enforcement.

1976   The International Covenant on Civil and Political Rights comes into force. As of May 2018, the Covenant has been ratified by 170 countries (including the United States and all members of the European Union) with another 6 having signed the Covenant but not ratified it and 21 others taking no action. Unlike the Declaration, the Covenant requires those countries who have ratified it to provide the Human Rights Committee with periodic reports as to their compliance with the Covenant's obligations, which are then made publicly available on the Committee's website.

1977   Amnesty International publishes *Torture in Greece*, a detailed look at the first trial of the torturers employed by the former Greek military regime. The book receives praise not only for contextualizing the trial but also for shedding light on the question of whether torturers are born or made.

1978   The European Court of Human Rights finds that while Britain's treatment of the IRA suspects in Northern Ireland was "inhuman and degrading," it did not rise to the level of torture and thus did not violate the Convention.

1981 The CIA trains Honduran army officers to use torture as an interrogation technique as the Agency and the Honduran government struggle against a leftist insurgency. As one officer tells *The New York Times* in 1988, his unit ended up turning into a death squad that murdered almost 120 people, including an American priest.

December 1984 The UN General Assembly unanimously approves the Convention against Torture. The treaty is an attempt to build on the work of earlier UN resolutions on the subject, as well as the International Covenant on Civil and Political Rights while closing the loopholes in each and providing an enforcement mechanism for its provisions. As of May 2018, 163 countries have ratified the Convention, including all major world powers except for India (which has been an unratified signatory since 1997).

1988 President Ronald Reagan signs the Convention against Torture and asks the U.S. Senate to ratify the treaty. The Senate declines to do so until 1994 and only acts subject to a reservation of rights that some observers feel eviscerates the treaty.

1995 President Bill Clinton begins the practice of "extraordinary rendition" or the transfer of suspected terrorists to third countries where they are likely to be tortured in violation of the Convention against Torture.

1996 The United States passes the War Crimes Act of 1996, which—for the first time—criminalizes "grave breaches" of the Geneva Conventions (including torture) committed by U.S. nationals anywhere in the world. Amendments in 1997 and 2006 expand its reach further.

January 2001 George W. Bush is inaugurated as president. He is expected to focus on education reform and domestic issues, leading many to fear that America will disengage from world affairs.

September 11, 2001 Teams of al-Qaeda hijackers seize four airplanes, crashing two of them into the World Trade Center in New York City and one into the Pentagon outside Washington,

D.C. A successful revolt by the doomed passengers on United Flight 93 prevents that team from hitting their intended target, believed to be either the White House or the U.S. Capitol, and the plane crashes in rural Pennsylvania. Almost 3,000 people are killed and 6,000 are injured in the worst terrorist attack in American history. That evening, Bush declares himself to be filled with "a quiet, unyielding anger."

September 17, 2001   Bush gives the CIA authority to detain suspected terrorists. Shortly thereafter, the CIA's lawyers begin to explore possible defenses to torture charges that could be brought under the Convention against Torture or the War Crimes Act.

January 2002   Department of Justice attorney John Yoo concludes that the provisions of the Geneva Convention do not apply to either al-Qaeda or Taliban prisoners, a view later endorsed by White House Counsel Alberto Gonzales.

February 7, 2002   Bush declares that the Geneva Conventions' prohibitions against torture do not apply to either al-Qaeda or Taliban detainees but orders they be treated "humanely."

March 2002   Abu Zubaydah is captured by Pakistani officials and turned over to CIA custody. The agency erroneously believes Zubaydah to be a top official of al-Qaeda and decides to use him as the first test subject for its new interrogation techniques. CIA interrogators waterboard him over eighty-three times and subject him to physical abuse, sleep deprivation, and stress positions, ultimately costing him an eye. They also repeatedly transfer him between a series of CIA black sites, or secret prisons, around the world until he is turned over to military custody at Guantanamo Bay in December 2006. As of May 2018, he has not been charged with any crime.

August 2002   Assistant Attorney General Jay Bybee advises the federal statute barring torture overseas only applied in cases of "grave" breaches of the Convention against Torture and that any prosecutions could be overridden as a violation of the president's power to make war.

November 2002   Al-Qaeda operative Abd al-Rahim al-Nashiri, who allegedly organized the attack on the U.S.S. *Cole* in 2000, is captured in the United Arab Emirates and turned over to the CIA. Agency interrogators subject him to waterboarding, sensory deprivation, isolation, and dietary manipulation but believe he is still holding back information; so they decide to use tactics the Agency has not approved. One CIA officer places al-Nashiri in a stress position for two days straight with his hands tied above his head. Later, the same officer blindfolds al-Nashiri, places a gun to his head and operates a cordless drill near his body. Other interrogators threaten to bring al-Nashiri's mother before him and rape her while he is forced to watch.

November 2002   Gul Rahman, who was captured in Afghanistan, becomes the first detainee to die in CIA custody after he is manacled to a wall by an Agency interrogator and forced to sit on a cold floor all night wearing only a sweatshirt.

March 2003   After his capture and transfer to CIA custody, Khalid Sheikh Mohammed, believed to be the mastermind behind the 9/11 attacks, is waterboarded 183 times in one month.

April 18, 2004   *CBS News* uncovers massive abuses of Iraqi prisoners by American forces at the Abu Ghraib prison outside of Baghdad. These include suspected Iraqi insurgent Manadel al-Jamadi, who dies after a CIA interrogator places him in a stress position, notwithstanding the five broken ribs al-Jamadi suffered during his capture by U.S. Navy SEALS. Another American soldier is photographed posing with al-Jamadi's corpse and giving a "thumbs up" sign.

November 2, 2005   *The Washington Post* reveals the existence of the CIA's network of secret prisons used to interrogate detainees.

November 2005   CIA leadership orders the destruction of videotapes showing the torture of Zubaydah, al-Nashiri, and others, including waterboarding.

December 30, 2005   The U.S. Congress passes the Detainee Treatment Act (DTA), which bars the military from using any interrogation techniques not listed in the U.S. Army field manual, which is a *de facto* ban on torture. The DTA bars the CIA and other government agencies from subjecting detainees to "cruel, inhuman, or degrading treatment or punishment" as defined by both the U.S. Constitution and the Convention against Torture.

June 29, 2006   In *Hamdan v. Rumsfeld*, the U.S. Supreme Court finds that Bush's military commissions set up to try suspected terrorists unconstitutional but holds—contrary to Yoo and Bybee's advice—that the protections of the Geneva Convention do apply to those in American custody.

September 7, 2006   Bush admits the existence of the CIA black sites and announces that all detainees have now been transferred to Guantanamo Bay. He also states that while the CIA used what he called "alternative" means of interrogation, "The US does not torture. I have not authorized it and I will not."

October 2006   In response to *Hamdan* and Bush's request, Congress passes the Military Commissions Act of 2006 (MCA), which codified Bush's earlier attempts to restrict the ability of detainees to seek relief via a writ of habeas corpus to federal courts and claims that no detainee may "invoke" the Geneva Conventions "as a source of rights."

July 20, 2007   Bush issues Executive Order 13440, in which he defined "Cruel, inhuman, or degrading treatment or punishment" as acts "prohibited by the Fifth, Eighth, and Fourteenth Amendments to the Constitution of the United States" (though not the CAT) and certified that the CIA's new techniques were in compliance with the Geneva Conventions and did not constitute torture.

June 2008   In *Boumediene v. Bush*, the U.S. Supreme Court strikes down the provisions of the MCA that restrict detainee access to habeas relief.

January 20, 2009   Barack H. Obama is inaugurated as president. In his address, Obama declares, "We reject as false the choice between our safety and our ideals." Watching from the audience, Bush looks tortured when Obama follows up with, "Our Founding Fathers, faced with perils that we can scarcely imagine, drafted a charter to assure the rule of law and the rights of man—a charter expanded by the blood of generations. Those ideals still light the world, and we will not give them up for expedience sake."

January 22, 2009   Obama issues Executive Order 13491, which revokes Bush's Executive Order 13440 and restricts CIA interrogators to techniques set forth in the U.S. Army field manual.

January 22, 2009   Obama also issues Executive Order 13492, which directs that the detention facility at Guantanamo Bay be closed "as soon as practicable, and no later than 1 year from the date of this order" with detainees to be transferred to the United States for criminal trial, held at other U.S. facilities, returned to their home country, or sent to a third country willing to accept them or released entirely. For a variety of reasons, this deadline is not met by the time Obama leaves office in January 2017.

May 29, 2010   Chelsea Manning is arrested by the U.S. military for disclosing hundreds of thousands of documents to WikiLeaks. The document dump becomes known as the Iraq War Logs.

July 2010   Manning is transferred to custody in Quantico, Virginia, at a military facility where she is forced to sleep in the nude and kept in solitary confinement twenty-three hours a day.

October 22, 2010   WikiLeaks releases 391,832 "Significant Action" reports prepared by U.S. Army personnel during the Iraq War from 2004 through 2009 provided to it by Manning. According to WikiLeaks founder Julian Assange, the files provide "compelling evidence" of war crimes committed by U.S.

forces in Iraq, including the slaughter of surrendering insurgents and several hundred reports of abuse that took place after the Abu Ghraib scandal. The Pentagon claims the disclosures will endanger the lives of American troops.

June 2011   U.S. attorney general Eric Holder announces that after investigating about one hundred cases of detainee abuse by American officials and agents, he is declining to bring criminal charges in any of them.

February 2012   The U.N. Special Rapporteur on Torture formally informs the United States that its treatment of Manning could constitute a violation of both the International Covenant on Civil and Political Rights and the Convention against Torture.

August 30, 2012   Holder confirms that he will not bring charges against anyone for the deaths of Rahman and al-Jamadi while they were American custody.

July 2013   At a military court martial, Manning is acquitted of the most serious charge against her—that of aiding the enemy—but convicted of other counts related to the disclosure of classified information to WikiLeaks. The Court awards her 112 days of credit on top of the time she had already served prior to trial because of the abuse she suffered at the hands of her jailers.

August 2013   Manning is sentenced to thirty-five years in prison for her disclosures to WikiLeaks, intensifying a campaign by her supporters for her release.

July 24, 2014   The European Court of Human Rights finds that Poland was complicit in the CIA's torture of Zubaydah and al-Nashiri because of its approval of the Agency black site on its territory. The Court orders Poland to pay each man $135,000 in damages.

January 17, 2017   Days before he leaves office, Obama agrees to commute Manning's sentence. She is freed on May 17, 2017.

January 30, 2018   Donald J. Trump issues Executive Order 13823, which formally revokes Obama's Executive Order 13492 demanding the closure of the Guantanamo Bay prison, even though the deadline set forth in Executive Order 13492 had already lapsed.

May 17, 2018 The U.S. Senate confirms Gina Haspel, who ran the CIA's black site in Thailand during part of Bush's term and drafted the cable ordering the Agency to destroy the videotapes that documented waterboarding and other torture, as a CIA director.

May 31, 2018 The European Court of Human Rights sanctions Romania and Lithuania for assisting the CIA's torture of Zubaydah and al-Nashiri by hosting black sites on their soil. Each country is ordered to pay $117,000 to both men.

March 8, 2019 U.S. District Judge Claude Hilton orders Chelsea Manning's arrest after she refuses to testify before a grand jury believed to be investigating WikiLeaks.

April 11, 2019 British authorities arrest WikiLeaks cofounder Julian Assange after the Ecuadorean embassy in London withdraws its grant of asylum to him. Shortly thereafter, the United States unseals an indictment charging Assange with various computer crimes in connection with the Iraq war logs. Manning is not listed as a defendant in that case.

April 22, 2019 A three-judge panel of the Fourth Circuit Court of Appeals upholds Judge Hilton's finding holding Manning in contempt for refusing to testify and declines to order her release.

May 9, 2019 Manning is released after the term of the grand jury she was subpoenaed for expires.

May 16, 2019 After she is subpoenaed for a new grand jury investigating WikiLeaks, Manning again refuses to testify. U.S. District Judge Anthony Trenga remands her to custody and fines her $500 for every day she is in custody up to thirty days—and $1,000 a day for every day she spent in custody defying the order to testify after that. As of November 2019, she remains in jail.

Glossary

Al-Qaeda   A right-wing organization that employs armed struggle and seeks the establishment of a Sunni Caliphate over the entire world. Formed in 1988 by Osama bin-Laden and several others, it became notorious in America following its 1998 bombings of the U.S. Embassy in Dar es Salaam, Tanzania, and Nairobi, Kenya, which it followed up in 2001 with the 9/11 attacks on the United States. On May 2, 2011, a U.S. Navy SEAL team killed bin Laden following an attack on his compound in Abbotabad, Pakistan. Following bin Laden's death, al-Qaeda has been overshadowed to some degree by competing groups like Daesh/Islamic State of Iraq (ISIL) in recent years but is still considered to be active by American officials.

Basanos   judicially supervised torture in ancient Greece. It was the only way slave evidence could be heard in litigation and the slave's owner could terminate the examination (i.e., the torture) of the slave by the adverse party at any time (since slaves were considered chattel, or property, rather than human beings).

Convention   a legally binding treaty between states (e.g., Convention against Torture).

Declaration   a statement of principles agreed to between states but which, unlike a convention or a treaty, is not legally enforceable.

Front de libération du Québec (FLQ)   a left-wing group that employs armed struggle and carried out attacks across the province of Quebec from the early 1960s until 1970. In 1968, Canadian prime minister Pierre Elliott Trudeau invoked the War Measures Act and placed the province under martial law following two high-profile kidnappings. This was the first time in Canadian history that the Act had been implemented during peacetime and led to allegations of the abuse of detainees by both Quebec and federal officials.

Informal torture   torture used outside the presence of a judicial authority, usually to gather information rather than to solicit in-court testimony or as a punishment.

Internal Security Unit (ISU)   a cadre of the Irish Republican Army charged with evaluating applicants for IRA membership and interrogating IRA prisoners who made statements while in British or police custody. Some ISU members have been accused of torture and murder, acts that certain observers believe was ordered by or at least tolerated by the British, who reportedly had penetrated the organization. See Irish Republican Army.

Irish Republican Army   A left-wing group that employed armed struggle and that, under various groupings and splinter organizations, has worked to evict the British from Ireland since the middle of the twentieth century. The British responded through a variety of measures, from mass internment without trial to targeted assassinations, which have been criticized by human rights advocates. Since the 1997 Good Friday Agreement, the main body of the IRA (the Provisional IRA) has observed a ceasefire and in 2005 formally abandoned the armed struggle, though some anti-Agreement dissidents continue to use violence against it and the British.

Jurisprudence   the expression of a country's or culture's legal philosophy. In some jurisdictions, like the United States and the United Kingdom, this is partially expressed through case law created by the courts; in others, it is defined exclusively by statutes enacted by the legislature, through executive decrees.

Reid Technique/Reid Interrogation   A nine-step process used by law enforcement officials to elicit confessions. Because the focus of the technique is to break the suspects' resistance and get them to confess rather than to persuade them to tell the truth, it is controversial as some contend it encourages false confessions.

Rendition or "Extraordinary Rendition"   The process of transferring a prisoner from one country to a recipient country he or she is likely to be tortured. This usually occurs outside of the formal extradition system and is banned by the Convention against Torture, but the United States has engaged in it since the U.S. Senate ratified the Convention under President Bill Clinton.

Torture (United Nations definition)   "Any act by which severe pain or suffering, whether physical or mental, is intentionally inflicted on a person for such purposes as obtaining from him or a third person information or a confession, punishing him for an act he or a third person has committed or is suspected of having committed, or intimidating or coercing him or a third person, or for any reason based on discrimination of any kind, when such pain or suffering is inflicted by or at the instigation of or with the consent or acquiescence of a public official or other person acting in an official capacity" (Convention against Torture, December 10, 1984).

Torture (U.S. definition)   "In order to constitute torture, an act must be specifically intended to inflict severe physical or mental pain or suffering and that mental pain or suffering refers to prolonged mental harm caused by or resulting from: (1) the intentional infliction or threatened infliction of severe physical pain or suffering; (2) the administration or application, or threatened administration or application, of mind altering substances or other procedures calculated to disrupt profoundly the senses or the personality, (3) the threat of imminent death, (4) the threat that another person will imminently be subjected to death, severe physical pain or suffering, or the administration or application of mind altering substances or other procedures calculated to disrupt profoundly the senses or personality" (Congress Record, 36198–36199).

Third Degree   a euphemism for the use of physical and mental torture by police, usually in the United States, to compel a prisoner to confess or to disclose information. The term is believed to have come from speculation about the initiation ceremony for a third-degree master Mason, which is rumored to have contained elements we could consider to constitute physical coercion.

Vagrancy   being without any visible means of support. Until the 1960s, laws against vagrancy were used by law enforcement in California as a way to arrest members of marginalized groups who were present in public, even though they were innocent of any crime.

Verschärfte Vernehmung   literally "enhanced" or "stricter" interrogation. It is the term for torture used in Nazi Germany that was designed not to leave physical evidence on the victim that it had taken place. Some of the ways it was implemented bore a strong resemblance to methods used by American police agencies up through the middle of the twentieth century. See also *Third Degree*.

Index

About the Author

Born in New York City back when it was legitimately danger-ous, Christina Ann-Marie DiEdoardo has been fascinated with history, particularly the tales of those society sees as outlaws, since she could first open a book. A dual citizen of Canada and the United States, she can claim a dubious ancestral connection to historical Irish pirates on the Canadian side of her family and a firmer one to Italian relatives who actively discourage such nosy questions on the other.

Christina spent ten years as an award-winning print reporter for a variety of newspapers in Missouri and California, talk-ing to people from criminal defense lawyers in San Diego to pro-democracy activists in Hong Kong and trying to do honor to their stories. She also was lucky enough to get her first seri-ous death threat connected with her work at a time when she was too young and inexperienced to take it as seriously as she should have.

Christina was part of the team of activists and lawyers who secured the repeal in 1998 of San Diego Municipal Code 56.19, the last enforced criminal ordinance in a major American city which targeted Trans people for simply appearing in public as their authentic selves. Shortly thereafter, she left journalism for the law.

After graduating *cum laude* with a juris doctorate from the William S. Boyd School of Law in 2005, Christina has worked as a criminal defense attorney in Nevada and California, where she has helped hundreds of people during the most challenging periods of their lives. That work gave her a deep appreciation of the gaps between what the American system of justice promises and what it delivers, which indirectly led to this book. Similarly, her Canadian heritage is why there's a considerable amount of Canadian content in this book regarding that country's involvement in torture, from the central government's struggle against the *Front de Libération du Québec* in the late 1960s to Omar Khadr in the early 2000s.

When not attempting to straighten out her clients' misunderstandings with law enforcement in California and Nevada, Christina serves her community as an advocate for criminal justice and social reform and as a historian. She stood with anti-fascist activists at all five Battles of Berkeley from January 2017 through August 2018, where she was hit with CS spray from fascists on two occasions and where she took a weapon away from a Nazi skinhead once. She also provides *pro bono* and reduced-fee legal services to a variety of charitable organizations and needy individuals in the Bay Area and elsewhere.

Christina wrote the "Resist" column, which covered local anti-fascist activism, for the *Bay Area Reporter*, the oldest continually published LGBTQ newspaper in the United States, from July 2017 through March 2019. Her previous published works include *Lanza's Mob: The Mafia and San Francisco* (ABC-CLIO, 2016), which was the first history of the Italian Mafia to focus on the activities of its San Francisco crime family.

She resides in San Francisco, California.